The MMPI:
Clinical Assessment and Automated Interpretation

David Lachar, Ph.D.
Institute of Behavioral Medicine
Good Samaritan Medical Center
Phoenix, Arizona

Published by

WESTERN PSYCHOLOGICAL SERVICES
Publishers and Distributors
12031 Wilshire Boulevard
Los Angeles, California 90025

Library of Congress Cataloging in Publication Data

Lachar, David.
    The MMPI: clinical assessment and automated interpretation.

    (WPS professional handbook series, no. 8)
    Bibliography: p.
    1. Minnesota multiphasic personality inventory.
1. Title. [DNLM: 1. Automatic data processing.
2. MMPI. W1W171F no. 8 1973 / WM145 L133m 1973]
BF698.8.M5L24   1974   155.2'8'3'   73-91237

ISBN 0-87424-134-0

Ninth Printing.................................... March 1985

In memory of my father.

CONTENTS

PREFACE

This book is intended to serve three purposes: (1) Provide a guide for teaching the MMPI or serve as a text for graduate students studying personality assessment; (2) Serve as a source book for clinicians who are faced with the task of applying MMPI data to clinical problems; and (3) Present an automated interpretation system in its entirety with the hope that it will stimulate study by others interested in automated assessment issues.

This volume is the result of my experience in introducing clinical psychology interns to MMPI interpretation as well as applying this inventory to various problems within a large teaching hospital. Part I is an introduction to the basic scales of the standard MMPI profile which has evolved from several revisions of lecture notes. Part II presents a compendium of accepted clinical interpretations from several sources and populations. Part III summarizes the results of the initial application of an automated interpretation program to a substantial, diverse clinical sample. Even though the interpretive system provided by this volume was designed to be computer implimented, it can also be easily utilized by clinicians without access to computer equipment.

Many individuals have given generously of their time and effort in bringing this work to completion. Frank Gallinaro and Roger K. Miller served as administrative assistants at various stages of the automated interpretation project and read early drafts of this manuscript.

The material presented in Part III represents considerable technical effort provided for the most part by the Biometrics Division of the School of Aerospace Medicine, Brooks Air Force Base, Texas. John W. Penn modified a scoring routine generously provided by Robert E. Lushene and programmed the entire interpretive system. John W. Penn, Joseph E. Braswell and Robert A. Balusek were responsible for the tedious task of processing test protocols and providing an efficient data retrieval system. Darwell E. Stowe provided the administrative support and optical scanning equipment which made this project possible. Phelps P. Crump and Vondal C. Hutchins provided data analysis assistance.

Many clinicians participated in the initial evaluation of this automated system. Special appreciation is extended to Russell L. Adams, James F. Corcoran, William J. Fisher, John P. Houlihan, Charles L. Jennings, William C. Koestline, Reed M. Larsen, Richard M. Nacewski, Donald R. Seidel, John C. Sparks and John R. Steigerwald for their substantial assistance in obtaining evaluated narrative interpretations.

The following friends and colleagues have read this manuscript and offered helpful advice: Malcolm D. Gynther, Richard I. Lanyon, Milton E. Strauss, Charles D. Maurer, John Breeskin and Charles T. Bisbee. It goes without saying, however, that I take sole responsibility for any inadequacies contained herein.

I also wish to thank my wife Barbara and daughter Ruth for their encouragement and support throughout this project.

Various materials found in this volume were reproduced with the generous permission of the following companies and individuals. I wish to thank them for their cooperation.

The Williams and Wilkens Company, publishers of P. A. Marks and W. Seeman, *An Atlas for Use with the MMPI: Actuarial Description of Abnormal Personality*, 1963, for permission to reproduce code type rules and mean profiles.

W. B. Saunders Company, publishers of H. Gilberstadt and J. Duker, *A Handbook for Clinical and Actuarial MMPI Interpretation*, 1965, for permission to reproduce code type rules and mean profiles.

Robert C. Carson for permission to reproduce much of his Manual of MMPI Interpretation published in J. N. Butcher, *MMPI: Research Developments and Clinical Applications*, 1969.

Malcolm D. Gynther for permission to reproduce code type interpretations developed from protocols obtained from state hospitals at the Missouri Institute of Psychiatry.

Zigfrids T. Stelmachers for permission to reproduce his "canned" MMPI interpretations used at Hennepin County General Hospital, Minneapolis.

The Psychological Corporation, and especially James H. Ricks of the Test Division, for permission to reproduce MMPI items, profile forms and T-score conversion tables.

The University of Minnesota Press for permission to reproduce Tables 6-9 of Appendix H, T-score conversions for adolescents from W. G. Dahlstrom, G. S. Welsh and L. E. Dahlstrom, *An MMPI Handbook. Volume I: Clinical Interpretation*, 1972.

DAVID LACHAR

Detroit, Michigan
November, 1973

I. AN INTRODUCTION TO THE BASIC SCALES

This section provides a basic orientation to the thirteen scales which are routinely scored. Data covering scale construction, scale composition and general principles of individual scale interpretation are presented. The validity scales (?, L, F, K) are first discussed in terms of indices of technical validity as well as personality characteristics which they may suggest. The ten clinical scales are then presented in their order of appearance on the standard profile sheet.

The original names of the clinical scales are only noted in passing. While the meaning and scope of each scale was being empirically determined, it became quite clear that the scale name tended to at least limit a scale's interpretation, if not to actually mislead. The scale name has also become less useful in communication of profile meaning as configural interpretation and the profile summary notation, the code, has become the primary approach to the MMPI. The recognition of profile codes, consisting of scale *numbers* in ordinal elevation position, has become essential in the communication of MMPI data. As a result, there is really no way to avoid the initial rote memorization of scale numbers and dimensions of scale correlates.

This section concludes with a systematic presentation of interpretive hypotheses from the clinical lore by elevation of individual scales. Though this data is mainly useful to illustrate the interpretive dimensions of each scale, it may also complement interpretations of profile codes listed in Sections II and III. In this regard, several points should be kept in mind: (1) Scores noted are K-corrected elevations, when appropriate; (2) Interpretation of a given scale is usually modified by other scale elevations, therefore, the hypotheses noted will apply most directly when the given scale is either a prominent or sole elevation in the clinical range; (3) The ranges noted for each scale are somewhat arbitrary and should not be interpreted in an absolute manner. That is, the interpretive hypotheses are not actually placed on an interval scale, rather, they represent an ordinal placement which is supported by substantial clinical experience and research data.

1

THE VALIDITY SCALES

SCALE ?

This "scale" is simply the total number of unanswered or double marked test items. Scores over 30 are often considered to invalidate a profile as missing data may lower clinical scales and change their interpretation. This principle is reflected by the rule for paragraph 2 (page 102) for the automated guide which omits the remainder of the narrative when Scale ? exceeds a score of 30.

Though many psychologists exclude the possibility of Scale ? exceeding 30 by requesting responses to all items, a protocol which contains a significant number of unanswered items suggests several interpretive hypotheses:

(1) Inability to respond to certain items because of reading difficulties, limited or poor comprehension, or significant confusion.
(2) An extremely obsessive, ambivalent or ruminative approach to test content.
(3) A defensive, highly guarded response set.
(4) An intentional lack of cooperation.
(5) Difficulty responding to items due to psychomotor slowing or lethargy which accompanies severe depression.

SCALE L

The Lie Scale is composed of 15 items, all scored in the false direction, expressing opinions and behaviors which, while valued in our culture, are actually found in only the most conscientious of individuals, if indeed they are found at all. Examples of items include:

I do not always tell the truth.   (F)
I would rather win than lose in a game.   (F)
I do not like everyone I know.   (F)
I get angry sometimes.   (F)

This scale was designed to identify a general, deliberate, evasive response set, though it is usually only successful with less sophisticated individuals.

Protocols with high L Scale scores are often associated with low clinical profiles. When clinical elevations occur, they are most likely on Scales 1, 2, 3 and 4 and tend to form neurotic profile configurations.

Elevations on this scale have been associated with several interpretive hypotheses:

(1) An intentional attempt to make a good impression and to deny faults.
(2) Psychological naivete often associated with limited cultural background and low IQ.
(3) Over-conventionality, rigidity, and over-evaluation of self worth.
(4) Neurotic characteristics, including the prominent use of the defenses of repression and denial, lack of insight and somatization.

Interpretive statements based on the elevation of the L Scale can be found on page 17. Hypotheses based on validity scale configurations are found on pages 34-42. The use of L Scale values to select a validity narrative paragraph for an automatically generated interpretation can be seen on page 102.

SCALE F

The Frequency Scale contains 64 items answered by normals in the scored direction no more than 10 percent of the time. These items express a broad spectrum of maladjustment; many items deal with peculiar thoughts and beliefs. Others reflect apathy, lack of interest in things and denial of social ties. F Scale items include:

My soul sometimes leaves my body.   (T)
Someone has been trying to rob me.   (T)
I believe my sins are unpardonable.   (T)
No one cares much what happens to you.   (T)
I am never happier than when alone.   (T)
I believe in law enforcement.   (F)
I usually expect to succeed in things I do.   (F)
I am troubled by attacks of nausea and vomiting.   (T)
I have used alcohol excessively.   (T)
My sex life is satisfactory.   (F)
Everything tastes the same.   (T)
My father was a good man.   (F)

Though many F Scale items are frank statements of psychiatric symptoms, they are seldom endorsed by patients and therefore less than 50 percent of these items appear on the clinical scales.

Increasing F Scale elevations are usually associated with increasing elevations of the clinical scales. As Scale F increases, high points on Scales 1, 2, 3, 4, 7 and 9 become relatively less frequent, while peak scores on Scales 6 and 8 become much more frequent.

Elevations on the F Scale indicate an atypical or deviant set of responses and suggest interpretive hypotheses related to both profile validity and personality characteristics:

(1) Clerical scoring errors.
(2) Lack of understanding of the assessment procedure and individual inventory items due to perceptual deficits, insufficient reading skills or limited intelligence.
(3) Lack of cooperation which results in an atypical response set (partial or all-random, all true, all false).
(4) A deliberate distorted description which claims fictitious mental symptoms ("fake bad") in an attempt to escape responsibilities.
(5) An exaggeration of existing difficulties to gain attention and assistance ("cry for help").

If (1) through (5) can be excluded, the degree of F Scale elevation is a good indicator of the severity of psychiatric disturbance (Blumberg, 1967). Increasing elevations often

accompany decompensation, while decreasing F Scale values often indicate good prognosis and symptom reduction accompanying therapy.

    (6) Moderate elevations are associated with unconventional thinking, sullen, rebellious personalities and emotional instability. Individuals with dramatic-theatrical life styles, "psychochondriacs," and those who are self-depreciatory or experience events "intensely" may score within this range.

    (7) F Scale elevation often accompanies severe stress.

    (8) Adolescents produce elevated scores which reflect age differences, youthful honesty ("let it all hang out"), and the turmoil which often accompanies an identity crisis.

    (9) High elevations may reflect the confusion and pervasive personality disorganization which results in acute psychotic reactions.

Interpretive statements related to F Scale elevation are given on pages 17-18. The central importance of the F Scale in selecting a validity statement for the automated program can be clearly seen on page 102.

SCALE K

The 30 item K Scale (McKinley, Hathaway & Meehl, 1948) is composed of 22 items which differentiated normal profiles obtained by defensive hospitalized psychiatric patients ("test misses") from those produced by normals. Eight items which improved discrimination of depressive and schizophrenic symptoms were added to form the final Correction Scale. Various fractions of this scale are added to the raw scores of 5 clinical scales in an effort to improve their validity when it may be impaired by a defensive response set.

K Scale items, in the scored direction, reflect denial of inadequacy in self, family, or circumstances, and a hesitance to criticize others. Examples of items include:

> At times I feel like smashing things. (F)
> It takes a lot of argument to convince most people of the truth. (F)
> I certainly feel useless at times. (F)
> I have very few quarrels with members of my family. (T)
> I frequently find myself worrying about something. (F)
> I often think, "I wish I were a child again." (F)

This scale measures approximately what Scale L was intended to measure, but it does so in a more subtle and effective manner.

High K Scale scores are usually associated with relatively lower clinical profiles, reflecting the respondents' defensiveness and guardedness. Low K Scale scores are associated with relatively high clinical profiles. High K Scale scores are often associated with profiles which peak on Scales 1, 3, and 4, while low K Scale scores are often obtained in protocols with peaks on Scales 6, 7, 8 and 9.

Interpretive hypotheses vary with scale elevation:

(1) Low elevations suggest:

    (a) A lack of normal defensiveness often associated with malingering or a "cry for help" (See elevation of Scale F).

    (b) Few functioning defenses, often associated with acute pathology.

    (c) An individual with a poor self-concept who is dissatisfied with his lot but is without the skills to bring about significant change. Pathology is relatively accessible for evaluation.

(2) Moderate elevations suggest:

    (a) Self-acceptance and good ego strength [44-55 T suggests improvement in status in a day treatment center and early release if rehospitalized (Ries, 1966). See also Sweetland and Quay (1953), and King and Schiller (1959).]

    (b) Appropriate defensiveness for college educated and middle or upper-class individuals.

(3) Moderate to marked elevations suggest:

    (a) A consistant effort to maintain an appearance of adequacy, self-control and effectiveness.

    (b) Rigidity and inflexibility with accompanying serious limitations in personal insight and understanding.

    (c) A defensive response set which may have significantly affected the clinical profile.

Moderate and greater K Scale elevations indicate the presence of a defensive structure which allows a person to function in spite of inner conflict. K Scale elevations associated with a psychotic process may reflect relative psychological stability. K Scale rises with successful psychotherapy or as defensiveness (knowing when not to admit to pathology or act crazy) increases.

Though the personality attributes associated with K Scale elevation help an individual to hold the confidence of others and facilitate interaction, these qualities may interfere with psychiatric evaluation and treatment. Persons with high K Scale elevation are often difficult to approach, unwilling to discuss personal inadequacies or accept the role of patient. This defensiveness may be linked to a more pervasive hysteroid denial (look for associated L Scale and Scale 3 elevation), or paranoid projection of blame.

NOTE: The K-correction procedure may or may not add to profile validity. Because the majority of the literature on the MMPI deals with K-corrected profiles, it has been suggested by many that the K-corrected profile be plotted as well as the non-K-corrected profile in those settings in which K-correction procedure has not been found helpful.

3

When K is not added to the clinical scales, the profile *must* be plotted using the T values found in Appendix A. These scale scores *cannot* be directly plotted onto the values of the standard profile sheets.

Protocols obtained from adolescents are usually scored using adolescent norms. These norms (Appendix B) are based on scale scores without the K-correction.

In those protocols where the K-correction significantly changes the shape of the non-K-corrected profile, the source of this variance should be kept in mind. For ex-ample, a Scale 8 elevation of 90 T which reflects 39 Scale 8 responses should be interpreted differently than the same elevation obtained by 23 Scale 8 items and 20 K-correction points. (That is, at least the former can be interpreted in a traditional manner with more surety than the latter as it at least reflects substantial Scale 8 item content.)

Interpretive statements related to K Scale elevation are given on page 18. The use of K Scale values to select a validity narrative paragraph for an automatically generated interpretation can be found on page 102.

THE CLINICAL SCALES

SCALE 1 (Hs/Hypochondriasis)

This scale (McKinley & Hathaway, 1940) contains 33 items expressing a variety of bodily complaints which were found to be characteristic of psychiatric patients with a diagnosis of hypochondriasis. Scale 1 is primarily a stable "trait" scale which reflects undue concern about health and a seeking of sympathy through exaggeration of vague and nonspecific physical complaints. Scale 1 elevation suggests the operation of somatization defenses and may also reflect somatic correlates of psychological discomfort.

These items describe physical complaints which are not restricted to any particular physiological system or part of the body. Scale 1 items reflect generalized aches and pains, specific complaints about digestion, breathing, thinking, vision and sleep, as well as peculiarities of sensation. A few items also relate to general health or competence. Scale 1 items include:

> I have a great deal of stomach trouble. (T)
> I hardly ever feel pain in the back of the neck. (F)
> I have a good appetite. (F)
> I am about as able to work as I ever was. (F)
> My sleep is fitful and disturbed. (T)
> I feel weak all over much of the time. (T)
> I seldom or never have dizzy spells. (F)
> I have numbness in one or more regions of my skin. (T)

When a primary or prominent elevation on Scale 1 is obtained within a psychiatric population, these characteristics may be present:

(1) The expression of psychological and emotional conflicts through somatic channels and a persistent preoccupation with physical integrity.
(2) A pessimistic, sour, whiny, complaining, passive-aggressive approach to the world which tends to make those around the patient miserable.
(3) Egocentricity, immaturity and lack of insight into the emotional basis for somatic preoccupations.
(4) Little psychological sophistication and a possibly limited, or typically average, intellectual level.
(5) Great skill in frustrating a series of physicians by simultaneously demanding attention and derogating or rejecting assistance offered.

Though individuals who have documented physical disease may produce protocols with some Scale 1 elevation (though depression, Scale 2, is a more frequent elevation), these elevations are seldom as high as those obtained by psychiatric patients who express psychological conflict in somatic equivalents. Those with bonafide physical disease do not obtain high elevations, usually no more than 55-65 T, because they only respond to the scale items which reflect their disability. Elevations of 65 T and more produced by physically ill patients suggest an overemphasis of bodily concern and a need for professional intervention in the form of reassurance and support at the very least.

Dahlstrom, Welsh & Dahlstrom (1972) suggest that a significant Scale 1 elevation may have these diagnostic implications:

(1) Various somatic reactions such as hypochondriasis and neurasthenia.
(2) Depressive reactions with important anxiety components, such as reactive depression, involutional melancholia and agitated depression.
(3) Hysterias, both anxiety hysteria and conversion hysteria.
(4) Anxiety reactions.

Individuals who obtain moderate Scale 1 elevations are often described as unambitious, lacking drive, stubborn and egocentric. Low scores often suggest alert, capable and responsible individuals who are effective in living.

Interpretive statements based on the elevation of Scale 1 can be found on page 19. The use of Scale 1 in isolation to select interpretive material for the automated program can be seen in paragraphs 17, 24A, 26A and 66. Other paragraphs within subroutine Code and Configuration make prominent use of Scale 1 variance.

SCALE 2 (D/Depression)

This scale (Hathaway & McKinley, 1942) contains items which were selected by contrasting depressed psychiatric patients mainly diagnosed manic-depressive depressed with a general sample. A small subset of correction items, added to increase scale accuracy, resulted in a 60 item scale.

In general, Scale 2 measures a state characterized by poor morale, moodiness and feelings of hopelessness and sorrow. Although this scale was constructed from a largely psychotic sample, these items reflect variations in mood regardless of underlying character structure or general adjustment. Scale 2 items deal with a lack of interest in things, apathy, denial of happiness or personal worth, inability to work, and physical symptoms.

Harris and Lingoes (1955) judgmentally separated five overlapping subclusters from Scale 2 items:

I. Subjective depression (D1/32 items):

> I have never felt better in my life than I do now. (F)
> My sleep is fitful and disturbed. (T)
> I don't seem to care what happens to me. (T)
> I am happy most of the time. (F)

II. Psychomotor retardation (D2/15 items):

> I have difficulty in starting to do things. (T)
> At times I feel like smashing things. (F)

5

III. Physical malfunctioning (D3/11 items):

I have a good appetite.   (F)
I feel weak all over much of the time.   (T)

IV. Mental dullness (D4/15 items):

My judgment is better than it ever was.   (F)
I find it hard to keep my mind on a task or job.   (T)

V. Brooding (D5/10 items):

I usually feel that life is worthwhile.   (F)
I certainly feel useless at times.   (T)

The K Scale is not added to Scale 2 because it contains a significant component of non-obvious items. Wiener (1948) separated these items into obvious and subtle subsets:

Examples of obvious (40) items:

I wish I could be as happy as others seem to be.   (T)
I certainly feel useless at times.   (T)
I cry easily.   (T)
I seem to be about as capable and smart as most others around me.   (F)
At times I am all full of energy.   (F)

Examples of subtle (20) items:

I am easily awakened by noise.   (T)
It takes a lot of argument to convince most people of the truth.   (F)
I am neither gaining nor losing weight.   (F)
I like to flirt.   (F)
I dream frequently about things that are best kept to myself.   (F)
I sweat very easily even on a cool day.   (F)

Scale 2 is a sensitive index of current mood; it characteristically reflects temporal variation in depressive symptoms. Changes in Scale 2 often occur with a variety of events, including adaptation to psychotic processes, removal of situational stress, a course of ECT or anti-depressant medication, and success in psychotherapy. Though the interpretation of Scale 2 elevation varies depending on the rest of the profile, it is an efficient index of immediate satisfaction and comfort in living.

Scale 2 is most frequently the highest scale in profiles obtained from psychiatric patients (Meehl, 1946). These patients readily recognize their own self-depreciation, moodiness and disposition to worry over even small matters. Here Scale 2 elevation generally reflects discomfort over failure to achieve life's satisfactions and acceptable adjustment.

Concern about suicide potential should increase with Scale 2 elevation, especially when Scales 4, 7 or 8 are also elevated. These additional scale elevations are frequently associated with suicidal behavior. Several sources suggest that extra care should be taken with those patients who obtain Scale 2 elevation without accompanying subjective or behavioral depressive symptoms ("smiling depressives") as they represent a possible suicide risk. Low base rates for suicide behavior will result in a great number of false positives, though they can be tolerated more easily than false negatives.

Scale 2 is often interpreted as a prognostic index. A moderate elevation suggests awareness of personal problems and motivation to change this state of affairs. Low elevation suggests that this individual's problems have been recognized only by others and are ego-syntonic and of no significant personal concern. This either has characterological implications or suggests reality distortion. Extreme Scale 2 elevations may reflect a severe lack of psychic energy or withdrawal which would make traditional talk psychotherapy inappropriate prior to chemotherapy or ECT (look for elevation in Scale 0 and low Scale 9).

Moderate Scale 2 elevation in normal populations suggests overcontrol, a slow personal tempo and a tendency to worry. They are often described as socially distant and reserved, moody, modest and sensitive.

Scale 2 elevation tends to increase with age and likely reflects increasing responsibilities and worries, and decreasing energy and assets.

Individuals who obtain low Scale 2 elevations are often seen as alert, cheerful, spontaneous and self-confident. They often easily form social relations and display a lack of inhibition which may lead to negative feelings in others.

Interpretive hypotheses based on the elevation of Scale 2 can be found on page 19. Scale 2 elevation is reflected in paragraphs 18, 27, 67-69 and 97 of the automated program. Other paragraphs within subroutine Code and Configuration make prominent use of Scale 2 variance.

SCALE 3 (Hy/Hysteria)

Scale 3 (McKinley & Hathaway, 1944) contains 60 items which differentiated psychiatric patients with conversion symptoms from normals. This scale was constructed to identify those individuals who are predisposed to use conversion symptomatology as a means of solving conflicts or avoiding responsibilities when under stress.

Harris and Lingoes (1955) identified five subclusters of items in Scale 3:

I. Denial of social anxiety (Hy1/6 items):

I find it hard to make talk when I meet new people. (F)
My conduct is largely controlled by the customs of those about me.   (F)

II. Need for affection (Hy2/12 items):

It is safer to trust nobody. (F)
I can be friendly with people who do things which I consider wrong. (T)
It takes a lot of argument to convince most people of the truth. (F)

III. Lassitude-malaise (Hy3/15 items):

I have periods of such great restlessness that I cannot sit long in a chair. (T)
I wake up fresh and rested most mornings. (F)
During the past few years I have been well most of the time. (F)

IV. Somatic complaints (Hy4/17 items):

I frequently notice my hand shakes when I try to do something. (T)
I have few or no pains. (F)
I have never had a fainting spell. (F)

V. Inhibition of aggression (Hy5/7 items):

Often I can't understand why I have been so cross and grouchy. (F)
I like to read newspaper articles on crime. (F)

An attempt was made to drop the somatic items to decrease the overlap with Scale 1; these items were retained, however, as it was found that they were necessary to maintain scale validity. The contradiction represented by Scale 3 item content (somatic complaints, denial of inadequacy in self and other, sadness and lack of satisfaction) reflects the general aspects of hysteria. Within normals, these two components are negatively correlated, that is, elevations under 70-75 T reflect either physical complaints or unusual social well-being. High elevations obtained by psychiatric patients, on the other hand, reflect the expression of both contents: the hysteroid defense mechanisms, repression and denial, and somatization.

Scale 3 is not K-corrected as it contains a subtle correction component which is characteristic of the syndrome. Weiner (1948) separated these items into obvious and subtle scales:

Examples of obvious (32) items:

I seldom or never have dizzy spells. (F)
Much of the time my head seems to hurt all over. (T)
Often I feel as if there were a tight band about my head. (T)
I do not tire quickly. (F)
My eyesight is as good as it has been for years. (F)

Examples of subtle (28) items:

I enjoy detective or mystery stories. (F)
I think most people would lie to get ahead. (F)
I have often lost out on things because I couldn't make up my mind soon enough. (F)
I drink an unusually large amount of water everyday. (F)
What others think of me does not bother me. (F)

In a general population, high Scale 3 elevations are fairly common for women, though infrequent for men. Individuals who obtain Scale 3 elevation are seen as friendly, enthusiastic, easily accessible, and socially active. These characteristics may be accompanied by a certain amount of immaturity, suggestibility and egocentricity. Low Scale 3 elevation, in contrast, often suggests an individual who is conforming, relatively unadventurous and socially restricted.

Within a general medical context, patients who obtain significant Scale 3 elevation often display anxiety attacks, sudden episodes of tachycardia, palpitation and headaches. Home and marital maladjustment are frequently noted.

The interpretation of Scale 3 largely depends on the configural relation of Scale 3 with other scales. An initial finding (McKinley & Hathaway, 1944), for example, was that when Scale 1 was elevated above Scale 3, the clinical picture usually included diffuse physical complaints and clear psychological components. When Scale 3 was elevated above Scale 1, however, physical complaints often paralleled or accompanied actual physical syndromes; these individuals usually appeared psychologically normal.

Scale 3 elevation varies over time and reflects the temporal changes in the intensity of defense mechanisms which mirror changes in the environment and variation in levels of internal stress.

Clinically, Scales 1, 2, and 3 and their relation to each other have been found to suggest many clinically useful hypotheses. These scales have been labeled the neurotic triad.

Several characteristics are suggested by Scale 3 elevation when obtained by psychiatric patients:

(1) The prominent use of repression and denial which makes insight improbable.
(2) An extremely naive and self-centered approach to the world.
(3) Social relations characterized as manipulative, demanding, outgoing, visible, superficial and immature.
(3) A rigidity and defensiveness which suggest a poor prognosis.
(5) Counterindication for psychosis or acting out behavior.

Interpretive hypotheses based on the elevation of Scale 3 can be found on pages 19-20. This scale solely determines the selection of paragraphs 19, 28, and 70-72 from the automated program.

SCALE 4 (Pd/Psychopathic deviate)

This scale (McKinley & Hathaway, 1944) contains 50 items which reflect a primary dimension ranging from constricted conformity to the antisocial acting out of impulses. The criterion group mainly consisted of individuals who had been hospitalized for psychiatric evaluation at the request of the courts due to their long history

of delinquent actions. Scale 4 was developed as an index to measure the predisposition to display characterological features such as impulsivity, low frustration tolerance and poor social adjustment, and is a fairly stable trait scale.

Scale 4 content ranges widely. The Harris and Lingoes subclusters provide a good indication of scale content:

I. Familial discord (Pd1/11 items):

At times I have very much wanted to leave home. (T)
I have very few quarrels with members of my family. (F)
My parents and family find more fault with me than they should. (T)

II. Authority problems (Pd2/11 items):

I have never been in trouble with the law. (F)
In school I sometimes was sent to the principal for cutting up. (T)
I have never been in trouble because of my sex behavior. (F)

III. Social imperturbability (Pd3/12 items):

I find it hard to make talk when I meet new people. (F)
I wish I were not so shy. (F)

IV. Social alienation (Pd4A/18 items):

I am sure I get a raw deal from life. (T)
No one seems to understand me. (T)
If people had not had it in for me I would have been much more successful. (T)

V. Self-alienation (Pd4B/15 items):

My hardest battles are with myself. (T)
I have not lived the right kind of life. (T)
Much of the time I feel as if I have done something wrong or evil. (T)

Wiener (1948) identified a subset of subtle items in Scale 4. Examples of these 22 items include:

I have been disappointed in love. (T)
At times my thoughts have raced ahead faster than I could speak them. (F)
I am neither gaining nor losing weight. (F)
I liked school. (F)
I am against giving money to beggars. (F)

When prominent Scale 4 elevations are obtained in a psychiatric patient population, several characteristics may be indicated:

(1) An inability to express anger in a modulated fashion.
(2) Impulsive behavior and limited inner controls.
(3) Nonconforming, rebellious, dissatisfied individuals who may engage in antisocial and self-defeating behavior in spite of adequate intelligence and opportunity.
(4) Inability to anticipate the consequences of one's behavior or profit from experience (including punishment and psychotherapy).

(5) Interpersonal relations which are quickly formed but shallow and lacking in true intimacy.
(6) General problems with authority.
(7) A tendency to project blame for current difficulties which may take on a paranoid tinge.
(8) Acting-out tendencies which may be evidenced by alcoholism, sexual promiscuity, marital difficulties and conflict with the law.

When Scale 4 is elevated, though not part of the primary scale elevation, it at least often suggests that the pathology suggested by other scales will be manifested in action; that is, pathology is likely to be more visible.

Scale 4 is a common high-point among a normal male population. These elevations are higher for adolescents which reflects age-appropriate parental or societal conflict and still growing inner controls. High Scale 4 in adolescence may well, however, reflect delinquent trends.

High Scale 4 elevation in normals usually reflects a sociable, adventurous, individualistic, assertive and active orientation which makes for high social visibility. High Scale 4 women are often seen as tense, striving, active, and lacking in internal control.

A low elevation on Scale 4, in contrast, suggests males with low drive and narrow interests who are seen as conforming, conservative and dependable. Women who obtain similar low elevations may also be seen as balanced, good-tempered and as having home and family interests. Some suggest (Carson, 1969) these elevations reflect low levels of heterosexual aggressiveness, rigidity and overidentification with social status.

Interpretive hypotheses which reflect Scale 4 elevation can be found on page 20. Scale 4 determines the selection of interpretive paragraphs 20, 29, and 73-75 of the automated program and also plays a prominent role in several subroutine Code paragraphs.

SCALE 5 (Mf/Masculinity-Femininity)

This 60-item scale (Hathaway, 1956) was constructed by contrasting male homosexuals and men described as feminine by the Terman and Miles I Scale with an in-general male group. Of secondary importance was the ability of these items to differentiate males from females. Scale 5 was originally designed to measure masculinity-femininity, but is still far from being a pure measure of this dimension.

These items are fairly heterogeneous and over 50 percent only appear on Scale 5. They express psychologically obvious content and can easily be manipulated by a respondent to express the sex role identification he wishes to present for evaluation. Pepper and Strong (1958) judgmentally formed 5 content subscales from these items:

I. Personal and emotional sensitivity (Mf1/15 items):

I am entirely self-confident. (F)
I think that I feel more intensely than most people do. (T)

My feelings are not easily hurt. (F)
I have often felt that strangers were looking at me critically. (T)

II. Sexual identification (Mf2/6 items):

I am very strongly attracted by members of my own sex. (T)
I wish I were not bothered by thoughts about sex. (T)

III. Altruism (Mf3/9 items):

Most people make friends because friends are likely to be useful to them. (F)
I frequently find it necessary to stand up for what I think is right. (F)

IV. Feminine occupational identification (Mf4/17 items):

I like collecting flowers or growing house plants. (T)
I enjoy reading love stories. (T)
I used to keep a diary. (T)
I think I would like the work of a librarian. (T)

V. Denial of masculine occupations (Mf5/10 items):

I like mechanics magazines. (F)
I think I would like the work of a building contractor (F)
I very much like hunting. (F)

Scale 5 is a quite stable index. Since this scale, when applied to females, is the inversion of the T range for males, clear elevations suggest a non-identification with the stereotyped masculine or feminine role.

In a normal male population, Scale 5 elevation may suggest imagination, sensitivity, a tendency to worry and a wide range of cultural interests. These men tend to be relatively passive; some are clearly described as effeminate. They may be seen as inner-directed, clever, curious, and possessing good judgment and common sense. Well-educated males score higher than those with less educational attainment. Those who obtain low scores, on the other hand, tend to have traditional masculine interests, prefer action to contemplation and tend to lack originality. They typically have a narrow range of interests and are often seen as adventurous, easy-going and rather coarse.

Behavioral correlates in a normal female population appear rather limited for Scale 5. High Scale 5 females are described as adventurous, aggressive, competitive and confident. Such elevations suggest mechanical and scientific interests and possibly discomfort in accepting the traditional feminine role. Some Scale 5 elevation is expected in the teens and from women from atypical cultural backgrounds. Females who obtain low scores place a great deal of emphasis on feminine interests. They are often described as sensitive, modest and may display a masochistic acceptance of discomfort.

Within male psychiatric samples, the relation of Scale 5 to the rest of the profile is important. In general, a prominent elevation of Scale 5 by itself is such an inadequate estimate of tendencies toward overt or latent homosexu-

ality that it is practically useless for this purpose. [However, a recent study by Manosevitz (1971) suggests that a majority of well-educated homosexuals score above a T score of 70 while heterosexual men matched for educational level do not.] An accompanying elevation of Scale 4, which exceeds Scale 3, however, may increase the probability of acting out of homoerotic impulses when they are present (Singer, 1970). Scale 5 elevation usually reflects a basic passivity and dependency. Accordingly, MMPIs obtained during marital counseling often include a Scale 5 discrepancy between the profiles of husband and wife which reflects sexual adjustment difficulties. (This pattern consists of a high Scale 5 husband and a low Scale 5 wife.)

Low Scale 5, especially when Scale 4 is elevated, may suggest a chest-thumping caricature of compulsive masculinity in which efforts to appear masculine seem overdone and inflexible. Carson (1969) suggests that this represents an identity conflict in which the individual may question his own masculinity.

Scale 5 elevation in a female psychiatric patient suggests a competitive, rebellious, dominating individual. Low Scale 5 elevations occur with some frequency in this population. These women are often described as highly constricted, self-pitying, fault-finding individuals who seem unable to tolerate pleasant experiences. They are often very difficult and manipulative in therapy. The simultaneous elevation of Scale 4, and perhaps Scale 9, may suggest a very critical and demanding individual or concern about the acting-out of sexual impulses.

Interpretive hypotheses based on the elevation of Scale 5 can be found on pages 20-21. Paragraphs 89-93 of the automated program are determined by Scale 5 elevation.

SCALE 6 (Pa/Paranoia)

This scale (Hathaway, 1956) contains 40 items which characterized a heterogeneous group of psychiatric patients with prominent paranoid features. The expressed purpose of Scale 6 was to evaluate the clinical picture of paranoia, which includes delusional beliefs, ideas of reference, feelings of persecution, influence and grandeur, pervasive suspiciousness, interpersonal sensitivity and rigidity.

Scale 6 appears fairly stable in a normal population, but is sensitive to fluctuations in paranoid characteristics in individuals within a psychiatric population. Scale 6 is a good example of an actuarial scale; its items correlate moderately to strongly with the clinical syndrome but very little with each other. This scale represents a rather heterogeneous group of items which range from frankly psychotic content to the denial of ulterior motives in others. Harris and Lingoes found three content clusters within this scale:

I. Persecutory ideas (Pa1/17 items):

Someone has been trying to poison me. (T)
I am sure I am being talked about. (T)

9

I have no enemies who really wish to harm me. (F)
Someone has control over my mind. (T)
I believe I am being followed. (T)

II. Poignancy (Pa2/9 items):

I feel uneasy indoors. (T)
Even when I am with people I feel lonely much of the time. (T)
At times I hear so well it bothers me. (T)

III. Naivete (Pa3/9 items):

Most people inwardly dislike putting themselves out to help other people. (F)
Most people are honest chiefly through fear of being caught. (F)
I tend to be on my guard with people who are somewhat more friendly than I had expected. (F)

The addition of K did not improve this scale's validity. Wiener (1948) identified obvious and subtle subclusters of this scale:

Examples of obvious (23) items:

I believe I am being plotted against. (T)
People say insulting and vulgar things about me. (T)
I have certainly had more than my share of things to worry about. (T)
Someone has been trying to influence my mind. (T)

Examples of subtle (17) items:

My mother or father often made me obey when I thought it was unreasonable. (F)
The man who provides temptation by leaving valuable property unprotected is about as much to blame for its theft as the one who steals it. (F)
Something exciting will almost always pull me out of it when I am feeling low. (F)

There are limited consistent behavioral correlates of Scale 6 in a normal population. Those who obtain Scale 6 elevation are often seen as sensitive, emotional, soft-hearted and prone-to-worry. Correlates of low Scale 6 scores are not consistent; males are seen as cheerful, balanced and decisive as well as self-distrusting, conscienceless, self-centered and wary with narrow interests. Females who obtain similar elevations are seen as conventional, balanced, mature and reasonable.

Scale 6 has relatively poor ability to discriminate paranoid characteristics; perhaps this is due to the frankly paranoid and socially unacceptable content of many of the items. Marks and Seeman (1963), for example, have noted that only 25 percent of the paranoid subjects catalogued in the Hathaway and Meehl Atlas obtained Scale 6 elevation above a T of 70. Thirty percent of these paranoid patients, in fact, obtained no scores above 70 T. These facts support well the general position that Scale 6 elevation is a relatively good inclusion sign, but has no validity in terms of an exclusion criterion. That is, though Scale 6 elevation suggests paranoid characteristics, the absence of this elevation does not preclude the presence of these characteristics. In fact, psychiatric patients who obtain extremely low scores are often described as stubborn, evasive and overly cautious about the way in which they describe themselves. Low Scale 6 may indeed be a paranoid index. (See paragraph 21 of the automated program.) This is especially true of rather bright hospitalized patients who obtain very low "normal" profiles.

This scale in general taps the dynamics of the defense mechanism of projection. Moderate elevations suggest excessive interpersonal sensitivity, secretiveness and a tendency to blame others for one's difficulties. Distrust, brooding, resentment and indirect hostility may be present.

When high elevations are obtained, it is sometimes useful to examine the individual Scale 6 item responses. In this way it may be possible to differentiate general characterological elements from psychotic and delusional content. Configural analysis is often helpful here. High Scale 6 also suggests suspiciousness, fixed beliefs, and perhaps delusional content and other paranoid signs. These patients characteristically have poor rapport in therapy. They are seen in this context as rigid and intellectually argumentative.

Interpretive hypotheses suggested by the elevation of Scale 6 can be found on page 21. Scale 6 determines the selection of paragraphs 21, 30, and 76-78 of the automated interpretive program. This scale is used in subroutines Code and Configuration.

SCALE 7 (Pt/Psychasthenia)

Scale 7 (McKinley & Hathaway, 1942) contains 48 items which were characteristic of a rather small group of obsessive-compulsive neurotics and correlated highly with a preliminary scale. This second construction approach of internal consistency added item homogeneity which gives this scale a greater saturation of general maladjustment variance than most other scales. The criterion group was characterized by excessive doubt and indecision, unreasonable fears, compulsions and obsessions.

Scale items appear to reflect the underlying personality structure of these individuals: anxiety and dread, low self-confidence and self-esteem, excessive sensitivity, moodiness and general inefficiency, rather than specific fears and behaviors which occur with relative infrequency among psychiatric patients. Comrey (1958) factored intercorrelations among Scale 7 items and described the resulting clusters with these labels: neuroticism, anxiety, withdrawal, poor concentration, agitation, psychotic tendencies, denial of antisocial behavior and poor physical health.

These items are for the most part face valid and obvious. Because of this characteristic, a defensive response set readily affects Scale 7 elevation; this explains the addition of 1 K when the profile is K-corrected.

Examples of Scale 7 items include:

I feel anxiety about something or someone almost all of the time. (T)
I am inclined to take things hard. (T)
I seldom worry about my health. (F)
I am afraid of losing my mind. (T)
Life is a strain for me much of the time. (T)
Almost every day something happens to frighten me. (T)
I have several times given up doing a thing because I thought too little of my ability. (T)
Sometimes some unimportant thought will run through my mind and bother me for days. (T)

Scale 7 elevation in a normal population is often obtained by men described as dissatisfied, verbal, individualistic and high-strung. Similar women are characterized as sensitive, prone to worry, emotional, high-strung, dissatisfied and conscientious. Low elevations are obtained by men described as balanced, efficient and capable in living, warm, self-controlled and relaxed. Low Scale 7 women are described as cheerful, balanced, relaxed, alert, confident and placid.

This scale is highly related to conventional measures of neurotic tendency and is a general measure of discomfort: anxiety, self-doubt, guilt, worry and rumination. Scales 7 and 2 are sometimes called the "distress" scales and are often elevated together. Most psychiatric patients who express problems in living obtain some Scale 7 elevation. Scale 7 is the best single index of anxiety.

High elevations reflect the ineffective use of the defense mechanisms of intellectualization, rationalization, isolation and undoing in an attempt to reduce anxiety and tension. Successful obsessive-compulsive systems may not be reflected in significant Scale 7 elevation. Moderate elevations suggest a perfectionistic orientation and a tendency to worry over even small matters.

As with Scale 2, some elevation on Scale 7 is described as an index of favorable prognosis, as it indicates sufficient discomfort with the present internal situation to provide motivation for self-evaluation and change. Very high elevations may indicate levels of agitation which preclude talk therapy. Here preliminary chemotherapy may be necessary to allow the individual to enter into effective psychotherapy. Initial low Scale 7 or decreasing elevations of Scale 7 in profiles with a psychotic configuration (especially high Scales 6 and 8) suggest poor prognosis. These profile characteristics suggest limited motivation and/or acceptance of pathological processes.

Within a general medical context, Scale 7 elevation is obtained by patients who over-react; they show extreme concern over any medical problem. Rigidity, anxiety, fearfulness and agitation are often combined with cardiac, GI and GU concerns.

Interpretive hypotheses based on the elevation of Scale 7 can be found on page 21. This scale determines the selection of paragraphs 22, 31, and 79-81 from the automated program. Other paragraphs within subroutine Code and Configuration make prominent use of Scale 7 variance.

SCALE 8 (Sc/Schizophrenia)

This is the longest of the clinical scales (Hathaway, 1956): 78 items which differentiated a heterogeneous sample of schizophrenic patients from normals. More effort was made to improve the validity of this scale than for any other scale because Scale 8 elevation was often obtained by non-schizophrenic patients. Attempts to construct scales from more homogeneous subgroups of schizophrenics were not successful.

The pattern of schizophrenia is quite varied and includes many contradictory behavioral features. Many Scale 8 items reflect unusual thought processes, lack of deep interests and apathy, feelings of social alienation, poor family relations, peculiarities of perception and reduced efficiency characteristic of the schizophrenic process. This scale includes one of the largest subsets of items dealing with sexual matters. Some scale items deal with difficulties in concentration and impulse control, fears and worries and general inability to cope.

The Harris and Lingoes subclusters provide a good example of Scale 8 content:

IA. Social alienation (Sc1A/21 items):

I have never been in love with anyone. (T)
I dislike having people about me. (T)
I get all the sympathy I should. (F)
I enjoy children. (F)
My people treat me more like a child than a grown-up. (T)
I loved my mother. (F)

IB. Emotional alienation (Sc1B/11 items):

Most of the time I wish I were dead. (T)
Sometimes I enjoy hurting persons I love. (T)
I believe I am a condemned person. (T)

IIA. Lack of ego mastery, cognitive (Sc2A/10 items):

I often feel as if things were not real. (T)
I have strange and peculiar thoughts. (T)
There is something wrong with my mind. (T)

IIB. Lack of ego mastery, conative (Sc2B/14 items):

Most of the time I would rather sit and daydream than to do anything else. (T)
I like to visit places where I have never been before. (F)
I cannot keep my mind on one thing. (T)

IIC. Lack of ego mastery, defective inhibition (Sc2C/11 items):

I have had periods in which I carried on activities without knowing later what I had been doing. (T)

I am so touchy on some subjects that I can't talk about them. (T)

At times I have a strong urge to do something harmful or shocking. (T)

III. Bizarre sensory experience (Sc3/20 items):

Once a week or oftener I feel suddenly hot all over, without apparent cause. (T)

Sometimes my voice leaves me or changes even though I have no cold. (T)

Peculiar odors come to me at times. (T)

I do not often notice my ears ringing or buzzing. (F)

I hear strange things when I am alone. (T)

These items are mainly obvious. Only 16 of 78 items are unique to this scale. The limited initial validity of this scale prompted, in part, the development of the K Scale. The figures cited below (Hathaway, 1956) suggest that K increased Scale 8 validity:

	Percent Correctly Labeled	
	Schizophrenic	Normal
Scale 8	31%	95.5%
Scale 8 with K-correction	59%	98.0%

Scale 8 elevation in a normal population has suggested few indications of pathology. Various male samples have been described with adjectives such as verbal, enthusiastic, frank, kind, conscientious, individualistic, prone-to-worry, and self-dissatisfied. They are often seen as having wide interests, general aesthetic interests, are imaginative and perhaps inventive. Problems in handling aggression and difficulties with self-control have been noted. High Scale 8 females have been described as sensitive, kind, modest, courageous, shy, dissatisfied and high-strung.

Low Scale 8 males are seen in general as controlled and restrained; they are described as submissive, compliant, conservative, balanced, conventional, responsible, adaptable and accepting of authority. They have also been characterized as emphasizing success and achievement in an attempt to gain status, power or recognition. Low Scale 8 females in a normal population have been described as both friendly and alert.

Scale 8 is possibly the most complex MMPI scale. Though this scale is quite valuable in the diagnosis of psychotic processes, it is often interpreted much too narrowly. (This is a good example of the reason for identifying clinical scales by their numbers rather than by their names, which can be misleading.) In general, this scale seems to tap the dimensions of schizoid mentation, feelings of alienation and being different, misunderstood, isolated and inferior, difficulty in expressing hostility, withdrawal, difficulties in communication and the extent to which an individual becomes lost in need-fulfillment fantasies. These patients have fundamental and disturbing questions about their own identity and often lack essential socialization skills and talents.

Scale 8 reflects temporal variations in the degree of an individual's contact with the real world. This scale appears to measure a general dimension of ego intactness-ego deterioration, as well as, within normal limits, indications of the presence of creativity, individuality and imagination.

Scale 8 elevation is often found in profiles with many scales above 70 T. Scales F, 4, 6, 7 and 9 often appear in elevation with Scale 8.

Though most schizophrenics score above 70 T, scores above this elevation are not, on any grounds, a sufficient basis to label an individual schizophrenic. Elevations of this scale up to 90 T are often obtained by agitated neurotics, adolescent adjustment reactions, pre-psychotics, and pseudoneurotic schizophrenics.

Interpretive hypotheses based on Scale 8 elevation are found on pages 21-22. Paragraphs 23, 32 and 82-84 of the automated program are solely related to Scale 8 elevation. Scale 8 also affects paragraph selection in subroutine Code.

SCALE 9 (Ma/Hypomania)

This 46-item scale (McKinley & Hathaway, 1944) reflects the characteristics of psychiatric patients with diagnoses of hypomania and mild, acute mania. Patients with more severe symptoms of mania were not included as such patients typically are unable to concentrate sufficiently on the Inventory task. The criterion group patients were characterized by a transitory affective disorder which often included overactivity, elated but unstable mood, and a flight of ideas. Though patients with mild symptoms are not easily differentiated from ambitious and energetic normals, cyclical periods of euphoria, increased irritability, and unproductive activity may suggest this syndrome. Several authors have suggested that this pattern is a defense against depression and noted that these traits frequently occur in characterological syndromes.

Scale 9 items are quite heterogeneous, reflecting expansiveness, activity level and excitement. Other less face-valid items describe moral attitudes and family relations as well as somatic concerns. Harris and Lingoes identified four content clusters in Scale 9:

I. Amorality (Ma1/6 items):

I don't blame anyone for trying to grab everything he can get in this world. (T)

I do not blame a person for taking advantage of someone who lays himself open to it. (T)

II. Psychomotor acceleration (Ma2/11 items):

When I get bored, I like to stir up some excitement. (T)

At times I feel that I can make up my mind with unusually great ease. (T)

At times my thoughts have raced ahead faster than I could speak them. (T)

III. Imperturbability (Ma3/8 items):

I never worry about my looks. (T)

It is not hard for me to ask for help from my friends even though I cannot return the favor. (T)

IV. Ego inflation (Ma4/9 items):

I am an important person. (T)

I have been inspired to a program of life based on duty which I have since carefully followed. (T)

I have at times stood in the way of people who were trying to do something, not because it amounted to much, but because of the principle of the thing. (T)

Wiener (1948) divided this scale equally into obvious and subtle components:

Examples of obvious (23) items:

At times I have fits of laughing and crying that I cannot control. (T)

I have met problems so full of possibilities that I have been unable to make up my mind about them. (T)

I have never done anything dangerous for the thrill of it. (F)

I have often had to take orders from someone who did not know as much as I did. (T)

Once a week or more often, I become very excited (T)

Examples of subtle (23) items:

A person should try to understand his dreams and be guided by or take warning from them. (T)

I sometimes keep on at a thing until others lose their patience with me. (T)

I believe women ought to have as much sexual freedom as men. (F)

I am afraid when I look down from a high place. (F)

When in a group of people, I have trouble thinking of the right things to talk about. (F)

Scale 9 elevation among a normal male population suggests sociable, energetic, open and forward individuals who are often described as expressive, individualistic, adventurous, enthusiastic, impulsive and curious. They were often noted to enjoy alcohol, have interests in national and political matters, and were often seen as generous and affectionate. High Scale 9 females were described as frank, courageous and idealistic. Descriptors generally formed a picture of high energy: talkative, enthusiastic and versatile.

Low Scale 9 males have been described as reliable, practical, balanced, mature, conscientious, and as showing good judgment and common sense. This general image of emotional stability is also seen within a normal female population. These low Scale 9 women were described as mature, balanced, temperate, alert, adaptable, clear-thinking, reasonable, orderly and practical.

Scale 9 is often interpreted as a measure of general energy level at the time of testing. This scale reflects a continuum ranging from low energy and inertia through a range of optimism and energy. Higher elevations suggest hyperactivity while extreme elevations suggest manic excitement and agitation.

Many manic patients are too flighty and unstable to complete an MMPI on entering the hospital. Once they have stabilized, they may show no appreciable elevation on Scale 9 at all, or may even show low scores which reflect their exhaustion or the accumulated effect of tranquilizers.

T scores of 60-70 usually suggest a pleasant, outgoing, enthusiastic individual. They may be seen as restless and uninhibited and perhaps tense and hyperactive. Scores above 70 T in a psychiatric population suggest, with increasing elevation, problems of poor control, narcissism, distractability, and superficiality. Difficulties in interpersonal relations and aggressive impulses as well as amoral behavior have been noted.

Low scorers in this population are often seen as listless, apathetic and lacking in drive. They often lack both self-confidence and optimism. A very low elevation may suggest a significant depression even when Scale 2 is not markedly elevated. (See paragraph 86 of the automated program.)

Interpretive hypotheses which reflect Scale 9 elevation can be found on page 22. Scale 9 determines the selection of interpretive paragraphs 33A and 34A of the automated program and also appears in several subroutine Code paragraphs.

SCALE 0 (Si/Social Introversion)

This scale (Drake, 1946) contains 70 items which were selected by contrasting college students scoring at the extremes on the social introversion-extroversion scale of the Minnesota T-S-E Inventory. Scale 0 was found to correlate in the low 70's with the original T-S-E scale and appeared to be a measure of social participation (Drake & Thiede, 1948).

The introversion-extroversion conceptualization of social orientation has been found popular by both mental health professionals and laymen alike. The social introvert becomes uncomfortable in social interaction, withdraws from these situations and often has limited social skills. The extrovert, in contrast, seeks and derives satisfaction from social interaction.

Scale 0 provides a fairly stable index of comfort in interpersonal relations. Many (26 of 70) of these rather face-valid items are unique to this scale. These items tap both social isolation and general maladjustment and self-depreciation. Graham, Schroeder and Lilly (1971) labeled the six factors which resulted when these items were

analyzed: (1) inferiority-discomfort, (2) lack of affilia-tion, (3) low social excitement, (4) sensitivity, (5) inter-personal trust, and (6) physical somatic concern. Scale 0 items include:

> Whenever possible, I avoid being in a crowd.   (T)
> I love to go to dances.   (F)
> If given the chance, I would make a good leader of people.   (F)
> I enjoy the excitement of a crowd.   (F)
> I am a good mixer.   (F)
> In school, I found it very hard to talk before the class.   (T)
> People often disappoint me.   (T)
> I shrink from facing a crisis or difficulty.   (T)
> I am not unusually self-conscious.   (F)
> I have often felt that strangers were looking at me critically.   (T)

Scale 0 elevation among normal males suggests these descriptors: modest, inhibited, lacking in self-confidence, conforming, lacking in poise and social presence, submis-sive, insecure, conventional and sensitive. Females who obtain Scale 0 elevation are often described as modest, shy, sensitive, prone-to-worry and self-effacing.

Males in a normal population who receive low Scale 0 scores are described as sociable, expressive, exhibition-istic, socially competitive, verbally fluent, ascendant with others, persuasive, manipulative and opportunistic. They often emphasize success and achievement to obtain status and easily arouse hostility in others. Women who obtain similar elevations are described as sociable, enthusiastic, talkative, assertive and adventurous.

Significant elevation in psychiatric samples suggests introverted, shy, socially inept persons who prefer to avoid social activity. They are withdrawn, aloof and anxious in their relations with others. The rest of the profile may clarify this elevation, suggesting a schizoid adaptation, neurotic withdrawal and self-depreciation, depression or just a general introverted orientation.

Though low scores may suggest interpersonal warmth and sociability, extremely low scores may suggest a flightiness and superficiality in relations.

Interpretive statements based on the elevation of Scale 0 can be found on page 22. Scale 0 determines the selection of paragraphs 36 and 94-96 and is found in two-point Code 2-0/0-2 (paragraph 50).

MODERATOR VARIABLES

Age. Several investigators have studied the relation between absolute and relative scale elevation and age. Aaronson (1958) sorted 871 cases listed in the *Atlas* (1951) by high point code. He found that Scales 1 and 2 are common high-points in older clinical samples, while Scales 4, 7 and 8 are more commonly found high-points in younger patients. Calden and Hokanson (1959) found that the absolute elevation of Scales 1, 2 and 3 increased with age in a sample of hospitalized male tuberculosis patients. Swenson (1961) presented MMPI data obtained from 95 nonpsychiatric individuals over 59 years. He found that Scales 0, 1, 2 and 3 were the most frequent high-point scales. The most frequent high-point was Scale 0 for females and Scale 3 for males. Scale 9 was the most frequent low-point scale, followed by Scales 6 and 4. Gynther and Shimkunas (1966) studied age effects in 420 psychiatric profiles, finding that the absolute elevation of Scales 4, 6, 8 and 9 decreased with age. An evaluation of high-point codes suggested that Scales 1, 2 and 3 were most often the highest clinical scales in older patients, while Scales 4, 6, 8 and 9 were most often the highest clinical scales in younger patients. Postema and Schell (1967) added further support to these findings by noting that hospitalized VA patients over 60 produced profiles dominated by elevations on the neurotic triad, while younger patients in this population did not produce profiles with this characteristic.

The relation between code-type frequency and age is suggested by data presented by both Marks and Seeman (1963) and Lachar (1968). In the former study, codes 2-7, 3-1, 3-2-1 and 2-3-1 were associated with the oldest patient samples, while 8-9, 2-7-4, 4-8-2, and 4-9 were associated with the youngest. The latter study noted that 1-2/2-1, 2-3/3-2, 2-7/7-2 and 1-3/3-1 were associated with the oldest samples, while 8-9/9-8, 4-9/9-4, 4-6/6-4 and 4-8/8-4 formed the youngest samples. The similarity between these two studies is especially significant if one considers the differences which exist between the two populations described by Marks and Seeman (university hospital) and Lachar (state hospital).

In general, the left side of the profile increases absolutely or in relation to the rest of the profile with age, while the right segment of the profile decreases with age. The findings support clinical impressions of the aging process: decreased assertiveness and energy level (Scales 4 and 9), increased dysphoria and social withdrawal (Scales 2 and 0) as well as an increased proclivity toward somatization (Scales 1 and 3).

Sex. High-point occurance by sex is given by Webb (1971). These data are cited in Section II. Of prime concern to a psychologist faced with MMPI data is whether code-type correlates vary by sex. Two studies (Marks and Seeman, 1963; Gynther, 1972(a)) suggest that they do not for descriptors which are equally applicable to both sexes. Except for the elevation and interpretation of Scale 5, the variable of sex is more likely to determine the relative proportion of code-types rather than their specific interpretation in a majority of instances.

Race and culture. Of primary concern to the clinician who is evaluating a minority group patient is the accuracy of the application of MMPI norms and clinical data obtained from primarily white, middle class samples. Several investigators have studied black *non-psychiatric* samples (Hokanson & Calden, 1960; McDonald & Gynther, 1963; Butcher, Ball & Ray, 1964; Harrison & Kass, 1967; and Gynther, Fowler & Erdberg, 1971). They have consistently found scale differences in black-white comparisons, blacks often scoring higher on Scales L, F, 1, 8 and 9. The Gynther et al. (1971) study of 88 black residents of an isolated black southern community is especially revealing. The most frequent high-point scale was 8 and the second highest was 9 for males and 6 for females. The mean profile for this sample fits the 8-9/9-8 code. Codes 8-6 and 8-9 were the most frequent for males and 6-8, 8-6 and 8-9 were the most frequent two-point codes for females. Application of the Goldberg index (1965) to this sample classified 84 of 88 profiles as psychotic.

A review of black-white differences in psychiatric samples (Miller, Knapp & Daniels, 1968; Costello, Tiffany & Gier, 1972; and Gynther, 1972(b)) supports the above finding of higher Scales L, F, 1, 8, and 9 in the black samples. Miller et al. (1968) found that within a VA mental hygiene clinic sample Scale 8 was more frequently the high-point among blacks, while Scale 5 was more frequently the high-point among whites. Codes 2-7/7-2 and 4-5/5-4 appeared more frequently among whites, while 1-8/8-1 appeared more frequently among the blacks. Costello et al. (1972) studied profiles obtained from black psychiatric patients in a university hospital sample. They found blacks more often obtained high-points on Scales 6 and 8, while white controls more often obtained high-points on Scales 5 and 0. Scale 8 was more often elevated in the black sample, while Scale 7 was more often elevated in the white sample. Two-point codes 2-7 and 4-7 were more often obtained by whites, while codes 8-6 and 2-4 were more often obtained by blacks.

Though there are obvious differences in scale elevation and profile configuration between black and white samples, it is still not clear whether these differences reflect test error (i.e., differences in test-correlate relations) or actual differences which exist between these groups. Some studies present data on this issue: Miller et al. (1968) present data to suggest that 1-8/8-1 obtained from blacks in their study did not reflect somatic delusions. Gynther et al. (1971) definitely support the position that black profiles must be interpreted differently, as 8-9/9-8 correlates (pages 186-192) certainly are not pervasive in a normal population. Gynther (1972(b)) also noted data to support this position. Though most of his two-point code interpretations were based on white

15

patients, he attempted to develop a F > 25 description for blacks as sufficient data was available for this patient cluster. He found that correlates descriptive of white patients were *not* descriptive of black patients. In fact, F > 25 for black patients suggested quite different behavioral correlates. My experience with the automated interpretation project presented in Section III supports this conclusion. Though this data has not been systematically collected, the interpretation of psychotic profiles obtained from black patients were often rated as highly inaccurate.

In summary, *it is important to handle profiles obtained from black psychiatric patients (and perhaps other minority and cultural groups) with utmost care.* A conservative approach which takes into account the above and incorporates the maximum sources of other test, history and interview data is strongly suggested. The need for further study of code correlates by race or culture will lead to more accurate assessment of these groups as well as to less unintentional discrimination and inappropriate disposition.

Intellectual level. Gynther and Shimkunas (1966) present a study which generally supports the basic interpretations made above on the relation between intellectual level and scale elevation. Admission of "feminine" interests (Scale 5) is positively related to intelligence and education, while both L and F Scale elevation are negatively related to intellectual level.

INTERPRETIVE HYPOTHESES BY SINGLE SCALE ELEVATIONS FOR AN ADULT PSYCHIATRIC POPULATION

THE VALIDITY SCALES

SCALE L

Elevation

36-55 T No consistent significance is given.

56-63 T A significant need to appear in a favorable light and to give socially approved answers regarding self-control and moral values is suggested. These individuals are often seen as overly conventional and socially conforming. They are often unaware of the impact that their behavior may have on others.

64-69 T The use of repression and denial, lack of personal insight, excessive rigidity or conscious deception may be indicated. An intentional defensive response set is usually only indicated by L Scale elevation in individuals with limited education, below average intellectual level or histories of socioeconomic or cultural deprivation. Look for psychological naivete, marked evasiveness and over-evaluation of moral worth.

Over 69 T Consider, along with the above:
(1) In the majority of instances, the excessive use of repression and denial in a naive and insightless manner. Lack of flexibility in adaptation and a poor tolerance for stress and pressure is suggested. A naive, hysterical view of the world and self is common. Neurotic profile patterns and lower social class placement are frequent correlates.
(2) Exceedingly scrupulous and conscientious individuals. Evaluate history for support of these characteristics.
(3) A conscious attempt to "fake good." Look for accompanying "submerged profiles." Clinical scales usually fall within the subclinical range but the resultant profile may suggest pathology.
(4) Scale L elevation may in rare instances suggest "pathological lying" in a sociopath or manic clinical picture. Look for elevation of Scales 4 and 9.

SCALE F

Elevation

44-54 T (1) This person is responding to inventory items in a rational and pertinent manner. Normals relatively free of stress who maintain a good adjustment score in this range. Similar individuals are often described as conventional and as possessing narrow interests.
(2) Scores in this range occasionally reflect a defensive individual's attempts to conceal significant psychopathology, emotional tension and distress ("fake good"). Elevations on Scales L and K support this hypothesis.

55-69 T The majority of normative and clinical studies fall within this range. Such scores, especially in the upper part of the range, suggest an independence of thought and negativeness. Such persons are often seen as moody, changeable, dissatisfied, opinionated, restless and unstable. Various clusters of individuals obtain similar elevations:
(1) Acute neurotics and character disorders.
(2) Normal individuals who are rather unconventional or unusual in some sense. This range may reflect specific current problems in social situations.
(3) Intact, defensive psychotics. Look for K Scale elevation 55-65 T.
(4) Situational stress reactions.
(5) Adolescent norms reflect a great disparity between normal adolescents and normal adults in their self-disclosure tendency. For example, the Minnesota 16-year-old sample obtained a 2 standard deviation limit of raw score 20 (males) and raw score 16 (females) which corresponds in the adult normative sample to T values of 88 and 80, respectively. This points out the need to utilize adolescent norms when evaluating patients under 18 years. Appropriate tables appear in Appendix B. Look for the "late adolescents" between 18 and 21 + years and adolescent turmoil which is often reflected in F Scale elevation.

70-80 T Elevations above 70 T suggest an increasing probability of ego dysfunction, disinterest, lack of cooperation or misunderstanding.
(1) This range reflects the unusual problems and feelings characteristic of psychosis or severe neurosis.
(2) Unusual or markedly unconventional thinking may be present.
(3) Sullen, anti-social, rebellious personalities of the schizoid type.
(4) Severe self-depreciation.
(5) With F Scale in this range and neurotic and psychotic scales elevated look for borderline state.
(6) Note F-K Index for probability of exaggeration or dissimulation.

Over 80 T Interpret this profile with caution, especially when Scale F exceeds 90 T. Possible sources for F Scale elevation:
(1) Lack of cooperation in the evaluation process which results in a random, all true or all false response set. Random sorts produce F Scale scores within the range 26 through 38. Look at the following section on Validity Scale Configurations for prototypic L-F-K patterns and related clinical profiles.
(2) Lack of understanding due to poor vision, inadequate reading skills or psychotic confusion.
(3) Faking Bad. This possibility should always be evaluated when there is some set of circumstances which might make an individual wish to look sick or sicker than he really is. Examples of such circumstances include disability determination, pre-court evaluation and draft

evasion. Malingering intent is most readily determined from a combination of some known incentive and the F-K Index. Note the following material for discussion of the F-K Index and examples of "fake bad" clinical profiles.

(4) "Cry for help" profile. Look for an elevated profile in which the distress scales (2 & 7) are higher than elevated psychotic scales (6, 8 & 9). Here the individual is telling the examiner how bad off he is by admitting to all sorts of problems.

(5) If (1) through (4) can be excluded, overt psychosis or other serious psychopathology is suggested. Scales 6 and 8 are often elevated. Look for a thought disorder and assorted clinical symptoms. Here degree of elevation is indicative of intensity of disturbance.

SCALE K

Elevation

27-45 T Similar patients have a poor self-concept and are self-dissatisfied and lacking in skills which would lead to improvement in their status. They tend to be overly critical and are rather blunt in speech and manner. Low K Scale elevation often suggests deteriorated defenses if accompanied by F Scale higher than 65 T. Elevation of the right side of the clinical profile is usual.

Interpretations may vary with socioeconomic status:
(1) Lower social class and adolescents characteristically obtain low K Scale elevations which reflect openness and self-criticism. K Scale here may be more of a class characteristic than an individual difference. Level of pathology here is best estimated from F Scale and clinical profile.
(2) Upper and middle-class patients who are moderately to severely disturbed (often acute) and manifest low ego strength and inadequate defenses (F Scale usually above 65 T). Prognosis for treatment is usually poor.

(3) Evaluate F-K Index for possibility of fake-bad response set.

46-60 T The typical normal and many psychiatric patients score in this range (allowing for social class variation). A balance in self-disclosure and self-protection is indicated. These individuals are free and open in their self-descriptions and willing to admit to socially acceptable limitations. These elevations are often indicative of adaptability, good ego strength, and a positive self-image.

61-72 T These individuals tend to minimize and overlook faults in themselves, their families and their circumstances. Mild to moderate defensiveness (with increasing elevation) and lack of insight.
(1) College graduates and upper-middle class or lower-upper class individuals regularly obtain 55-65 T which is indicative of effective defenses. Over 65 T suggests a certain degree of prudence, circumspection and minimization of difficulties in living.
(2) Moderately to highly defensive normals who are not college educated nor of high social class.
(3) Neurotics with hysteroid characteristics who may be adequately defended. Other neurotic disturbances where defensive maneuvers are somewhat effective. In general, with the exception of hypochondriacs and hysterics, neurotics with well-functioning defenses do not show up for evaluation. It is only when there is a failure of the defenses with a consequent experience of anxiety and tension that the defenses become exaggerated and rigid. (Look for elevations on Scales 1 and 3.)

Over 72 T Severe defensiveness. Resistance to psychological evaluation and lack of personal insight are often characteristic. These individuals are rigid and inflexible and intolerant of the possibility of deviance in themselves or in the deviant attitudes and behavior of others. Rejection of the role of patient and poor response to treatment is often characteristic. See the K + profile type under "Indeterminant" Profiles, page 95.

THE CLINICAL SCALES

SCALE 1   (Hs/Hypochondriasis)

Elevation

21-49 T   Few body complaints and little concern about health is indicated. These individuals are often alert, capable, optimistic and effective in living.

50-59 T   Realistic concern about body functioning and the expression of few physical symptoms is suggested. Medical patients with specific physical symptoms typically obtain similar elevations.

60-74 T   The expression of a significant concern about body functioning is indicated. Diffuse, vague, and non-specific somatic complaints and concern about health are usually suggested, though more focalized symptoms may be indicated with higher elevations. Patients with physical pathology who score over 65 T tend to overemphasize or overreact to their difficulties and may, in fact, control unacceptable impulses through somatization defenses.

75-84 T   A prominent concern about physical integrity and the presence of a large number of somatic complaints is suggested. Somatization defenses in these individuals are not effective; they often plead for treatment while rejecting and derogating any assistance. A sour, complaining attitude and the indirect expression of hostility are often characteristic.

Over 84 T   Along with the above characteristics are probably a great number of chronic, fixed and organized somatic complaints and body preoccupations. Functional pain, fatigue and weakness often occur in individuals who may display symptoms for every organ system.

SCALE 2   (D/Depression)

Elevation

28-44 T   Probably cheerful, enthusiastic, optimistic, active, and outgoing (Look for low Scale 0). Some who score in this range display a lack of inhibition which arouses hostility in others.

45-59 T   Such elevations reflect a life perspective with an average balance of optimism and pessimism, energy and enthusiasm.

60-69 T   This individual is likely to be mildly depressed, worrying, and pessimistic. This mood state may be the result of transient situational pressures or reflect a more stable and pervasive characteristic.

70-79 T   This range suggests levels of depression which are clinically significant. Similar individuals tend to worry over even minor issues. Psychiatric patients often score in this range. The discomfort reflected by this elevation may provide the necessary motivation to suggest a favorable prognosis. If signs of depression are absent here and at higher elevations, evaluate patient for suicidal tendencies.

Over 79 T   Similar patients are severely depressed, worrying and pessimistic. Indecision and social withdrawal may be characteristic as well as anorexia and sleep disturbance. Feelings of inadequacy and self-depreciation may reach a delusional quality. At high elevations, psychomotor slowing and extreme apathy may be characteristic.

SCALE 3   (Hy/Hysteria)

Elevation

24-44 T   A denial of good interpersonal relations and a negative, cynical approach to people in general may be suggested. These individuals may be described as conforming and lacking in tact if not socially withdrawn. Elevation of Scale 0 supports this poor social skills/people-avoidance pattern.

45-59 T   No consistent significance is given.

60-69 T   Two general patterns occur frequently:
(1) If Scale 1 is similarly elevated, and Scale 2 is about 10 T less than Scales 1 and 3, well functioning hysterics are common. A tendency toward somatization during periods of stress is suggested.
(2) If Scale 3 exceeds Scale 1 by at least 10 T, the characteristics of a hysteroid personality are more likely prominent than are somatic symptoms. These individuals are often described as naive and self-centered; they need to see themselves in a favorable light and lack insight into their interpersonal relations.

70-75 T   Elevations above two sigma suggest immature, egocentric, suggestible and demanding individuals with hysteroid characteristics and repressive defenses.
Some general points to consider for elevations above 70 T:
(1) The ineffective use of repression may be suggested by (A) elevations on Scales 1 and/or 2, or (B) increasing elevation of Scale 3.
(2) Individuals who obtain a Scale 3 elevation above 75 T are rarely psychotic, regardless of other scale elevations.
(3) Scale 3 elevation may modify the interpretation of acting-out potential suggested by Scale 4. When Scale 3 exceeds Scale 4, this potential is likely to be either suppressed or to occur episodically in a blandly insightless fashion (See paragraphs 51, 51A and 51B, page 127 for example.)
(4) Increasing elevations on Scale 3 reflect increasing likelihood of the presence of strong dependency needs, social immaturity and an inability to handle the experience of hostility toward others. Strong demands for affection, support and attention are often expressed by unconscious stratagems.

76-85 T   In addition to the above, these characteristics are suggested:
A strong tendency to develop circumscribed conversion symptoms after extended periods of tension. Presenting complaints may include headache, backache, chest pains, abdominal distress, weakness and dizziness, and fainting. These symptoms *may* be based on some actual organic

pathology. A long history of insecurity, immaturity and a well-established tendency to physical complaint may be characteristic.

Over 85 T Individuals who are incredibly immature, egocentric and demanding, and possess an amazing capacity for repression and lack of insight often score in this range. Fixed notions as to the organic bases for symptoms are likely. Somatic symptoms may not fit patterns of actual organic pathology. Symptoms are often chronic and adhered to with great rigidity.

SCALE 4 (Pd/Psychopathic deviate)

Elevation

20-44 T Suggests conventional and conforming individuals who may be seen as passive and non-assertive. They may be seen as moralistic and may possess a narrow range of interests.

45-59 T Characteristics of over-control and restraint are less likely. A reasonable level of conformity to social regulations can be expected.

60-69 T Suggests a mildly independent and non-conforming individual, though impulsivity and grossly inappropriate expression of feelings may not be present. They are often energetic and active. A history of minor difficulties with societal limits and expectations may occur.

70-79 T Such individuals are often seen as rebellious, resentful and non-conforming. A limited frustration tolerance and dissatisfaction with current social adjustment is likely. Impulsivity and acting-out tendencies are generalized or appear in the behavioral areas indicated by other scale elevations. These individuals often form relationships which are characterized as shallow and superficial. A history of, as well as current involvement in, conflicts with society may be present.

In Bright Average and above, and college-educated groups, the more malignant aspects of this description may be modified by intellectual ability. An easy manner and good social techniques in casual ties are suggested. In general, high intellect is a contraindication of impulse control deficit. When such individuals do act-out, however, they are more successful at evading detection and censure.

Over 79 T In addition to the above, prominent high elevations may suggest the classical picture of the psychopath. Poor social judgment, inability to profit from experience, antisocial behavior, and significant conflict with authority figures may be indicated. Such individuals usually only care about others to the extent that they may be used to further their personal ends.

SCALE 5 (Mf/Masculinity-femininity)

Elevation

MALES

26-40 T Suggests an emphasis on masculinity. These men prefer action to contemplation, lack originality and have a rather narrow range of interests. They may be seen as easygoing, adventurous and rather coarse. The addition of Scale 4 elevation suggests a chest-thumping, aggressive caricature of a "real he-man." Here an over-emphasis on physical strength and athletic prowess is suggested.

41-59 T Such scores reflect an average middle class male vocational and avocational interest pattern.

60-69 T Aesthetic interest patterns, imagination, sensitivity and a deviation from the culturally stereotyped masculine interest pattern are suggested. Similar elevations in high Scale 1 profiles emphasize passivity. (Here Scale 4 is usually low.)

Elevations over 65 T are clarified by additional demographic and clinical data. College or seminary students and the college educated most frequently obtain elevations in this range as well as those individuals in literary and artistic vocations.

70-79 T In general, such elevations suggest an intelligent, imaginative, sensitive and prone-to-worry individual with a wide range of interests. A basic passivity is often indicated.

On occasion, a male who over-emphasizes his sexual and athletic prowess may obtain such elevations. In such cases, Scale 5 elevation may suggest a conflict in sexual identity and a possible reaction formation against passivity. In other individuals this passivity is overt and ego-syntonic. Such men are often unable to direct and control their own lives and often present marital problems because they are unable to satisfy the needs of their marriage partners.

Over 79 T A fussy, effeminate and extremely passive and submissive orientation is suggested. Strong artistic interests may be present. Conflict with sexual identification and homoerotic trends may be suggested; overt homosexuality becomes a *possibility*, especially if Scale 4 exceeds 70 T.

FEMALES

20-40 T Such elevations are often obtained by passive, submissive, yielding women. They are often highly constricted, self-pitying and fault-finding individuals. Low Scale 5 is often associated with neurotic triad elevation. When Scale 4 elevation accompanies Scale 5 in this range, concern with possible acting-out of sexual impulses becomes likely.

41-55 T An average middle-class female vocational and avocational interest pattern is suggested. Scale 5 is often the low-point scale in profiles obtained from females.

56-65 T Such elevations may suggest a rather active, assertive and competitive interactional approach, especially with scores above 60 T.

Over 65 T These women are often confident, spontaneous and somewhat uninhibited. They are often found in occupations and activities which are traditionally masculine. These women may be revolting against the traditional female role and may feel uncomfortable when placed in reciprocal heterosexual situations. Dominant, aggressive and tough become increasingly likely characteristics with increasing elevations, especially if Scale 4 is elevated. Scale 5 is rarely a high-point in profiles obtained from females.

SCALE 6 (Pa/Paranoia)

Elevation

27-44 T These individuals are often described as stubborn, touchy, and difficult. Over-sensitivity and interpersonal antagonism may be present.

Note: Extremely low scores, especially when the profile low-point, often indicate a well-developed suspiciousness which leads to denial of paranoid personality features. These profiles are often obtained from individuals with a high probability of psychopathology but essentially normal MMPI profiles. Such patients, in contrast to high-scorers, are usually distinguished by their cautiousness, suspiciousness, distrust and denial, and are better put together in their relations with others. They are better able to judge what constitutes socially acceptable self-descriptions than are those patients who obtain high Scale 6 elevations. These patients may have the same behavioral characteristics as the high Scale 6 patient.

45-59 T Scores in this range suggest adequate regard and consideration for others, a flexible approach and no undue sensitivity. Individuals who score in the upper segment of this range (55-59 T) have been described as aware, sensitive and discerning.

60-69 T These elevations suggest the increasing probability of over-sensitivity, rigidity and feelings of being limited and pressed by social and vocational aspects of one's life space. Outright suspiciousness, distrust, brooding and resentment over real and imagined wrongs may be present. These individuals are often very effective in expressing hostility in an indirect fashion.

70-79 T Projection of blame and hostility may be a prominent feature. These individuals are often also described as rigid, stubborn, touchy, difficult and over-sensitive. Their defenses cause them to misperceive many social stimuli. Clear paranoid features may be evident.

Over 79 T Within this range a differentiation should be made between more characterological features and frankly delusional elements through clinical exam and examinations of individual Scale 6 item responses. If the profile is valid, a disabling level of pathology may be present. In addition to the above, these patients are often described as presenting ideas of reference and feelings of persecution and maltreatment. (Individuals in an actual bind who are rather naive may, though rarely, obtain a high Scale 6 elevation.) The concurrent elevation of Scale 4 "activates" Scale 6 characteristics and increases the probability of more overt, direct and intense expression of anger and resentment.

SCALE 7 (Pt/Psychasthenia)

Elevation

20-44 T Self-confidence, the absence of worries and a relaxed attitude toward responsibilities are suggested. Such elevations are infrequent in clinical populations, especially those who are self-referred.

45-59 T These individuals usually possess an adequate capacity for the organization of work and living without undue worry and self-doubt.

60-74 T Such elevations suggest conscientious, perfectionistic, orderly and self-critical individuals who tend to worry over minor problems. Increasing elevations above 60 T indicate the increasing probability of significant anxiety, indecision and tension. The inefficient though prominent use of rationalization and intellectualization becomes more likely with increasing elevation above 70 T.

75-84 T In addition to the above, these patients are often described as religious, moralistic, worrisome, apprehensive, rigid and meticulous. They are often intensely dissatisfied with their life and particularly their social relations. Moderate to severe levels of anxiety and tension may make routine life tasks difficult. Rule out obsessions, compulsions and phobias.

Over 84 T High elevations suggest agitated rumination, fearfulness and the likelihood of fixed obsessions, compulsions or phobias. Disabling guilt feelings may be present. Severe levels of anxiety and tension may make even simple routine life tasks impossible. The clear use of intellectualization, isolation and rationalization presents no relief; constant rehashing of problems and their possible solutions leads only to the continuation of their present misery.

SCALE 8 (Sc/Schizophrenia)

Elevation

21-44 T Such elevations suggest interest in people and practical matters. These individuals are often described as conventional, accepting of authority, concrete, controlled and unimaginative.

45-59 T Such individuals are likely to display a normal combination of practical and theoretical interests.

60-74 T Statements made within this range are varied and should be selected taking into consideration the total profile and configuration:

(1) At the lower end of this range and also in fairly benign or neurotic profiles, such elevations often suggest that such persons tend toward abstract interests to the neglect of interest in people and practical matters. These individuals may be creative and fairly imaginative in their approach to tasks. They may be seen by others as fairly aloof and uninvolved, especially if Scale 0 is elevated. A good number of adolescents who are seen for evaluation obtain such elevations.

(2) In the 65-75 T range, it is often difficult to judge whether general alienation or blatant psychotic content is being endorsed. Elevation on Scales F and 6 support the latter. Here it is often useful to evaluate individual scale items.

(3) Moderate elevations, especially if other psychotic signs are present (high Scales F, 4, 6, 9, depressed neurotic scales) suggest a schizoid social adaptation and possibly the presence of rather unique, if not unusual, ways of looking at the world.

Over 74 T

(1) Most individuals who obtain such elevations show, at minimum, a schizoid mentation; they may appear rather unusual, unconventional and eccentric to acquaintances but may be able to maintain an adequate social and vocational adjustment. The above is especially likely in more benign clinical profiles.

(2) These patients are often seen as socially introverted; they relate poorly and tend to escape from reality pressure and their own unacceptable impulses into need-fulfillment fantasies. Such individuals are often at a loss to know what is expected of them in even the simplest of interpersonal situations.

(3) Increasing elevations, in valid profiles, suggest with increasing likelihood the presence of a thought disorder, confusion and strange thoughts, beliefs and actions.

(4) If F-K exceeds 12, rule out malingering, clear signs of secondary gain, and a "cry for help" profile.

SCALE 9 (Ma/Hypomania)

Elevation

21-44 T Scores in this range are typical for older (65+) individuals, though such elevations usually reflect a low energy and activity level for others. They are often seen as listless, apathetic, low in drive and difficult to motivate. Hospitalized patients who are taking massive doses of tranquilizers often score in this range.

Low scores, especially under 40 T, suggest depression even if there is only slight Scale 2 elevation. Moderate or higher Scale 2 elevation here suggests apathy, phlegmatism and inertia.

45-59 T Normal energy and activity level are suggested.

60-69 T These individuals are often seen as pleasant, energetic, enthusiastic, sociable and have a pleasant outgoing temperament and broad interests. They are pretty happy with the way they are: optimism, independence and self-confidence are suggested. (Look for relatively low scores on Scales 2 and 0.)

In the 65-75 T range, it is difficult to differentiate by profile data alone the ambitious, energetic individual who is full of plans and leads a productive life, and the hypomanic who is ineffective in everyday activities due to hyperactivity of thought and action.

70-85 T With increasing elevation, there is an increasing probability of maladaptive hyperactivity and agitation, and an insufficient capacity for delay which is often accompanied by irritability and a ready anger at minor obstacles and frustrations. Such individuals are often seen as restless, impulsive and as having scattered interests and energies. These individuals often form quick, superficial relations and manifest intense but short-lived enthusiasm for their various plans and undertakings.

Over 85 T Manic excitement or agitation may be indicated, depending on profile configuration. Such persons are often expansive, distractible, unpredictable and may show hyperactivity (such as pacing) and flight of ideas. Exaggerated feelings of self-worth and self-importance are not uncommon.

SCALE 0 (Si/Social introversion)

Elevation

25-44 T Such elevations suggest warm, sociable, outgoing and rather gregarious individuals. Very low scores (25-39 T) are suggestive of such persons who may be adept at making positive social contact with many people, but operate on a superficial and perhaps rather insincere level. Social dependency and a high need for social approval may be indicated.

45-59 T A capacity to maintain rewarding social relations is suggested.

60-69 T Similar individuals are likely to be reserved in unfamiliar social situations and hard to "get to know." Scores above 64 T suggest the descriptors shy, timid and retiring.

Over 69 T Socially introverted, shy and socially inept individuals often score in this range. Such persons tend to be rather withdrawn, aloof and anxious in their social interactions. Worry, lack of confidence, moodiness and neurotic traits also occur with frequency. (Look for elevation on Scales 2, 7, and 8.)

II CONFIGURAL PROFILE INTERPRETATION

This section provides an introduction to some of the issues involved in profile classification and interpretation. Coding, configural interpretation and the effect of base rates are discussed in some detail.

The majority of this section covers a compendium of code-type interpretations. The major sources of these interpretations are discussed first and this discussion is followed by a numerical index of code types. Because this section allows easy location of relevant interpretive data, the reader may find it to be the most valuable portion of this work.

The material on validity scale configuration and the issue of malingering are discussed next. These data are presented here rather than in Section I since in a majority of situations the validity scales are considered in combination before profile configuration interpretation is attempted. The eight prototypic L-F-K patterns presented cover all general combinations of clinical interest.

The remainder, and majority, of this section covers code-type interpretations. All code-types are placed in numerical order in the diagnostic category with which they are the most associated, e.g., "neurotic," "characterological," "psychotic," or "indeterminate." The reference population is also noted as well as the source of interpretation, whenever possible. This order of subject matter was determined to be the most versatile over the past three years. Students can read through a section and begin to grasp the concept of "families of profiles/ codes" in terms of similarities of descriptors. The practicing clinician can consult the Index and then evaluate interpretations, finding the best match in terms of reference group to his patient. Major interpretive paragraphs of the automated program (Section III) are also referenced for easy use.

CODING

The MMPI code is the numerical summary notation which presents the basic characteristics of the validity and clinical scales. As the scale numbers are arranged in decreasing elevation, the first two or three numbers indicate the highpoint code, especially if these scales exceed 69 T. The code allows reconstruction of the profile within 5 T for each scale. This reconstruction is easily accomplished by placing each scale at the midpoint of its elevation range.

The procedure outlined below is essentially the Welsh Extended Code (Welsh, 1948). My experience, however, has suggested a compromise between the original Hathaway and the Welsh approach to validity scale notation. This approach retains the profile order of Scales L, F and K as in the Hathaway Code (Dahlstrom, Welsh & Dahlstrom, 1972) while substituting elevation symbols for raw scores, as in the Welsh Code.

CODING DIRECTIONS:

(1) Arrange the ten clinical scales in order of descending elevation.

(2) Place the elevation symbol after those scale numbers which fall within that 10 T-point range:

range	elevation symbol
Over 99 T	**
90 - 99 T	*
80 - 89 T	"
70 - 79 T	'
60 - 69	—
50 - 59	/
40 - 49	:
30 - 39	#
Under 30 T	no symbol

(3) Place L, F, K (symbols) at the end of this code, each followed by the appropriate elevation symbol.

(4) Underline all clinical scale numbers which are within one T-score of each other.

(5) Coding Example:

```
scale 1 2  3  4  5  6  7  8   9  0  L  F  K
T     45 89 62 64 60 67 96 103 65 70 30 80 45
```

Code: 8**7*2"0'69435-1: L#F"K:

(6) The code is often placed at the beginning of a solitary MMPI interpretation or within the interpretation of a test battery preceeding the MMPI interpretation.

Format:

MMPI interpretation: (8**7*2"0'69435-1: L#F"K:)

CONFIGURAL INTERPRETATION

The three broad profile characteristics reflected in MMPI interpretation are (1) elevation, (2) shape and (3) scatter.

Elevation. Interpretations based on absolute scale elevation reflect the *principle of intensity*. The higher the elevation of a given scale, the greater the likelihood that the patient resembles those on which the scale was constructed. Also, the elevation of a scale indicates the severity or intensity of the "problem" that is represented by that scale. The previous section (pages 17-22) on Interpretive Hypotheses by Single Scale Elevations clearly illustrates the principle of intensity.

Interpretation by absolute scale elevation was an early approach to profile interpretation. The principle of intensity appeared to have some merit for neurotic configurations but did not for psychotic codes. The automated screening program used at the Mayo Clinic is primarily based on single scale elevation characteristics (Marks & Seeman, 1963, pp. 307-311). Such an approach does not take into account the modifications suggested by other scale elevations and may, indeed, result in an interpretation with blatant contradictions.

Shape. The MMPI code is basically a notation of relative scale elevation. The *principle of dominance* suggests that scales which achieve the highest elevation both (1) represent those traits most characteristic of a given patient and (2) modify the interpretation of other scale elevations. The function of this principle is clearly demonstrated throughout the following material: "profile types" defined by total profile characteristics, high-point codes which classify profiles according to single, pairs or triads of highest profile scales (usually those over 69 T) as well as interpretations associated with validity scale shapes. The utility of the principle of dominance is clearly illustrated in the richness and consistency of the interpretations which are associated with profile shape.

Scatter. Scatter is a little more difficult to define and utilize. It basically refers to the amount of elevation variance. In rather simplistic terms, one can suggest that increased scatter is associated with increased ease of profile classification. For example, knowing that Scales 2 and 4 are profile high-points does not as clearly classify this protocol as would be the case if Scales 2 and 4 are also at least 10 T above all other clinical scales and therefor form a *distinct* pattern. Conversely, constricted scatter decreases the ease of profile classification and may decrease the level of certainty a clinician places on his final interpretations.

Example of Configural Interpretation: The following profiles illustrate several interpretive issues. They were obtained from a 26-year-old married female with 15 years of education. The first (- -) was obtained as part of a voluntary evaluation in an outpatient psychiatric clinic, the second (—) approximately one month later during a period of hospitalization:

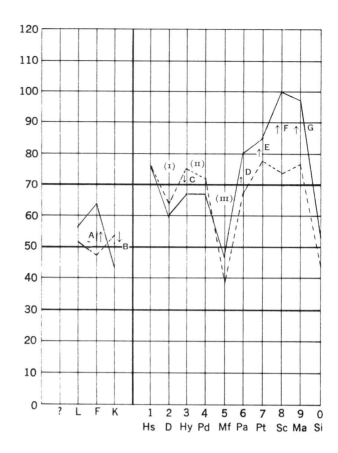

1st Administration (- -). The validity configuration suggests that the inventory task was completed in an appropriate fashion. Scales L and K suggest some ego strength and circumspection about expressing blatant deviancy. Though this is technically a 7-9/9-7 profile, other scales (1 and 3) obtain similar elevations, while Scales 4 and 8 almost reach the same level. The 1-2-3 configuration (I) suggests a tendency to somatize when under stress. The relation between Scales 3 and 4 (II) suggests inhibition of acting out behavior, and the Scale 3 elevation is contraindicative of psychotic behavior. The 4-5-6 configuration (III) suggests indirect expression of hostility. Scales 7 and 9 occur as highpoints in outpatient females once in 200 cases (Webb, 1970). This scale configuration suggests the presence of anxiety, tension and worry (Scale 7) as well as restlessness, agitation and a heightened energy level (Scale 9). Though this code may be suggestive of manic-depressive symptoms, this rare code definitely would suggest careful evaluation and continual observation as well as possible chemotherapy to reduce tension and anxiety.

2nd Administration (—). The validity configuration suggests a change in response style characterized by an increase in admission of symptoms and deviant traits (A) as well as decreased defensiveness and ego strength (B). The clinical configuration can easily be classified as an 8-9/9-8 profile due to the relative elevation of these scales and the resultant increased scatter. This profile fits the rules for the Marks & Seeman 8-9/9-8 Profile Type. Profile Type correlates suggest the acute onset of a syndrome which includes the psychotic characteristics

of a thought disorder, withdrawal and decreased efficiency and reality testing. A scale-by-scale comparison of the clinical profiles supports the 8-9/9-8 code interpretation: a Scale 3 decrease (C) increases the likelihood of acting out behavior. The general elevation of the right side of the profile suggests the increased likelihood of paranoid characteristics and mentation (D), tension and anxiety (E), thought disorder and alienation (F) and heightened activity level, restlessness, hyperactivity and manic symptoms (G).

These interpretations are well supported by clinical data. Initial clinic contact was precipitated by increasing feelings of discomfort and dissatisfaction. A history of tension headaches was present. The patient was hospitalized as the result of an acute manic episode (her first) which included hyperactivity, grandiosity, religiosity and a general activity level and irritability which made management extremely difficult. A loosely knit delusional system was evident during the brief acute phase which subsided rapidly with chemotherapy.

BASE RATES

A clinician's accurate interpretation of MMPI profiles is largely influenced by his knowledge of the distribution of (1) test characteristics, (2) patient characteristics and (3) referral processes present in the population he studies.

Test characteristics. A knowledge of the relative frequency of profile characteristics, such as code-types, *in a given setting*, has the value of informing the clinician of the interpretive tasks he is most likely to face. It may well be that a dozen or so two-point codes will account for the majority of profile patterns. These codes can then be studied in detail and the accuracy of various interpretations can be evaluated in some systematic fashion.

In certain settings a specific profile code, such as 4-9/9-4 in correctional or drug rehabilitation facilities, will appear with such a frequency that identifiable subclusters of three- or four-point codes may be quite easily studied. Similarly, an infrequent profile may be associated with infrequent characteristics or may suggest the need for greater-than-usual scrutiny of psychometric data.

Patient characteristics. The degree to which one can accurately infer a given characteristic from a psychometric instrument is related to the frequency to which this characteristic occurs. That is, it is difficult to establish reliable psychometric-criterion relationships for an infrequently occurring criterion. On the other hand, knowledge of criterion base rates for a given population may greatly modify more traditional interpretations of profile data. This is especially true in those cases in which the traditional interpretation would imply extremely infrequent descriptors. Examples of this include a within-normal-limits admission profile obtained from a state hospital patient or a 4-9 profile over 80 T obtained from a medical student during a routine group administration. The usually accepted interpretation of the former as suggesting the absence of psychological problems and the latter as reflecting psychopathic, characterological de-

fects will not likely be accepted as these descriptors occur infrequently in these populations. Such data are more likely to be interpreted as a test "miss" in the former case, while the 4-9 profile would best be interpreted as reflecting an individual who is adventurous, energetic, active and socially facile.

Referral processes. The accuracy of traditional MMPI interpretations relies upon the previous functioning of certain societal referral and selection pressures. The referral process increases the probability that certain patient characteristics will be observed in a given population. For example, a recent study by the author of the entering freshman class of a military academy revealed many spike 4, spike 9 and 4-9/9-4 profiles. A study of the social histories of these young men did not in any way support the traditional interpretations of these profile configurations. This is because the traditional interpretation of these patterns assumes that the behaviors of those individuals who obtain such patterns have been seen as deviant by some societal agency which subsequently refers them for a psychiatric evaluation. That is, the referral process acts as a sieve to increase the likelihood of certain pathology in the population studied and hence decreases the rate of false positive errors in interpretation of the resulting psychometric data.

Another example of the role of referral processes is the correct identification of false negatives. A case in point would be the interpretation of within-normal-limits admission profiles in a given psychiatric unit. If all patients receive a careful evaluation by professional staff before admission, such profiles would most likely be correctly identified as test misses. A high L and/or K would support an interpretation of defensiveness. The 60-70 T elevations of such profiles are also more likely to be interpreted, or perhaps "over-interpreted," in contrast to profiles obtained in a screening situation. On the other hand, a within-normal-limits admission profile obtained in a setting with a variety of loosely defined referral sources may, indeed, correctly suggest an inappropriate admission.

GENERAL ISSUES OF INTERPRETATION

1. *Use of auxiliary data.* A generally accepted approach to profile interpretation is first to evaluate the protocol *blindly*; that is, the clinician takes into account only setting of evaluation, sex, age, education and marital status, collects all relevant, interpretive hypotheses and integrates them. This interpretation is then followed by a further analysis which includes referral data and any available clinical material. Here the clinician attempts to integrate all relevant data and respond to specific questions.

Psychologists differ to the extent to which they separate these two interpretive phases. Some strictly present a two section interpretation, while others present only an integrated report which combines normative data and individual application. The specific approach is not really that important, though it is crucial for the clinician to *clearly recognize the sources of his interpretations.* If profile interpretation is synonymous with feedback of referral data, the product may appear very accurate but be of no real value.

2. *Reference group.* Most traditional interpretations assume that the person to be evaluated is self-referred or other-referred to a mental health facility for existing psychological problems. Most interpretive data has been obtained from adult, Caucasian, lower- to middle-class patients seen in VA and teaching hospital settings. MMPI profiles obtained from patients who deviate significantly from these reference groups, or more specifically, the reference group noted by a specific interpretation, should be interpreted with caution using all other available data. Examples of such patients include those with organic brain syndromes referred from neurology or neurosurgery, patients from atypical cultural backgrounds such as blacks and foreign nationals, and adolescents.

3. *Rote memorization.* One distinct advantage of the nature of MMPI interpretive data is the systematic fashion in which it is organized in relation to the profile code or highpoint. Rote memorization of the wealth of interpretive data available in the literature is not a necessary interpretive skill. Even the most experienced clinicians frequently refer to references and atlases as interpretive aides. Differentiation of the experienced from the inexperienced occurs in his grasp of applications and limitations of this psychometric instrument. The experienced clinician can separate those profiles which are easily interpreted in his setting with accuracy from those which pose interpretive questions, and knows where to look for help in dealing with these difficult profiles.

4. *Professional responsibility.* The apparently simple format of the MMPI leads some inexperienced clinicians to simplistic absolute judgments which are totally inappropriate. An example in point would be the interpretation of the profiles presented in Figure 7 (page 37) as indicative of paranoid schizophrenia. MMPI interpretation requires the same level of professional integrity, responsibility and confidentiality as does any assessment procedure. The ease of administration and scoring and the recent appearance of automated interpretation schemes make these issues even more crucial. These test characteristics and interpretation systems increase the availability of such interpretations and, though they help meet a manpower need, clearly increase the opportunities for their improper use. This is especially true as these interpretations are, for the most part, relatively *blind* — they do not take into account demographic variables, local base rates or referral questions and are therefore more open to error and inappropriate application by inexperienced clinicians.

MAJOR SOURCES OF INTERPRETATIVE DATA

1. Dahlstrom, Welsh and Dahlstrom (1972) present in their chapter on configurations a composite of general clinical and research data on frequent two-point codes. This monograph, the *MMPI Handbook,* is the most comprehensive work available on this personality inventory. This volume contains invaluable material on all useful scales and interpretive procedures for the MMPI. It is a "must" for all clinicians who are seriously interested in MMPI interpretation.

2. Carson (1969) presents in J. N. Butcher's monograph his Interpretive Manual to the MMPI. This author presents a synthesis of his experience and that of C. A. Cuadra and C. F. Reed. This manual presents fundamental general interpretations for the clinical student whose experience with the test in a clinical setting is in the beginning stages. The majority of the two- and three-point interpretations found in this manual are presented below.

3. Marks and Seeman (1963) were the first to answer Meehl's (1956) challenge to construct an actuarial personality "cookbook." This effort resulted in descriptions of psychiatric patients based on a set of independently defined profiles. These 16 profiles identified 78 percent of the voluntary, adult, university hospital sample. Though the majority of patients studied were female, these investigators found that the descriptive correlates did not differ by sex for any of these profiles. They furthermore suggest that the descriptors presented are equally applicable to male and female patients. The descriptions presented are primarily based on the five most similar Q-sorts obtained on female psychiatric patients who met the rules for a given profile type.

Application. Marks and Seeman suggest that F Scale in excess of 25 excludes a given profile from this classification system. Though the mean profile may provide visual configural properties to aid in profile classification, the fulfillment of the profile rules should take priority over a given profile's similarity to the mean profile. The first rule for each code type must always be met, though the descriptive material may apply to profiles in which one or perhaps two of the latter rules are not strictly satisfied. The material presented here on these code types is essentially my interpretation of the extremely complex and rich data presented in the Marks and Seeman monograph. Those clinicians who function within the psychiatry departments of general teaching hospitals are especially urged to study this 1963 monograph in detail.

4. Stelmachers. This refers to two sources of interpretive material: (1) course notes obtained at a formal course on the MMPI taught by Z. T. Stelmachers at the University of Minnesota and (2) "canned" interpretive statements which were significantly influenced by initial Marks and Seeman data and have been applied at Hennepin County General Hospital (Minneapolis, Minnesota) for several years.

5. Gilberstadt and Duker (1965) and Gilberstadt (1970) present a cookbook of 19 code types for the interpretation of MMPI profiles obtained from male VA psychiatric patients. The code types were selected as clinical experience suggested that they had power as cardinal types in representing trait clusters. Data drawn from nine or ten classical cases comprise the primary data pool for each code-type vignette. Descriptors include traits and symptoms whose frequency differed from a general psychiatric sample as well as characteristics applicable to more than 49 percent of a given code type.

Application. The authors suggest that profiles should not be interpreted by their system if Scale L exceeds 60 T, Scale F exceeds 85 T, or Scale K exceeds 70 T. When a patient is older than 60 or his verbal IQ is less than 105, the clinician should use caution in applying these descriptors. Gilberstadt and Duker (1960) suggest that profiles which deviate from the specified rules are generally interpretable within this system. They suggest that the inferences made from single scale or pair-wise scale deviations from the basic configuration could be used to modify the interpretation of the profile. These profile types suggest interpretations which are only appropriate for male patients. Clinicians who work in VA settings would be well advised to study these sources.

6. Gynther and his colleagues (1973) at the Missouri Institute of Psychiatry have recently completed a cross-validated actuarial interpretation system for state hospital patients based on two-point codes. These narratives are based on the analysis of many potential descriptors obtained from over 3000 patients who were evaluated by the Missouri hospital system over a four-year period. Profile interpretations by sex or high-point code are presented in those cases in which separation of two-point data by these variables resulted in replicated differences in the descriptors which were identified.

Application. This interpretive material will be most applicable to MMPIs obtained from inpatients in public mental health facilities. The correlates may also be applicable to outpatients in public mental health facilities, especially if they have become outpatients after having been hospitalized. In state hospital settings this system should provide interpretive statements for about 60-70% of white patients. Two limitations are placed on protocol validity: (1) interpretations are not given if omissions exceed 60 and (2) when Scale F exceeds 25 (100 T) a special interpretation is made in place of a two-point interpretation.

7. Lachar (1968) provides some data on two-point code correlates in a state hospital which may complement the Gynther et al. data. Mean profiles are presented to aid in identification of frequent profile configurations.

COOKBOOK UTILITY

Though expectations of the value of the actuarial approach to personality assessment were initially quite high, the application of current cookbooks to other than the original construction samples has led to rather conservative and disappointing results.

Marks & Seeman (1963) classified 78% of their construction sample. Similar university hospital samples, however, obtained classification rates of 17% (Sines, 1966), 22% (Pauker, 1966) and 22% (Briggs, Taylor & Telegen, 1966), using the Marks & Seeman system. The last study is especially representative of expected classification as this sample size was 2875. Application in state hospital populations resulted in hit rates of 22% (Shultz, Gibeau & Barry, 1968), 23% (Gynther, 1972), 27% (Payne & Wiggins, 1968) and 28% (Huff, 1965). Other populations studied have included a state prison— 15% (Owen, 1970), outpatient alcoholics—28% (Fowler & Coyle, 1968) and military—30% (Porier & Smith, 1971).

Though Gilberstadt & Duker (1965) did not report classification data on their construction sample, several studies have applied their rules to various samples. Vestre & Klett (1969) were able to classify 33% of a three-year VA sample. State hospital studies resulted in 29% (Payne et al., 1968) and 25% (Shultz et al., 1968). Other samples include outpatient alcoholics—27% (Fowler et al., 1968), military population—33% (Porier et al., 1971) and a state prison—34% (Owen, 1970).

A proposed solution to this problem of low hit rates was the simultaneous use of both the Marks & Seeman and Gilberstadt & Duker systems. This approach increased application to 36% (Meikle & Gerritse, 1970), 43%

(Shultz et al., 1968), 48% (Fowler et al., 1968), 49% (Payne et al., 1968) and 51% (Porier et al, 1971). Another approach has been various rule relaxation procedures. This classification scheme for the Marks & Seeman cookbook has accommodated 70% of a large university hospital sample (Briggs et al., 1966) as well as 47-62% of state hospital samples (Payne et al., 1968; Gynther, 1972; and Shultz et al., 1968). Two studies have employed rule relaxation of the Gilberstadt & Duker code types with state hospital samples which resulted in coverages of 56% (Shultz et al., 1968) and 57% (Payne et al., 1968).

It is important to consider the limitations of these two methods which increase application rates of cookbooks. Application of Gilberstadt & Duker to females or application of cookbooks in general to samples which vary in characteristics from the construction samples is quite questionable. Rule relaxation procedures should be considered with similar caution. Since it is not certain whether profile-behavioral correlate relations hold in these cases, blind profile interpretation should be avoided whenever possible.

These cookbook application studies support, more than anything else, the need for the development of skill in clinical interpretation of MMPI profiles. A conservative, and perhaps pessimistic, expectation would be possible interpretation of 25-50% of obtained profiles by these two systems. Another issue which limits these approaches is the relevance of cookbook data. If the clinician is requested to answer specific questions rather than provide a general personality description, he may not find the needed information in these systems. It is impossible at this time to determine if this is due to limitations of the test or of present cookbooks.

INDEX OF CONFIGURAL INTERPRETATIONS

[1]indicates page on which material begins.
[2]indicates general section in which material placed: (N) "Neurotic" Profiles, (P) "Psychotic" Profiles, (C) "Characterological" Profiles and (I) "Indeterminate" Profiles.

VALIDITY SCALE CONFIGURATIONS

Figure 1. High Scale L

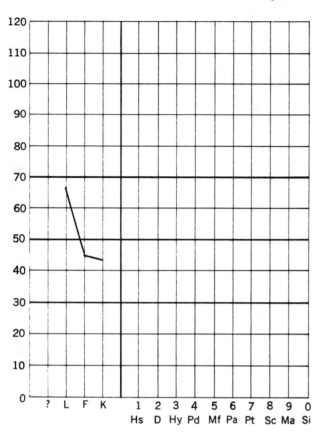

This pattern usually reflects the attempts of a naïve person to look good. These individuals usually have little education and come from lower socioeconomic backgrounds. Such attempts to look good are usually ineffective. Look for elevations on the neurotic triad (Scales 1, 2, 3) and a low Scale 5 (male).

Figure 2. High Scale K

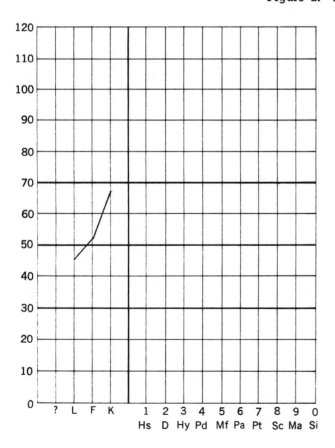

This pattern suggests sophisticated defensiveness and evasion or "conforming responses" from educated or upper socioeconomic status individuals. Look for subclinical profiles and a possible elevation on Scale 5 (male).

Figure 3. High Scales L & K

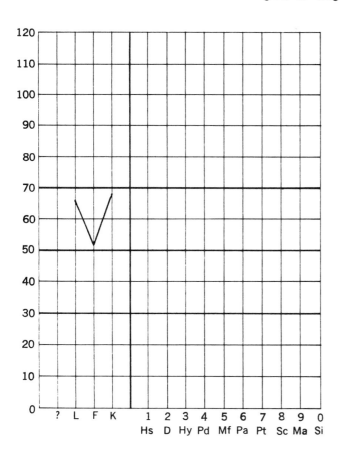

This pattern suggests an attempt to avoid or deny unacceptable feelings, impulses and problems. This pattern is usually obtained from normal defensives or hysterics and hypochondriacs. Look for elevation on Scales 1 & 3, with the rest of the profile low. Deliberate defensiveness and falsification may be suggested. A flattened "V" in psychotic patients suggests the presence of only mild behavioral disturbance (Gross, 1959).

Figure 4. Moderate Scale F

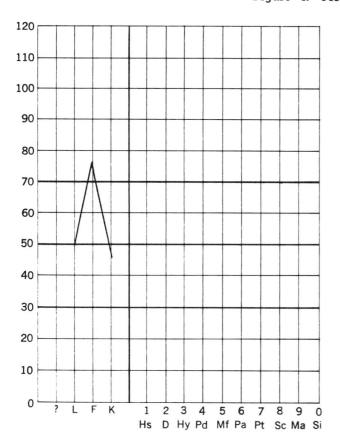

This pattern is usually obtained by character disorders and psychotics, seldom by neurotics. It reflects symptomatic status or other sources of variance noted under Scale F (See pages 17-18). In psychotic patients these L and K Scale levels suggest an acute disturbance in an individual with a relatively good premorbid social adjustment. Open admission of pathology, a poor self-concept, lability and dysphoria may be present. A similar configuration with a somewhat lower F Scale, and Scales L and K above 50 T in a psychotic population suggests chronic maladjustment and ineffective defensiveness (Gross, 1959).

Figure 5. K-corrected Profiles Expected Theoretically for Males (—) and Females (- -) Responding Randomly. F score near 32, L & K exceed 50 T.

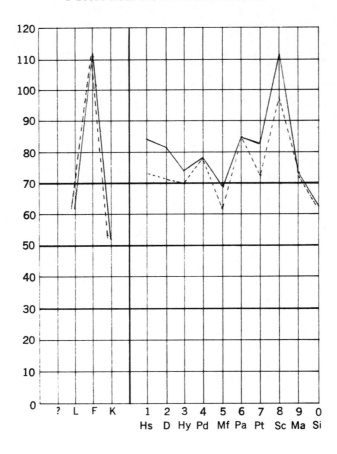

Figure 6. Very High Scale F, Scales L & K Under 50 T.

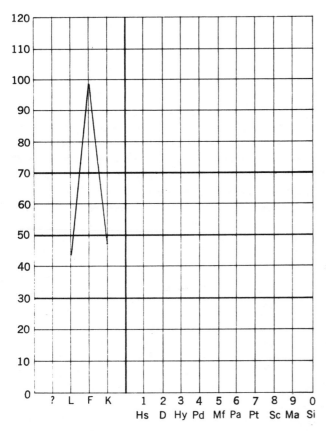

These hypotheses may be true:

(1) This is an all-true pattern (See Figure 7).
(2) This is a "cry for help" profile.
(3) Male adolescents, individuals experiencing an acute disturbance, and very unguarded individuals may obtain this pattern.
(4) This is a "fake bad" profile. F-K Index exceeds 11. See discussion below.

Figure 7. K-corrected Profiles Expected for Males (—) and Females (- -) Answering Each Item True.

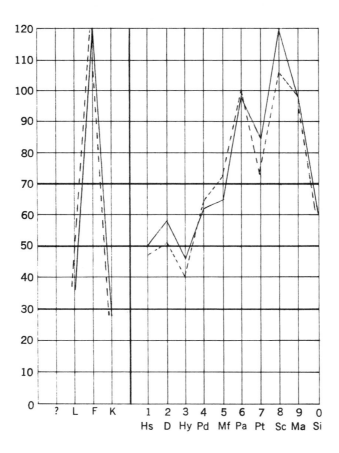

MALINGERING

Test subjects who are motivated to appear inadequate, incompetent or psychiatrically involved or who seek to escape responsibilities through apparent psychiatric disability often produce elevated F Scale scores in addition to high-ranging scores on the clinical scales. These individuals lack the experiential referents that determine the characteristic interpretations and responses to the inventory items. This absence of basic feelings, attitudes, and sensibilities leads the deliberate fakers to *overrespond* on the basis of a rough stereotype and to endorse many statements that a bona fide patient would not usually accept. An elevated F Scale and depressed K Scale are the usual result of this overinclusion response set.

Here an F-K Index (Gough, 1950) of 12 or more, with clear indications of additional gain, should lead to a careful evaluation for dissimulation. Type of setting is important here in establishing the most accurate cutting point of F-K. For example, an F-K of 9+ or 12+ will identify a majority of fakers or exaggerators in an outpatient setting, while mislabeling acute psychotics in an inpatient facility. (See item 3 under Figure 6.) In settings which evaluate and treat such psychotics, an F-K of more than 16 may be more efficient.

If the MMPI is interpreted blindly and without additional testing, the degree to which faking bad is suspected should be indicated. If the interpreter is quite certain that an individual is attempting to present a false negative psychiatric picture, this should be noted and no further interpretation given.

A brief interview, mental status notes, or additional tests (usually projective) are useful in determining malingering, as the interpreter can judge whether the pathology expressed on the MMPI is consonant with, for example, an obtained Rorschach or Holtzman protocol.

A related issue which is more difficult to resolve is raised by the bona fide psychiatric patient who is motivated to accentuate or exaggerate his psychiatric involvement. Here the profile pattern may appear valid and consonant with the patient's presenting complaints and background data. Here an elevated F Scale may lead the clinician to interpret profile elevation conservatively and to include additional measures of personality.

"Fake bad" profiles are often obtained from young men in the military who wish to obtain some assistance in manipulating the system. Several examples of such profiles are presented below to illustrate various profile configurations:

Figure 8.   The Case of J.L.B.

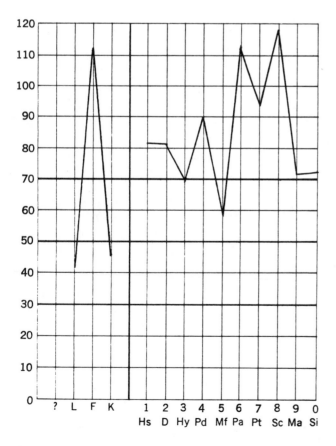

J.L.B. was a 23-year-old male who was awaiting a court martial from the Navy. His lawyers said that he was not competent to stand trial, though medical officers who had examined him felt that J.L.B. was putting on an act to appear crazy. He obtained an F-K of 27, showed no signs of organicity or a thought disorder throughout an extensive psychometric battery and presented a general picture which included average intelligence and characterological features.

Figure 9. The Case of C.

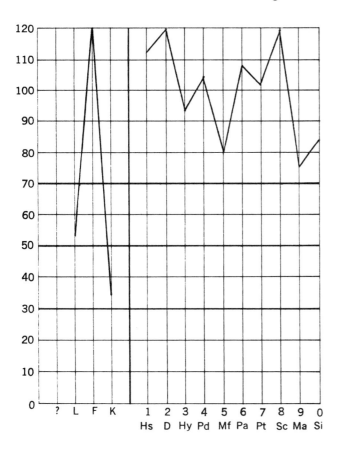

C., an 18-year-old, married male, was first seen three months prior to this MMPI administration. At that time he expressed dissatisfaction with his military job, his marriage of one month and boredom with life in general. A multitude of complaints included vegetative signs of depression, lower back pain and difficulty in concentration. At that time the patient produced an invalid MMPI. At the time of this administration he came into the clinic requesting a discharge from the military due to "flashbacks." He refused any medical treatment for his "drug problems." This MMPI has an F-K of 45.

Figure 10. The Case of D.K.

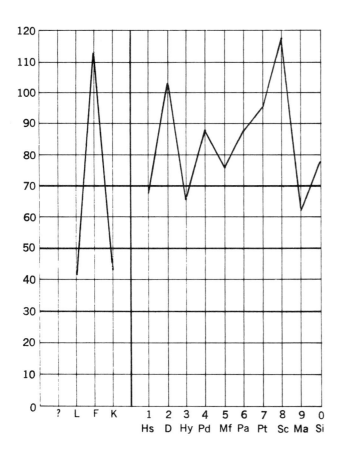

D.K. was a 24-year-old male with three years of college. His referral read, "Patient appears mildly depressed and anxious. He is dissatisfied with military life and appears to gain little satisfaction from social activities. He does not appear suicidal." Interview and additional psychometrics presented a picture compatible with a diagnosis of situational adjustment reaction with underlying depression, anxiety and immaturity.

The following case (S.W.K.) illustrates the exaggeration of difficulties rather than dissimulation:

Figure 11. The Case of S.W.K. First Administration (—) and Second Administration (- -)

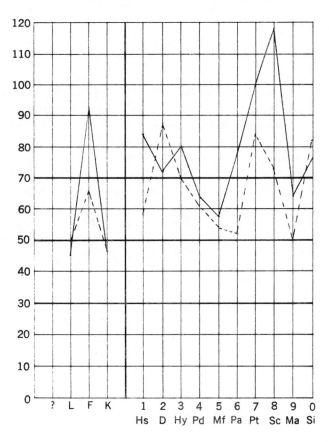

S.W.K. was a 19-year-old male with a high school education who was having difficulty adjusting to his job. He appeared very nervous and seemed to genuinely desire help with his problem rather than a discharge. He had already discussed this problem with a chaplain, his supervisor and a doctor at the dispensary. Presenting complaints included sleep disturbance, nervous stomach and increased irritability. Diagnostic impression from interview data was anxiety neurosis. The first administration of the MMPI immediately followed this interview. The resultant profile did not agree with the clinical impression. Here an F-K of 12 can be interpreted, in light of the interview, as a "cry for help." The second MMPI was obtained immediately after the first. The instructions differed from the first administration as S.W.K. was reassured as to availability of help for his problems as well as told to be as accurate as possible with his self-descriptions, being careful not to exaggerate his problems. The 270 profile obtained correlates well with interview data.

Figure 12. High Scales L & F

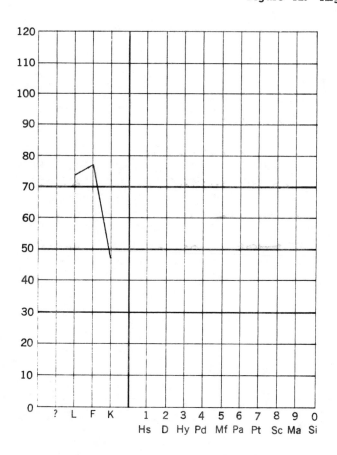

This pattern suggests a deviant response set. Here the patient denies mildly negative content but admits to very negative content. This pattern is often indicative of psychosis or of patients from low socioeconomic backgrounds who are quite defensive about their problems. Look for elevated psychotic scales (6, 8, 9) and the distress scales (2, 7).

Figure 13. High Scales F & K

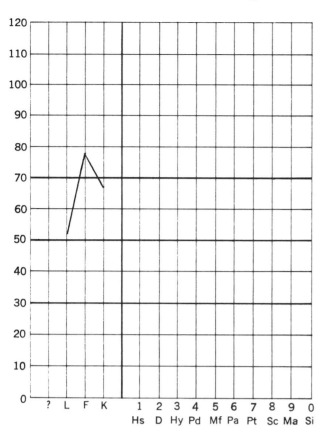

This pattern may suggest: (1) An acute disturbance with rather intact defenses, or (2) A severely disturbed individual who is defensive but still looks quite sick. The equilibrium between open pathology and defensive structure is likely to be unstable and unpredictable. If Scales F and K are above 70 T, extreme lack of insight and poor prognosis are suggested. Look for elevated Scales 2 and 7.

Figure 14. High Scales L, F & K

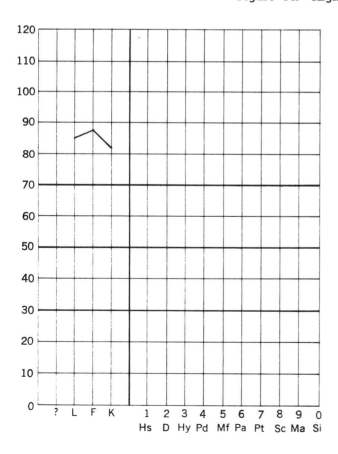

This validity pattern often suggests an all-false response set (see Figure 15). This pattern may also be obtained from severely agitated or deteriorated psychotics.

41

Figure 15. K-corrected Profiles Expected for Males (—) and Females (- -) Answering Each Item False

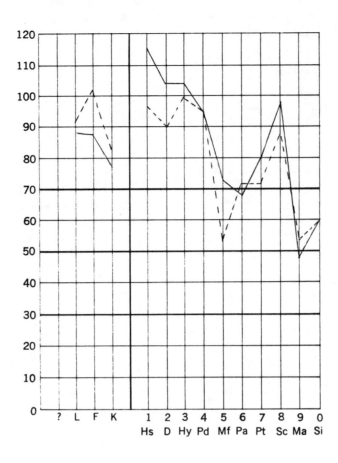

"NEUROTIC" PROFILES

High-point Scale 1

Scale 1 is profile high-point in 6.3% of males and 4.1% of females in a general psychiatric sample (Webb, 1971).

1 Spike

(GENERAL) When Scale 1 exceeds 70 T and is elevated in isolation, a long history of exaggerated physical complaints and sympathy-seeking is suggested. These individuals are usually immature, insightless and narcissistic. They use somatization and repression to cope with tensions and conflicts. Physical complaints may be used to control others and to channel disguised hostility.

Automated Interpretation

See paragraph 24 (page 117).

1-2/2-1

This two-point code represented 3.82% of males and 1.71% of females in a sample of over 12,000 psychiatric outpatients (Webb, 1970).

(1-2/2-1 GENERAL: Dahlstrom, Welsh & Dahlstrom, 1972) Two-thirds of these individuals show prominent somatic concern. Here Scales 3 and 7 play an important subordinate role. These individuals are seen as irritable, depressed, shy and seclusive. Pain is a prominent feature and complaints center around the viscera. A chronic pervasive emphasis on physical symptoms and physiological processes and lack of psychological insight is suggested.

(1-2 "pure" GENERAL: Stelmachers) Medical symptoms, pain, fatigability and over-evaluation of minimal complaints are likely. If Scales 1 and 2 are around 100 T or higher, a history of somatic concern and free-floating anxiety may be suggested. 1-2 patients are usually neurotic and anxious. Underlying depression is associated with somatic concerns. Somatization and passive dependency are characteristic. Diagnostic Impression: Psychophysiological Reaction (Hypochondriasis).

(1-2 COUNSELING BUREAU: Drake & Oetting, 1959) College men who request counseling and obtain the 1-2 pattern were seen as tense and insecure in social situations. Though somatic concern was not a prominent characteristic, these men were described as unhappy, worried, introverted and lacking in heterosexual social skills.

Physical complaints (e.g., headache) were more prominent among female college counselees than among men, especially when Scale 5 was low. They were described as depressed, worried, anxious, indecisive and lacking in self-confidence. They were similar to male counselees as they were also described as socially insecure, shy and self-conscious. They also lacked heterosexual social skills.

(1-2/2-1 STATE HOSPITAL WHITE MALES: Gynther et al., 1973) Patients of this kind are more likely to be diagnosed alcoholic and less likely to be diagnosed as psychotic than patients generally. They usually are considered to have a definite drinking problem at the time of admission and are often acutely intoxicated at that time. Their drinking history usually includes previous hospitalization or arrest. Their recent history may include benders and blackouts. Current social problems arising from drinking may take the form of job absenteeism, job loss, or family difficulties.

Other current symptoms which may be encountered are multiple somatic complaints associated with major interference with functioning due to physical problems and poor personal hygiene. Trouble sleeping is usually present.

These characteristics occur *less* frequently among 1-2/2-1 males than among other state hospital patients: fragmentation of thought, flat affect, withdrawal and impaired insight and judgment.

(1-2/2-1 STATE HOSPITAL WHITE FEMALES: Gynther et al., 1973) Patients of this kind are more likely to be diagnosed as alcoholic than female patients generally. They may have a definite drinking problem at the time of admission and may be acutely intoxicated at that time. Their drinking history may include benders and blackouts. Current social problems arising from drinking may take the form of job absenteeism, job loss or family difficulties.

Other current symptoms which may be encountered are multiple somatic complaints associated with major interference with functioning due to physical problems and poor personal hygiene. Trouble sleeping may be present.

These characteristics occur *less* frequently among 1-2/2-1 females than among other state hospital patients: fragmentation of thought, flat affect, withdrawal and impaired insight and judgment.

(1-2/2-1 STATE HOSPITAL: Lachar, 1968)
Mean Male (- -) & Female (—) Profiles

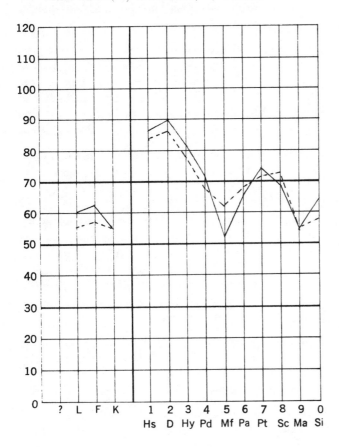

The 1-2/2-1 code was the 12th most frequent (n=88) in this sample and was obtained by more male patients (64.7%) than female patients. Three-quarters were married or widowed. The modal diagnosis in this sample was Reactive Depression. Diagnostic frequencies: Psychoneurotic—43%, Schizophrenic—23%, Other psychotic—13%, Personality Disorder—10% and Brain Syndrome—7%.

Automated Interpretation

(1-2/2-1) See paragraph 37 (pages 120-121).

1-2-3

(1-2-3 GENERAL) These are "old-fashioned somatizers." These patients are neurotic, depressed, clinically anxious and display the fatigue syndrome (loss of interest, apathy and tension). Somatic symptoms are often associated with the autonomic nervous system. Somatic symptoms may appear instead of affective signs. These patients often say, "My nerves bother me." Their self-descriptions may be labeled an "organ recital."

(1-2-3 GENERAL: Stelmachers) Patients with this profile type demonstrate somatic overconcern manifested by hypersensitivity to minor dysfunction and numerous complaints without adequate physical pathology. They typically have a chronic and unabating history of hypochondriacal trends. Their symptoms are likely to involve pain, weakness and fatigability. The prime defense mechanism is repression, the patient usually exhibiting lack of insight and self-understanding. Anxiety level is probably rather high.

Despite frequent visits, the medical status of these patients remains relatively constant and unchanging. Nevertheless, such visits usually result in short-lived and symptomatic relief. Impression: Hypochondriasis, Anxiety Reaction.

(1-2-3 Profile Type; VA MALES: Gilberstadt & Duker, 1965) Mean Profile (n=11)

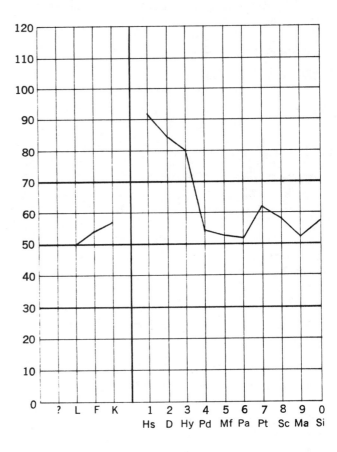

1-2-3 Profile Type Rules (Gilberstadt & Duker, 1965):

1. Scales 1, 2 and 3 over 70 T.
2. Scale 1 exceeds 2 which exceeds 3.
3. No other scales over 70 T.
4. Scale L less than 66 T, F less than 86 T, K less than 71 T.

Most descriptive diagnosis: Psychophysiological Reaction. Modal diagnoses: Anxiety Reaction; Depressive Reaction. Characteristics & rate of occurrence: Abdominal pain (45%), Anorexia, nausea, vomiting (45%), Blindness, eye complaint (36%), Dizziness (64%), Ear complaints (buzz, click, ring) (27%), Headache (64%), Insomnia (36%), Irritable (45%), Nervousness (64%), Sexual difficulty (27%), Weak, tired, fatigued (45%), Worrying (55%) and Anxiety (55%).

44

These patients present somatic symptoms which usually have their origin in the autonomic nervous system. They react to life's stresses with physiological symptoms rather than affect. They often lack aggressiveness and sexual drive. Their social histories are characterized by stability at work and in marital adjustment.

1-2-3-7

(1-2-3-7 Profile Type; VA MALES: Gilberstadt & Duker, 1965) Mean Profile (n = 11)

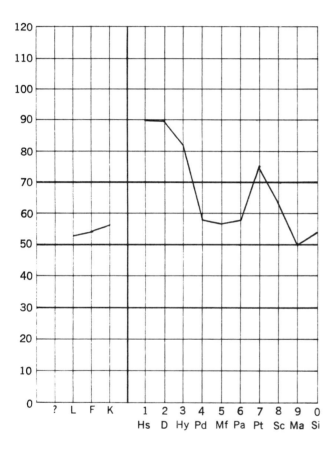

1-2-3-7 Profile Type Rules (Gilberstadt & Duker, 1965):

1. Scales 1, 2, 3 and 7 over 70 T.
2. Scales 1 and 2 greater than 3.
3. Scales 1, 2 and 3 greater than 7.
4. Scale 9 less than 60 T.
5. Scale 0 less than 70 T.

Most descriptive diagnosis: Psychophysiological Reaction with anxiety in a Passive-dependent Personality.
Modal diagnosis: Psychophysiological Reaction.
Characteristics & rate of occurrence: Anorexia, nausea, vomiting (36%), Anxiety (82%), Back pain (36%), Dependent (73%), Epigastric complaints (45%), Inadequacy feelings (36%), Nervousness (73%), Numbness (36%), Passive (45%), Tension (64%), Worrying (36%) and Depression (64%).

These patients focus on chronic symptoms which usually have their origin in the autonomic nervous system. Actual organic pathology is represented as well as hypochondriacal trends.

Weak, moody, fearful and highly inadequate are characteristic descriptors. When these patients regress, they become unable to cope with everyday stress and responsibility. This adjustment may lead to chronic unemployment and many unproductive years. If the patient's wife is strong and protective, he may take on the role of a weak, helpless child. Inadequate interpersonal relations may be characteristic. Similar patients may become dependent on alcohol or drugs.

(1-2-3-7 Group I; VA: Halbower, 1955) This code-type represented 16% of a VA sample. Rules: 1-2-3 slope above 70 T; Scales 4, 6 and 9 below 70 T; Scale 9 a low point; Scale 8 less than Scale 7 by at least 3 T, Scale 7 above 70 T and Scale F less than 70 T and greater than or equal to Scales L and K. Somatization or psychophysiological mechanisms, complaints of pain, weakness and fatigability are likely. These patients are hypersensitive and overevaluate minor dysfunctions. A prominent lack of insight and use of repression are suggested. These patients are likely to be described as passive-dependent. They typically internalize anxiety and conflict.

1-3/3-1

This two-point code represented 3.65% of males and 5.24% of females in a sample of over 12,000 psychiatric outpatients (Webb, 1970).

(1-3/3-1 GENERAL: Carson, 1969) In general, an elevation of Scale 3 decreases the probability of the overtly pessimistic, complaining attitudes often associated with the high Scale 1 person. When Scale 3 is higher than Scale 1, denial and repression may even allow expression of hysteroid and optimistic attitudes.

When the 1-3/3-1 code occurs with relatively lower Scale 2 ("conversion V"), a specific syndrome is often observed. Such individuals have a strong need to interpret their circumstances in a logical and socially acceptable manner. Psychological conflicts are often manifest in somatic displacements or socially acceptable psychological symptoms. Hysteroid mechanisms often obscure the function of such symptoms.

1-3/3-1 configuration, when Scale K is elevated and Scales 2, 7 and 8 are down, suggests an extremely defensive person who presents himself as normal, responsible and without significant fault. Suggestions of any weakness or unconventionality in their character may be quite threatening. They often see themselves as contributing significantly to the needs of others. They do not tolerate well the role of a patient.

(1-3/3-1 "Working Conversions" GENERAL) If Scale 1 is more than Scale 2 by at least 5 T, and Scale 3 is more than Scale 2 by at least 10 T, a "working conversion" may be indicated. Such individuals often emphasize, but fail to show any real concern about their somatic symptoms. Symptomatic depression and anxiety are usually conspicuously absent with egocentricity, immaturity and dependency conspicuously present. This configuration is usually found in moderately elevated or normal profiles. The 1-3's are differentiable from the normal reference group by the frequency and extremity of their denial of troubles or inadequacies. It seems clear that many of the individuals who obtain this pattern and who do not manifest emotional difficulties at the time are remaining symptom-free at some considerable effort and cost in emotional control and repression.

1-3's have shallow social relationships and usually project a pollyana, "everything's right with the world" attitude. As little or no insight is present, psychological intervention is likely to be futile. Such cases are best handled by general practitioners with support from mental health specialists.

Pain is a frequent complaint, and is often localized in the extremities, rather than the trunk. If pain is localized in the trunk, it is usually not associated with the viscera. Look for classical secondary gain.

In general, the higher the elevation of the "V", the more rigid are the defenses supporting this adjustment. A "V" above 80 T suggests that much of the individual's psychic energy is involved in warding away anxiety and that such defenses are not working well (especially when F is significantly higher than L & K). A rise in Scale 7 will support this latter interpretation.

(3-1 "Hysterical Characters" GENERAL) If Scale 3 is at least 80 T and Scale 1 falls between 60-70 T, repression, exhibitionism and a frank exploitation of social relations is likely. As Scale 1 approaches Scale 3 in elevation, discrete conversion symptoms become ever more probable. Scale 6 is not infrequently elevated, reflecting hostility of which the person has little if any insight.

(3-1 GENERAL: Dahlstrom, Welsh & Dahlstrom, 1972) The long-standing tension states characteristically are associated with insecurity, immaturity and a tendency to develop symptoms under stress. When physical symptoms appear, they are relatively restricted and specific both in location and nature, in contrast to 1-3 patients.

(3-1 GENERAL: Stelmachers) This profile suggests complaints of and preoccupation with somatic symptoms which represent emotional conflict and seem to produce secondary gains for the patient. There is likely to be some surplus anxiety and nervousness which is not taken care of by the somatic preoccupations. Depressive reactions, if they occur, are apt to be of short duration and to be expressed by crying, tearfulness or emotional lability rather than by sustained depressive mood and self-depreciatory trends. Patients with such profile types are described as being self-centered, selfish and emotionally immature, as being socially demanding and tending to exploit social relationships.

Defense mechanisms typically used are denial and repression. Their social interactions tend to be shallow and superficial and lack genuine emotional involvement. They clearly prefer a medical explanation for their symptoms and tend to reject psychological interpretations and psychiatric inquiry. Their insight into their motivations and dynamics is characteristically poor. Prognosis for any type of psychiatric treatment is guarded. Diagnostic Impression: (1) Conversion Reaction; (2) Psychophysiological Reaction.

(3-1/1-3 Profile Type; TEACHING HOSPITAL: Marks & Seeman, 1963)
Mean Female Profile (n=20)

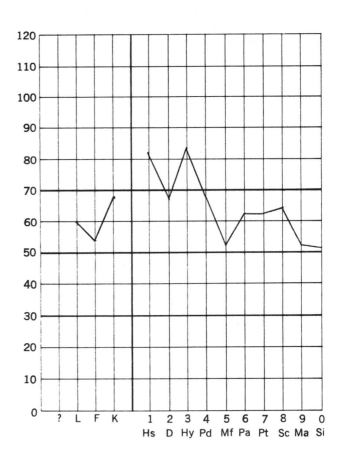

3-1/1-3 Profile Type Rules (Marks & Seeman, 1963):

1. Scales 3 and 1 over 70 T.
2. Scale 1 minus 2 more than 10 T.
3. Scale 3 minus 2 more than 10 T.
4. Scale 3 minus 4 more than 10 T.
5. Scale 5 above 45 T.

6. Scale 8 cannot exceed 7 by more than 4 T.
7. Scales 9 and 0 less than 70 T.
8. Scale K greater than F, F less than 60 T.

A majority (77%) of these patients are diagnosed as psychoneurotic (Conversion/Psychophysiologic). They present themselves as physically ill and obtain appreciable "secondary gain" from their symptoms. A great variety of symptoms is suggested: weakness, fatigue, dizziness, sleep disturbance, back pain, headache, nausea, numbness, tremor, etc. These patients are depressed, tense, perplexed and anxious; their physical complaints often represent psychological conflicts. Socially appropriate behavior is often associated with insecurity, a need for affection and attention, demands for sympathy and a tendency toward over-control of needs and impulses. Conflict about emotional dependency may be suggested. A majority of these patients received only psychotherapy, which resulted in some improvement for 75%.

3-1/1-3 Mean Discharge Profile (n=18)

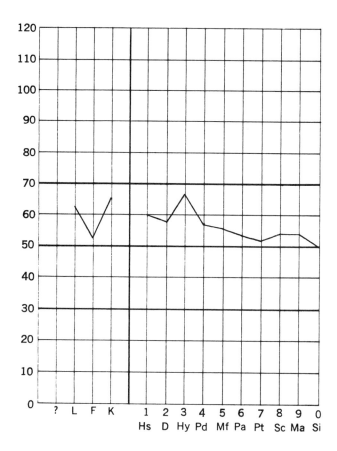

(1-3-2 Profile Type; VA MALES: Gilberstadt & Duker, 1965) Mean Profile (n=19)

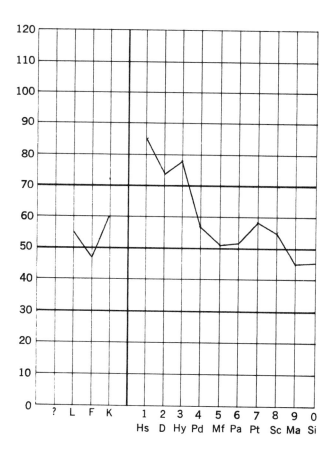

1-3-2 Profile Type Rules (Gilberstadt & Duker, 1965):

1. Scales 1, 2 and 3 over 70 T.
2. Scales 1 and 3 greater than 2.
3. No other scales over 70 T.
4. Scale 2 minus 7 at least 5 T.
5. Scale 9 less than 61 T.

Most descriptive diagnosis: Psychoneurosis, Conversion Reaction with depression.
Modal diagnoses: Psychophysiological Reaction; Anxiety Reaction.
Characteristics & rate of occurrence: Anorexia, nausea, vomiting (26%), Back pain (32%), Chest pain (26%), Dependent (42%), Headache (37%), Irritable (42%), Passive (32%), Tension (47%), Weak, tired, fatigued (37%) and Anxiety (53%).

These patients are sociable, extroverted and display a hysteroid, passive-dependent character. They are well-liked until reactive depression leads to irritability and "chuck-it-all" symptoms. Their use of repression and denial often leads to strong rejection of the premise that their symptoms have a psychological etiology. Psychosomatic illness or conversion symptoms follow periods of stress. They are highly conforming and are seen as conventional in both work habits and in marital adjustment.

47

(1-3/3-1 Group III; VA: Halbower, 1955) Rules: Scales 1 and 3 more than 69 T; Scale 2 less than Scales 1 and 3 by at least 10 T; Scale K or L more than Scales ? and F; Scale F less than 66 T; Scales 4 through 0 less than 70 T; and Scale ? less than 20 (raw). The patients who obtain this pattern are seen as displaying somatization or psychophysiological reaction. Secondary gain was often obtained from symptoms. They were described as very self-centered and selfish, dependent and demanding in their personal relations. They were often emotionally labile and displayed unpredictable self-control. Rationalization, blaming others, projection and acting out are noted. Such individuals are frequently seen as poorly motivated for intensive psychotherapy and described as passive-aggressive and deficient in heterosexual drive.

1-3/3-1 Research

Gilberstadt & Jancis (1967) found that medical patients who obtain 1-3/3-1 profiles exhibit a high incidence of psychological symptoms such as nervousness and hypochondriasis. These patients are similar to 1-3/3-1 psychiatric patients in that they also display somatic symptoms (cardiovascular and musculoskeletal) and physiological instability. The authors conclude that both psychiatric and general medical patients who obtain a 1-3/3-1 configuration are drawn from the same population with respect to their main parameters of character or personality. Their division into medical or psychiatry patients is determined by factors apparently not measured by MMPI variance.

Of 50,000 profiles obtained by medical patients at the Mayo Clinic (Schwartz & Krupp, 1971), 8% obtained a 1-3/3-1 profile. These 4,000 cases were about evenly divided between males and females. Though profile elevation did not appear related to frequency of functional diagnosis in a sample of 120 profiles, 37.5% received a functional diagnosis, while 75% of the patients received a diagnosis which at least noted a functional component.

A study of 178 medical patients from the Mayo population who obtained a 1-3/3-1 profile following the Halbower Group III rules found that the proportion who received psychiatric diagnoses varied with the age of the patient (Schwartz, Osborne & Krupp, 1972). In general, a conversion "V" was more likely to be associated with psychological diagnoses in younger patients. There was also a trend for female patients to receive more functional-psychologic diagnoses and fewer pure organic diagnoses than males. The table presented below may assist the clinician in establishing a probability level of psychiatric involvement when a 1-3/3-1 profile is obtained in a general medical/psychiatric consultation setting:

1-3/3-1 Diagnosis by Sex and Age

Age	N		Psychologic %		Mixed %		Organic %	
	M	F	M	F	M	F	M	F
60 +	16	11	12.5	27.2	25.0	36.4	62.5	36.4
50-59	27	26	11.1	26.9	29.6	34.6	59.3	38.5
40-49	27	30	29.6	33.3	22.2	36.7	48.2	30.0
30-39	12	20	75.0	65.0	16.7	10.0	8.3	25.0
< 30	4	5	50.0	60.0	25.0	40.0	25.0	0.0

A recent study (Shaw & Mathews, 1965) suggests that the conversion "V" pattern characterized patients who presented physical complaints which were unsubstantiated upon examination, while patients whose complaints *were* substantiated obtained profiles within normal limits suggestive of mild reactive depression.

(1-3/3-1 STATE HOSPITAL WHITES: Gynther et al., 1973) This type of patient may display an unusual amount of bodily concern, often in the form of multiple somatic complaints, sometimes reaching the proportions of hypochondriasis. However, it should be noted that real physical problems are sometimes the cause of the patient's concern.

(1-3/3-1 STATE HOSPITAL: Lachar, 1968)
Mean Male (- -) & Female (—) Profiles

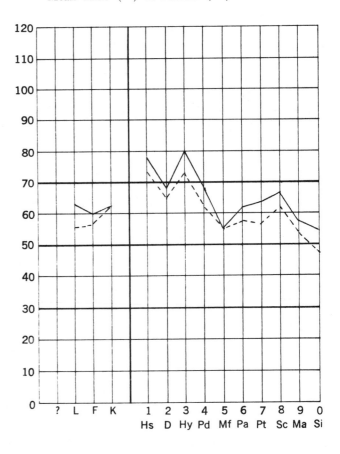

The 1-3/3-1 code was the 13th most frequent (n=82) in this sample and was obtained by more female patients (70.8%) than male patients. The modal diagnosis in this sample was Personality Trait Disturbance. Diagnostic frequencies: Psychoneurotic—27%, Personality Disorder —27%, Schizophrenic—27% and Other Psychotic—7%.

A true conversion hysteric today is rare indeed—and more so in the case of males. Increased medical sophistication of the general public has led to physical complaints that are either vague or often parallel specific syndromes. In any case, an individual's attitude toward his symptoms and opportunity for secondary gain should be scrutinized.

Automated Interpretation

(1-3/3-1) See paragraphs 38, 38A and 85 (pages 121-122, 140).

1-3-7

(1-3-7 Profile Type; VA MALES: Gilberstadt & Duker, 1965) Mean Profile (n=12)

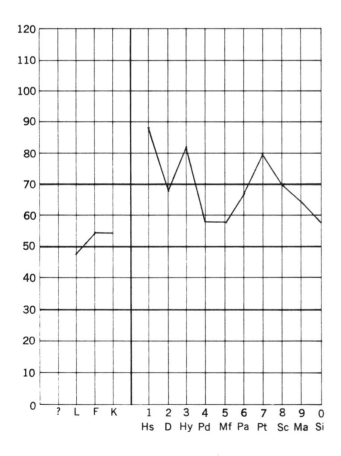

1-3-7 Profile Type Rules (Gilberstadt & Duker, 1965):

1. Scales 1, 3 and 7 highest profile elevations.
2. Scales 1 and 3 over 70 T.
3. Scale 7 over 65 T.
4. Scale 1 minus 2 at least 10 T.
5. Scales K, 4 and 0 less than 70 T.

Most description Diagnosis: Psychoneurosis, Anxiety Reaction, chronic with somatization.
Modal Diagnoses: Mixed Neurosis; Anxiety Hysteria; Phobic Reaction.
Characteristics & rate of occurrence: Anorexia, nausea, vomiting (42%), Anxiety (67%), Cardiac complaint (42%), Depression (75%), Dyspnea, respiratory complaint (50%), Epigastric complaints (58%), Father punishing (33%), Fearful (42%), Financial status poor (58%), Headache (42%), Hostile (42%), Insomnia (42%), Leg or knee pain (42%), Nervousness (83%), Passive (33%), Tension (75%), Weak, tired, fatigued (42%) and Wife pregnant or postpregnant (42%).

These patients appear physiologically unstable and show vascular instability. A predisposition to react to stress with physiological breakdown may exist from childhood. They often display severe anxiety and panic attacks and may be phobic about illness. They are often rigid and consequently adapt poorly to environmental changes. Similar patients are unable to accept aggressiveness in themselves or others.

These patients often have a poor vocational adjustment and have trouble settling down into a vocational role. They are unrealistic about work and finances and demand vocational and financial help. These passive-dependent, immature men often marry attractive, adequate wives.

1-5/5-1

This two-point code represented .36% of males and .08% of females in a sample of over 12,000 psychiatric outpatients (Webb, 1970).

(1-5/5-1 GENERAL) Although uncommon, the elevation of Scales 1 and 5 together appears to point up the passivity and the fussy, complaining attitude of these patients. Somatic complaints are likely much in evidence.

1-7/7-1

This two-point code represented .65% of males and .26% of females in a sample of over 12,000 psychiatric outpatients (Webb, 1970).

Automated Interpretation

See paragraph 41 (page 122).

High-point Scale 2

Scale 2 is profile high-point in 20.4% of males and 18.8% of females in a general psychiatric sample (Webb, 1971).

2 Spike

(GENERAL) This pattern often suggests acute depressive reactions to environmental stress. A good response to psychotherapy is indicated.

Where Scale 2 is the only elevated scale, a reactive depression is probable even when depressed feelings are denied, as in so-called "smiling depression." When Scale 2 is very highly elevated (over 90 T), it generally serves to pull up the other clinical scales. The major symptomatic feature, however, is depression. Suicidal ideation and tendencies should be ruled out, even when behavioral depression is limited or absent.

(2 Spike; GENERAL: Stelmachers) This profile suggests a relatively clearcut and uncomplicated reactive depression of moderate to severe proportions. The patient is likely to suffer from feelings of inadequacy and lack of self-confidence. He would characteristically have strong self-depreciatory trends, be generally pessimistic about the future and would be prone to be bothered by strong guilt feelings.

This patient would seem to be a good psychotherapy candidate and could be expected to show significant improvement within a relatively short period of time.

Automated Interpretation

See paragraph 27 (page 117).

2-3/3-2

This two-point code represented 3.10% of males and 5.77% of females in a sample of over 12,000 psychiatric outpatients (Webb, 1970).

(2-3/3-2 GENERAL: Dahlstrom, Welsh & Dahlstrom, 1972) Depression, tension, weakness and apathy, inadequacy, self-doubt, bottled-up emotion and general over-control are typically descriptive of this group. They lack interest and involvement. They tolerate unhappiness and have accepted a low level of efficiency. These patients are poor risks for psychotherapy; they lack insight, are resistant to psychological interpretations and seldom seek help. Women show many physical symptoms, but men have more delimited physical symptoms (such as physical effects of prolonged tension) and appear more immature. These patients are either neurotics of some form or psychotic depressions. Frigidity and resultant marital disharmony are frequently seen in women, while ulcers are frequently seen in men.

(2-3/3-2: GENERAL) Elevations of Scales 2 and 3 point toward the ineffective use of repressive defenses and hysteroid mechanisms. Such individuals may show symptoms of apathy, dizziness and lowered efficiency as well

as symptomatic depression. 2-3's are much like 2-1's, but show greater immaturity, inadequacy and inefficiency. Little hope for behavioral change is indicated.

(2-3/3-2 STATE HOSPITAL WHITES: Gynther et al., 1973) Patients of this kind are more often described than patients generally as showing depressive symptomatology, especially sadness, depressed mood, and decreased activity.

(2-3 STATE HOSPITAL WHITES: Gynther et al., 1973) Other findings that occur with increased frequency are feelings of helplessness and multiple somatic complaints.

These characteristics occur *less* frequently among 2-3's than among other state hospital patients: depersonalization and blocking.

(3-2 STATE HOSPITAL WHITES: Gynther et al., 1973) These characteristics occur *less* frequently among 3-2's than among other state hospital patients; depersonalization and blocking.

(2-3/3-2 STATE HOSPITAL: Lachar, 1968)
Mean Male (- -) & Female (—) Profiles:

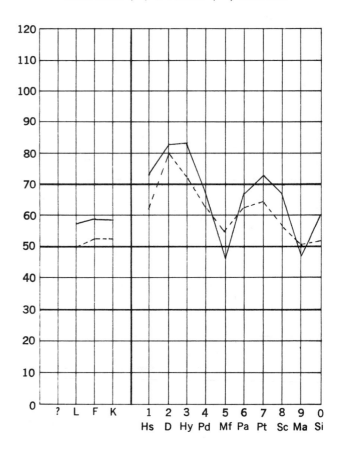

The 2-3/3-2 code was the 9th most frequent (n = 140) in this sample and was obtained by more female patients (72.9%) than male patients. The modal diagnosis was Reactive Depression. Diagnostic frequencies: Psychoneurotic—50%, Schizophrenic—10%, Other Psychotic—27%, Brain Syndrome—7% and Personality Disorder—6%.

Automated Interpretation

See paragraph 44A and 44B (pages 123-124).

2-3-1/2-1-3

(2-3-1 GENERAL: Stelmachers) This profile suggests a chronic neurotic condition with mixed symptomatology. The patient exhibits at least moderate distress syndrome (depression, tension, nervousness, anxiety) plus multiple somatic complaints, especially headaches and insomnia. Among men the physical complaints appear to be more delimited and concentrated in the upper GI tract. Hysteroid features are prominent in the patient's personality and a substantial secondary gain from the physical symptoms is usually the rule. This patient is apt to be easily threatened and to demand much sympathy.

The patient can be expected to suffer from fatigue and exhaustion, loss of interest, involvement and initiative. (In women patients the fatigue syndrome is sometimes replaced by restlessness and agitation.)

Persons with such profiles have often learned to tolerate great unhappiness and a high level of discomfort and, consequently, have poor motivation for help and poor response to treatment. They frequently operate at a lowered level of efficiency for considerable periods of time.

The majority of patients of this type receive psychiatric diagnoses of either depressive reaction or psychophysiological reaction, although a strong minority are classified as psychotic depressions.

(2-3-1/2-1-3 Profile Type; TEACHING HOSPITAL: Marks & Seeman, 1963)

Mean Female (—) and Male (- -) Profiles (n=20)

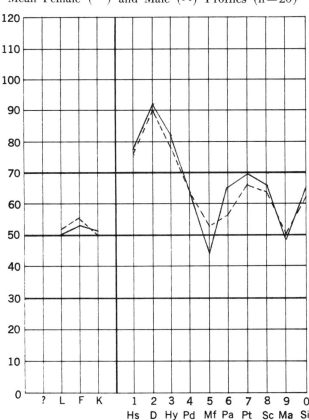

2-3-1/2-1-3 Profile Type Rules (Marks & Seeman, 1963):

1. Scales 2, 3 and 1 greater than 70 T.
2. Scale 2 minus 1 more than 5 T.
3. Scale 2 minus 3 more than 5 T.
4. Scales 7 and 0 lower than 2, 3 and 1.
5. Scale 8 cannot exceed 7 by more than 4 T.
6. Scales 9 and 0 less than 70 T.
7. Scale 0 greater than 9.
8. Scales L, F and K less than 70 T.

A majority (54%) of these patients are diagnosed as psychoneurotic (Depressive/Psychophysiologic) though a significant proportion (30%) are labeled psychotic (Depressive) or Brain Syndrome (17%—Chronic). This is a relatively chronic adjustment pattern including multiple neurotic complaints and hypochondriacal tendencies. These patients are depressed, tense, anxious, worried and manifest somatic complaints such as headache, nausea, chest pain, anorexia and weakness. Hysteroid features are suggested as well as secondary gain from symptoms. The majority (93%) of these patients displayed some improvement with treatment. Energizers were used most frequently (25%) in this code type.

2-3-1/2-1-3 Mean Discharge Profile (n=24)

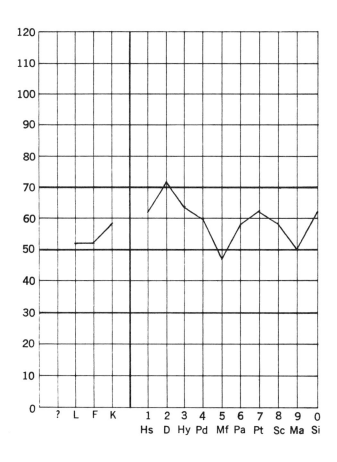

51

3-2-1

(3-2-1 GENERAL: Stelmachers) This profile indicates a mixed neurotic pattern with depressive trends and somatization predominating. A high level of anxiety with insomnia and anorexia usually accompanies the clinical picture. Patients falling into this category tend to suffer from periodic hysterical attacks consisting of palpitation, sweating, abdominal cramps, episodes of fear, fatigue and exhaustion. Women patients are often reported to be sexually frigid, to have marital difficulties and to be prone to develop menopausal disturbances. Men are more likely to be in chronic anxiety states with the physical effects of prolonged tension and worry, such as gastric distress and ulcers. Lack of psychological insight and the resistance to psychiatric interpretations are typical of this group of patients.

The majority of patients receive either psychophysiological reaction or depressive reaction diagnoses (approximately equal frequency). A minority are labeled passive-aggressive. Diagnostic Impression: (1) Psychophysiologic Reaction; (2) Depressive Reaction.

(3-2-1 Profile Type; TEACHING HOSPITAL: Marks & Seeman, 1963)
Mean Female Profile (n=20)

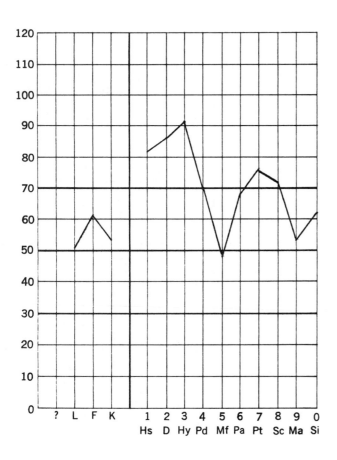

3-2-1 Profile Type Rules (Marks & Seeman, 1963):

1. Scales 3, 2 and 1 over 70 T.
2. Scale 1 cannot exceed 2 by more than 4 T.
3. Scale 3 cannot exceed 1 by more than 14 T.
4. Scale 3 cannot exceed 2 by more than 9 T.
5. Scale 8 cannot exceed 7 by more than 4 T.
6. Scales 7 and 0 less than 3, 2 and 1.
7. Scales 9 and 0 less than 70 T.
8. Scales L, F and K less than 70 T.

Diagnostic impressions vary within this code type: psychoneurotic (39%—Psychophysiologic), psychotic (35% —Depressive), personality disorder (17%—Passive-aggressive) and brain syndrome (9%—Chronic). Half of these patients have had similar episodes. They are described as manifesting multiple neurotic symptoms and hypochondriacal tendencies. They are intropunitive, self-defeating and admit to feelings of hopelessness, inferiority and perplexity. Symptoms and complaints include anxiety, poor concentration, insomnia, tension, depression, tearfulness, sexual difficulty, nausea, back pain, constipation and diarrhea. Secondary gain is often associated with somatic symptoms. Response to treatment: no change (29.4%); small improvement (41.2%); and decided improvement (29.4%).

3-2-1 Mean Discharge Profile (n=28)

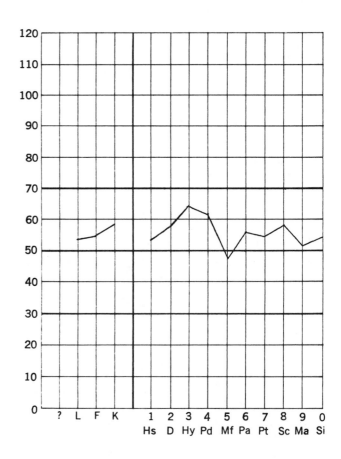

2-7/7-2

This two-point code represented 8.61% of males and 6.41% of females in a sample of over 12,000 psychiatric outpatients (Webb, 1970).

(2-7/7-2 GENERAL: Carson, 1969) This common psychiatric pattern reflects self-devaluation, intropunitiveness, tension and nervousness. Some elevation on Scales 2 and 7 is desirable in candidates for psychotherapy as this usually indicates internal distress with motivation for change, as well as some introspective bent. Extreme elevations, however, often mean that the individual is so agitated and worried that he cannot settle down to the business of psychotherapy. Other forms of therapeutic intervention become necessary.

(2-7 GENERAL: Stelmachers) This profile type is found with great frequency among psychiatric patients and is rare among normals. It represents multiple neurotic manifestations, including the distress syndrome (nervousness, anxiety and depression), the neurasthenic syndrome (weakness, fatigue, lack of initiative) and a pervading lack of self-esteem and self-confidence. Their anxiety is typically quite manifest clinically. Psychic conflicts can be expected to be represented in hypochondriacal tendencies and somatic complaints, especially cardiac symptoms, insomnia and anorexia. Patients with such profiles are likely to be pessimistic worriers, guilt-ridden and intropunitive, generally fearful and obsessively preoccupied with their personal deficiencies, the latter being in a disturbing conflict with their typically perfectionistic and meticulous attitudes and their strong motive for personal achievement and recognition. To frustration they characteristically respond by self-blame and neurotic guilt feelings. Diagnostic Impression: (1) Anxiety Reaction; (2) Depressive Reaction; (3) Obsessive-compulsive Reaction.

Some of these 2-7s turn out to be quite resistant to change with psychotherapy in spite of the generally good prognosis often associated with this pattern. They may, in fact, become psychological invalids and professional patients going from one therapist to another. In males, the presence of an elevated Scale 5 may be a poor prognostic sign for improvement.

(2-7 Profile Type; TEACHING HOSPITAL: Marks & Seeman, 1963)

Mean Male (- -) and Female (—) Profiles (n=20)

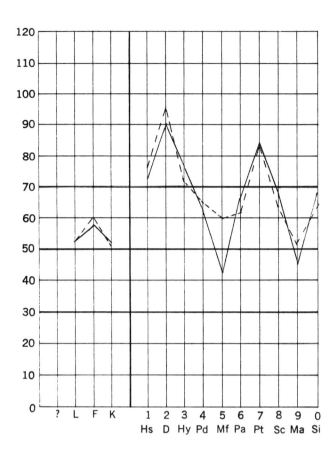

2-7 Profile Type Rules (Marks & Seeman, 1963):

1. Scales 2 and 7 greater than 70 T.
2. Scale 2 greater than 7.
3. Scale 2 minus 8 more than 15 T.
4. Scale 7 greater than 1 and 3.
5. Scale 7 minus 4 more than 10 T.
6. Scale 7 minus 6 more than 10 T.
7. Scale 7 minus 8 more than 10 T.
8. Scale 9 less than 60 T.
9. Scales L, F and K less than 70 T.

A majority (56%) of these patients are diagnosed as psychoneurotic (Depressive/Anxiety) though a significant proportion (36%) are called psychotic (Depressive). Multiple neurotic manifestations and somatic symptoms are suggested. These patients are also depressed, admit to feelings of hopelessness, inferiority and guilt, show signs of tension and anxiety and display fears or phobias. They are often seen as serious, anticipating problems, perfectionistic and compulsively meticulous. Frustration is resolved in intropunitive maneuvers. Other symptoms include sleep disturbance, neurasthenia, religiosity, weight loss and worry. Most of these patients are married and have attained a good marital adjustment. This code is the highest IQ sample of Marks & Seeman; above average school achievement is noted. Therapy outcome: small improvement (42%); decided improvement (42%) and no change (16%). Energizers and ECT were occasional treatment approaches.

2-7 Mean Discharge Profile (n=24)

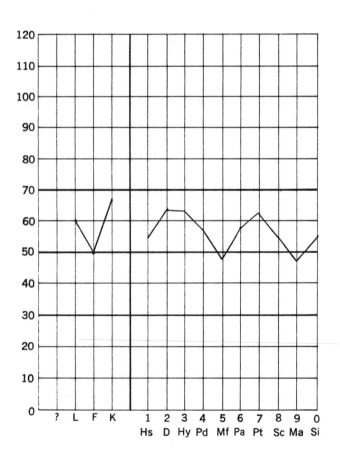

(2-7 (3) Profile Type: VA MALES: Gilberstadt & Duker, 1965) Mean Profile (n=13):

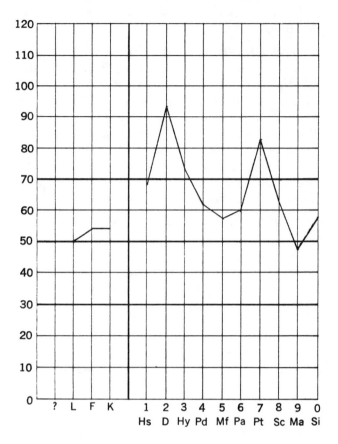

2-7 (3) Profile Type Rules (Gilberstadt & Duker, 1965):

1. Scales 2 and 7 over 70 T.
2. Scale 2 greater than 7.
3. Scale 7 minus 8 at least 15 T.
4. Scale 0 less than 70 T.
5. Scales 4 and 6 less than 80 T unless Scales 2 and/or 7 do not exceed 85 T, in which instance Scales 4 and 6 less than 70 T.

Most descriptive diagnosis: Psychoneurosis, Anxiety Reaction.

Modal diagnoses: Obsessive-compulsive Neurosis; Depressive Reaction.

Characteristics & rate of occurrence: Anorexia, nausea, vomiting (38%), Anxiety (85%), Cardiac complaint (23%), Depression (85%), Insomnia (46%), Nervousness (69%), Obessions (30%), Tension (69%), Weak, tired, fatigued (38%) and Worrying (46%).

These patients are vulnerable to accumulated stress. When anxiety becomes intolerable, they become depressed, clinging, dependent, self-depreciatory, lose confidence, feel inferior and become overwhelmed. Somatic correlates of anxiety are likely present.

Such individuals often set high standards of performance for themselves and do achieve. They are chronically anxious and strive to do well. They are capable of forming emotional ties.

(2-7 (3) GENERAL: Carson, 1969) Similar individuals are likely to present docile, markedly dependent interpersonal behavior with a tendency to inspire nurturant and helpful attitudes in others. The poignant helplessness of these persons not infrequently causes even experienced therapists to engage in nonfunctional protective maneuvers. Clinically, this type of problem is usually seen in the context of an anxiety or phobic reaction of relatively severe proportions.

(7-2 GENERAL) In most 2-7/7-2 profiles the Scale 2 elevation is greater than Scale 7. Where Scale 7 is greater than Scale 2, however, tenseness, indecision, anxiety and agitation tend to be more pronounced than when Scale 2 is greater than Scale 7.

(2-7/7-2 STATE HOSPITAL WHITES: Gynther et al., 1973) A critical characteristic of patients of this kind is that they are more likely to have suicidal thoughts than patients generally. (These patients are likely to be older, male and on a voluntary commitment as compared to other code-types within this population.)

(2-7 STATE HOSPITAL WHITES: Gynther et al., 1973) Other depressive symptoms that are more likely to occur include loss of interest and feelings of worthlessness.

These characteristics occur *less* frequently among 2-7's than among other state hospital patients: hostility, especially angry outbursts and unrealistic hostility, antisocial ideation, impaired insight and judgment, delusions of persecution and reference, evasiveness, labile affect and increased motor behavior.

(7-2 STATE HOSPITAL WHITES: Gynther et al., 1973) Another depressive symptom that is more likely to occur is feelings of worthlessness.

These characteristics occur *less* frequently among 7-2's than among other state hospital patients: hostility, especially angry outbursts and unrealistic hostility, antisocial ideation, impaired insight and judgment, delusions of persecution and reference, evasiveness, labile affect and increased motor behavior.

(2-7/7-2 STATE HOSPITAL: Lachar, 1968)
Mean Male (- -) & Female (—) Profiles

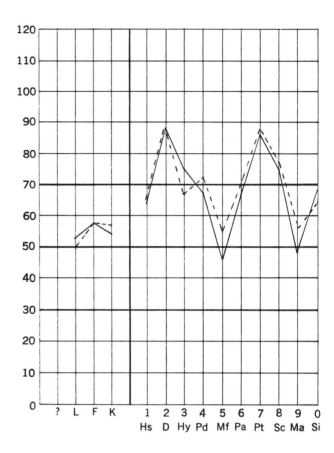

The 2-7/7-2 code was the 5th most frequent (n = 167) in this sample. The modal diagnosis was Reactive Depression. Diagnostic frequencies: Psychoneurotic—37%, Schizophrenic—10%, Other psychotic—30%, Personality Disorder—10% and Brain Syndrome—10%.

Automated Interpretation

See paragraph 47 (page 125).

2-0/0-2

This two-point code represented 1.75% of males and 5.14% of females in a sample of over 12,000 psychiatric outpatients (Webb, 1970).

(2-0/0-2 GENERAL) Tendencies toward withdrawal and social isolation are suggested. Shyness, timidity, self-isolation and marked social introversion are characteristic. Feelings of inadequacy in social situations and a real ineptitude and lack of skill in social interaction often accompany their introverted attitudes.

(2-0 GENERAL: Stelmachers) This profile suggests a relatively mild but chronic and characterologically deeply ingrained depression in a socially introverted and withdrawn person. In interactions with other people, the patient can be expected to demonstrate considerable insecurity and lack of social skills, especially with the opposite sex. The patient is also likely to be unhappy and prone to excessive worry. The patient may have learned to accept a considerable amount of depression as an integral part of himself, which may detract from the motivation and capacity to change. Should the patient be more than usually depressed at the present time, he could be helped to return to his "maintenance level" of depression.

(2-0/0-2 VA MALES: Gilberstadt & Duker, 1965) Look for withdrawn, schizoid personalities.

Automated Interpretation

See paragraph 50 (page 126).

High-point Scale 3

Scale 3 is profile high-point in 6.8% of males and 10.9% of females in a general psychiatric sample (Webb, 1971).

3 Spike

(GENERAL: Carson, 1969) Elevations on Scales 3 and K when Scales F and 8 are low are characteristic of affiliative, constrictedly over-conventional people. Such individuals in their relations with others show an over-determined striving to be liked and accepted. Characteristically they maintain an unassailable optimism and emphasize harmony with others at the expense of any internal value system. They are made extremely uncomfortable in situations demanding angry response, independent decision or the exercise of power. When these people do show up in the clinic, which is infrequent, they are most resistant to

considering that their difficulties may be within themselves. It is also a remarkable fact that even in the face of catastrophic failure they often maintain that "things are going fine." They seem to be quite without the equipment for tolerating feelings of defeat.

Automated Interpretation

See paragraph 28 (pages 117-118).

High-point Scale 7

Scale 7 is profile high-point in 7.3% of males and 4.7% of females in a general psychiatric sample (Webb, 1971). 1971).

7 Spike

(GENERAL) Although it is rare for isolated spikes to occur on Scale 7, interpretive statements by elevation noted above in interpretation by single scale elevation are applicable.

This is a rare profile. Phobias and compulsions are suggested. Some of these patients are called obsessional psychotics because of their bizarre behavior.

Automated Interpretation

See paragraph 31 (page 118).

7-0/0-7

This two-point code represented .36% of males and 1.08% of females in a sample of over 12,000 psychiatric outpatients (Webb, 1970).

(7-0/0-7 GENERAL) Although uncommon, this code suggests a serious generalized social inadequacy which is greater than when Scale 0 is elevated alone. The individuals are often described as anxious, ruminative, indecisive and depressed.

"PSYCHOTIC" PROFILES

Extreme 1 Spike

(GENERAL) When Scale 1 is more than 85 T and 10-20 T above Scales 2 and 3, schizophrenia is frequently indicated. This is especially true if Scale 8 is also elevated in the clinical range. Look for somatic delusions.

1-2-3 & 8 Spike

(VA MALES: Gilberstadt & Duker, 1965) When Scales 1, 2, 3 and 8 are all above 70 T, look for probable somatic delusions.

1-3-8/8-3-1/3-1-8

(GENERAL) This code is essentially a conversion "V" elevated with a peak on Scale 8 (usually above 80 T). This is essentially a schizophrenic profile.

(1-3-8 (2) Profile Type; VA MALES: Gilberstadt & Duker, 1965) Mean Profile (n=9)

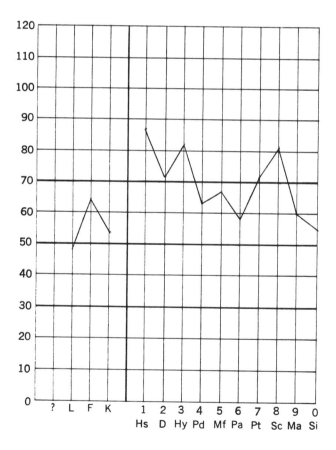

1-3-8 (2) Profile Type Rules (Gilberstadt & Duker, 1965):

1. Scales 1, 3 and 8 highest profile elevations.
2. Scale 8 over 70 T.
3. Scale 5 over 60 T.
4. Scale 4 less than 80 T.

Most descriptive diagnosis: Schizophrenic Reaction, Paranoid type.
Modal diagnoses: Anxiety Reaction in a Paranoid Personality; Schizophrenic Reaction, Chronic Undifferentiated type.
Characteristics & rate of occurrence: Agitated (33%), Compulsive (33%), Father mentally ill (22%), Financial status poor (44%), Religious (33%), Suicidal preoccupations (44%), Depression (67%) and Heavy drinking (56%).

These patients often display schizophrenic symptoms: thought disturbance and blocking, bizarre sexual concern and compulsions, ambivalence or open hatred, especially toward fathers, and religiosity and religious delusions. They may be described as emotionally flat, suspicious, jealous and paranoid. They may develop states of agitation in which they become restless, overbearing, demanding, excitable, loud and short-tempered. Similar patients may disclose fears regarding homosexuality and select masculine occupations (e.g., machinist) in order to deny psychosexual passivity.

Periods of severe depression and suicidal preoccupation are noted. These patients may display regressive psychotic behavior following periods of drinking. Somatic symptoms and hypochondriacal concerns, when present, seem to defend against florid outcroppings of schizophrenia.

1-6/6-1

This two-point code represented .15% of males and .19% of females in a sample of over 12,000 psychiatric outpatients (Webb, 1970).

(1-6/6-1 VA MALES: Gilberstadt & Duker, 1965) When Scales 1 and 6 are the high-point and Scale 4 is less than 70 T, look for paranoid schizophrenia.

Automated Interpretation

See paragraph 40 (page 122).

1-8/8-1

This two-point code represented 1.30% of males and .87% of females in a sample of over 12,000 psychiatric outpatients (Webb, 1970).

(GENERAL: Carson, 1969) With very high scores on Scale 8, an elevation on Scale 1 is often associated with somatic delusions.

Automated Interpretation

See paragraph 42 (pages 122-123).

8-1-2-3

(8-1-2-3 (7-4-6-0) Profile Type; VA MALES: Gilberstadt & Duker, 1965) Mean Profile (n=6)

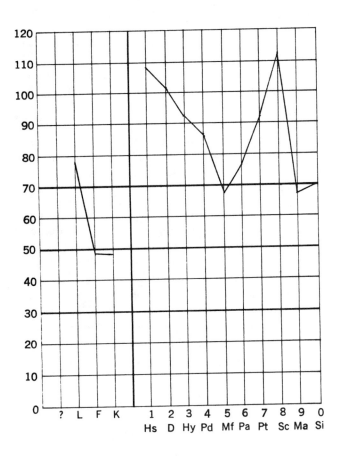

8-1-2-3 (7-4-6-0) Profile Type Rules (Gilberstadt & Duker, 1965):

1. Scales 1, 2 and 8 greater than 80 T.
2. Scale 1 > 2 > 3.
3. Scale 8 greater than 7.
4. Scale F less than 85 T.
5. Scale L may exceed 70 T.
6. IQ may be below average.

Most descriptive diagnosis: Schizophrenic Reaction, Simple type.
Modal diagnoses: Paranoid or Chronic Undifferentiated Schizophrenia; Anxiety Reaction in a Schizoid Personality.

Characteristics & rate of occurrence: Hostile (50%), Inadequacy feelings (50%), Poor work adjustment (100%), Schizoid (50%), Blunted, inappropriate affect (50%), Dependent (50%) and Tension (50%).

These patients exhibit extreme inadequacy in all areas of their lives. Presenting complaints may include flat affect, withdrawal, confused thinking and borderline somatic delusions. They are usually single (83%) and obtain a very poor adjustment in marriage. A nomadic adjustment and floating from one job to another are noted.

2-7-8

(2-7-8 GENERAL: Stelmachers) This is one of the most frequent profile types among psychiatric patients and is only rarely found among normals. The psychopathology indicated by the MMPI is likely to involve multiple neurotic manifestations and to be chronic and long-standing. The predominant symptom picture includes the distress syndrome (depression, anxiety, nervousness) and strong obsessional characteristics. The depression is mainly expressed by feelings of hopelessness. The patients with such profile types tend to be self-analytical and ruminatively introspective. They are typically intellectualizers who are over-ideational in their approach to solving emotional problems. They complain of concentration and thinking difficulties, are apt to suffer from excessive indecision, doubts and vacillation. They are described as being fearful worriers who lack self-esteem and are prone to engage in suicidal ruminations. They also frequently exhibit the neurasthenic syndrome (weakness, fatigue, loss of interest and initiative). Their basic personality pattern is often said to be schizoid, the patients tending to withdraw, to be socially introversive and distant.

The majority of these patients are severe obsessive-compulsives and only a small proportion decompensate into the kind of psychosis which is sometimes called schizophrenia. Very sick 2-7-8's can improve with brief, directive and goal-directed psychotherapy which encourages real-life achievements and de-emphasizes further introspection and self-analysis. Other therapeutic approaches may produce negative results. As these patients become anxious again, a few "recharge" treatment sessions may be needed though long-term, ongoing and reconstructive therapy is strongly counterindicated. Diagnostic Impression: (1) Obsessive-compulsive Reaction, severe; (2) Pseudoneurotic Schizophrenia.

(2-7-8 Profile Type; TEACHING HOSPITAL: Marks & Seeman, 1963)

Mean Male (- -) and Female (—) Profiles (n=20)

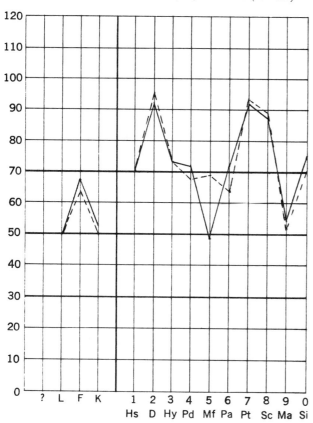

2-7-8 Profile Type Rules (Marks & Seeman, 1963):

1. Scales 2, 7 and 8 over 70 T.
2. Scale 2 minus 1 more than 15 T.
3. Scale 2 cannot exceed 8 by more than 14 T.
4. Scale 7 minus 4 more than 10 T.
5. Scale 7 minus 6 more than 10 T.
6. Scale 8 cannot exceed 7 by more than 4 T.
7. Scales 7 and 8 greater than 1 and 3.
8. Scale 9 less than 70 T.
9. Scale 0 over 70 T.
10. Scales L and K less than 70 T, F less than 80 T.

The majority (58%) of this profile type sample were diagnosed psychotic (Schizophrenic) though a significant element (33%) were labeled psychoneurotic (Anxiety/ Obessive-compulsive). Presenting symptomatology includes tension, anxiety, fearfulness and difficulty concentrating. Depression, worry, loss of interest and an obsessional-ruminative, perfectionistic orientation are associated with suicidal ruminations (65%).

Similar patients display multiple neurotic symptoms, feelings of hopelessness, manifestations of anxiety, fears and phobias. They overreact to minor problems and appear on mental status as tearful, crying, agitated or perhaps apathetic. Somatic correlates of anxiety, weakness and easy fatigability are noted. These patients may be seen as shy, inhibited and withdrawn. They fear emotional commitment, avoid making decisions and are consciously guilt-ridden, self-condemning and self-accusatory. Response to treatment: no change (25%); small improve-

ment (25%) and decided improvement (50%). Tranquilizers were used in 44% of this sample.

2-7-8 Mean Discharge Profile (n=22)

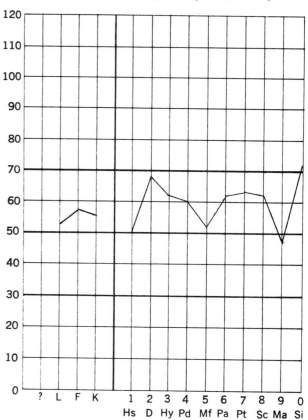

(2-7-8 (4-0-1-3-5-6) Profile Type; VA MALES: Gilberstadt & Duker, 1965)

Mean Profile (n=22)

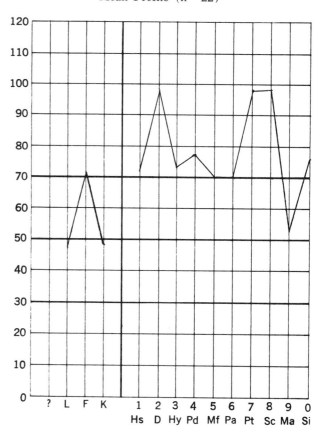

59

2-7-8 (4-0-1-3-5-6) Profile Type Rules (Gilberstadt & Duker, 1965):

1. Scales 2, 7 and 8 over 70 T.
2. Scale 2 minus 8 less than 15 T.
3. Scales 7 and 8 separated by less than 20 T (unless any of Scales 2, 7 or 8 greater than 100 T).
4. If Scale 7 is high-point, include only if all other scales less than 90 T and 7 does not exceed 2 by more than 5 T.
5. Scale 0 greater than 9.
6. Scale 9 less than 70 T.
7. Scale 2 greater than 1 by at least 11 T.
8. Scale 6 less than 80 T.

Most descriptive diagnoses: Pseudoneurotic or Chronic Undifferentiated Schizophrenia.

Modal diagnoses: Anxiety Reaction or Depressive Reaction in a Schizoid Personality.

Characteristics & rate of occurrence: Blunted, inappropriate affect (41%), Depression (87%), Difficult concentration (28%), Fearful (32%), Ideas of reference and persecution (32%), Inadequacy feelings (37%), Indecision (23%), Inferiority feelings (37%), Ruminations (28%), Schizoid (46%), Weak, tired, fatigued (32%) and Withdrawn, introversive (51%).

These patients are often described as ambivalent, shy, indecisive, quiet, withdrawn, obsessive, ruminative and sensitive. They are unable to love and frequently (86%) are unmarried. Characteristics may include severe depression, fatigue, weakness, insomnia, apathy and strong feelings of inadequacy and inferiority. Somatic correlates of anxiety and peculiar "neurologic" symptoms involving gross musculature may be present. These patients may show an interest in reading and ruminating about obscure subjects or religion. Presenting symptoms may include bizarre thinking, flat affect, ideas of reference and brief, acute psychotic episodes.

2-8/8-2

This two-point code represented 6.65% of males and 4.85% of females in a sample of over 12,000 psychiatric outpatients (Webb, 1970).

(2-8/8-2 GENERAL: Dahlstrom, Welsh & Dahlstrom, 1972) These individuals tend towards withdrawal and dissociation. The resulting status is often that of confusion, marked inefficiency and inability to concentrate. Although very infrequent, anxiety and agitation may be pronounced. Where there is such anxiety and depression, this reflects the profound inner turmoil of a person grappling with highly conflictual problems to which he can see no satisfactory solution. It is more typical of these patients that they are described as "resigned" to their psychosis.

Where both these scales are greater than 75 or 85 T, such patients are seen as psychotic, typically psychotic depressives and somewhat less frequently as schizophrenics. Depression, anxiety, confusion, withdrawal, guilt and agitation are frequent in the clinical picture.

(2-8 GENERAL: Stelmachers) This profile suggests rather severe depression with accompanying anxiety and agitation, leading to a fear of loss of control. In addition to being depressed, the patients with such profile types exhibit a marked psychological deficit as evidenced by a general loss of efficiency, periods of confusion, retarded stream of thought, a stereotyped approach to problem solving, forgetfulness, and noticeable difficulties with concentration. Occasionally the clinical picture includes hysterically determined somatic symptoms of an atypical variety. Unlike the hysteric, however, patients in this category are typically unsociable, interpersonally sensitive and suspicious. The majority of these patients receive psychotic diagnoses, predominantly psychotic depressions and schizo-affective disturbances. A good proportion of them are preoccupied with suicidal thoughts. Diagnostic Impression: (1) Psychotic Depressive Reaction; (2) Schizophrenic Reaction, Schizo-affective type.

Some of these females become psychotically depressed following a dissociative episode during which they did something bad (such as infanticide). This pattern may include fluctuation between a dissociative state in which there is no recollection of the bad deed and psychotic depression which follows the return of their memory about what they have done.

(2-8/8-2 Profile Type: TEACHING HOSPITAL: Marks & Seeman, 1963)

Mean Male (- -) and Female (—) Profiles (n=20)

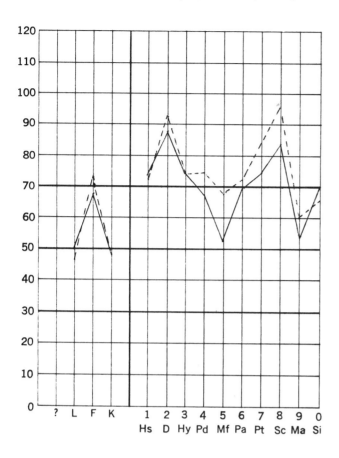

2-8/8-2 Profile Type Rules (Marks & Seeman, 1963):

1. Scales 2 and 8 over 70 T.
2. Scale 2 minus 8 less than 15 T.
3. Scale 7 greater than 4 and 6.
4. Scale 8 greater than 1 and 3.
5. Scale 8 greater than 7 by at least 6 T.
6. Scale 9 less than 70 T.
7. Scale 0 greater than 9.
8. Scales L and K less than F.

Patients who obtained this profile type received predominantly (70%) psychotic (Schizophrenic, schizoaffective) diagnoses. Other diagnoses: Brain Syndrome (15%—Acute) and Psychoneurotic (10%—Mixed). Similar patients distrust people in general, keep them at a distance, avoid close interpersonal relations and are afraid of emotional involvement. Depression, retarded thought, emotional lability, anxiety, obsessive thinking and suicidal ruminations are suggested. They may present themselves as physically sick and obtain secondary gain from their symptoms. Complaints may include sleep disturbance, memory loss, weakness, easy fatigability and dizziness.

These patients may be described as irritable, resentful, tense and high-strung. They may be rather defensive and manifest conflict over self-control and self-assertion. Conflicts about sexuality may be suggested. In treatment, tranquilizers (24%) and energizers (18%) were used. The discharge profile reflects the relative chronicity and stability of these symptoms. Treatment outcome: decided improvement (15%); small improvement (54%) and no change (31%).

2-8/8-2 Mean Discharge Profile (n=18)

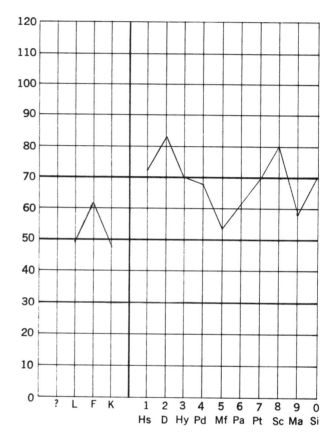

(2-8/8-2 STATE HOSPITAL WHITES: Gynther et al., 1973) Patients of this type are likely to show symptoms of depression. Depressive mood, soft voice, reduced speech and suicidal thoughts or attempts may be present. Not uncommonly, the suicidal ideation is in the form of a specific plan for suicide.

(2-8 STATE HOSPITAL WHITES: Gynther et al., 1973) Somatic delusions and a tendency to withdraw from personal interaction may also be evidenced.

(8-2 STATE HOSPITAL WHITES: Gynther et al., 1973) In addition, one or more symptoms are frequently present that are usually associated with a schizophrenic process, such as blocking, auditory hallucinations, delu-

sions of persecution, a tendency to withdraw from personal interaction and somatic delusions.

(2-8/8-2 STATE HOSPITAL: Lachar, 1968)
Mean Male (- -) & Female (—) Profiles

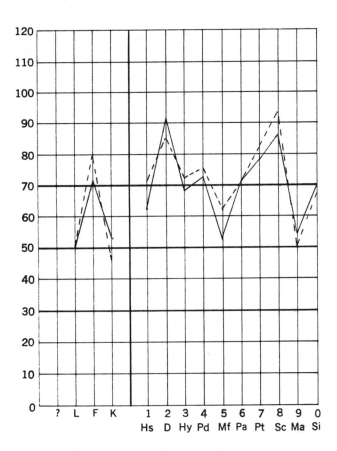

The 2-8/8-2 code was the 6th most frequent (n=158) in this sample. Half of this sample had never married. The modal diagnosis was Psychotic Depressive Reaction. Diagnostic frequencies: Schizophrenic—27%, Other Psychotic —23%, Psychoneurotic—30%, Brain Syndrome—13% and Personality Disorder—7%.

Automated Interpretation

See paragraph 48 (pages 125-126).

3-8/8-3

This two-point code represented .53% of males and 1.55% of females in a sample of over 12,000 psychiatric outpatients (Webb, 1970).

(8-3 GENERAL: Stelmachers) This profile suggests a moderate amount of distress syndrome (depression, anxiety and nervousness) plus some discharge of anxiety into somatic complaints, especially headaches and insomnia. The patient can be expected to be generally fearful, emotionally vulnerable and a chronic worrier. The patient tends to be basically quite dependent and immature and possesses schizoid characteristics. In addi-

tion to this, the patient is likely to have difficulties with thinking and concentration, to suffer from autistic episodes and emotionally inappropriate behavior. There may be present a more pervasive thought disturbance, a tendency to have peculiar and unconventional associations as well as outright delusions. Psychotic reactions in this group are typically accompanied by noticeable regression, behavior disorganization and bizarre associations. Diagnostic Impression: (1) Schizophrenic Reaction; (2) Dissociative Reaction.

(8-3/3-8 Profile Type; TEACHING HOSPITAL: Marks & Seeman, 1963)
Mean Female Profile (n=20)

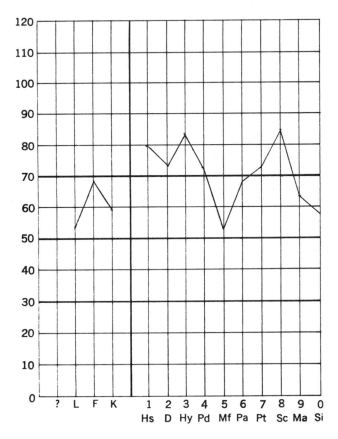

8-3/3-8 Profile Type Rules (Marks & Seeman, 1963):

1. Scales 8, 3 and 1 over 70 T.
2. Scale 3 minus 1 less than 10 T.
3. Scale 3 at least 6 T more than 2.
4. Scale 3 cannot exceed 8 by more than 4 T.
5. Scale 8 minus 7 more than 5 T.
6. Scale 8 minus 9 more than 10 T.
7. Scale 9 greater than 0.
8. Scale 0 less than 70 T.

This code-type sample was diagnosed psychotic (Schizophrenic/Manic depressive) 48%, psychoneurotic (Dissociative/Mixed) 43% and personality disorder (Schizoid) 10%. These patients manifest unusual and unconventional

thought processes including delusional thinking and ruminative and over-ideational thought processes. Difficulty in concentration and poor memory are noted. Thought processes are often described as autistic and irrelevant. Regression is a characteristic defense mechanism.

Somatic complaints include headache, blurred vision, numbness, sleep disturbance, chest pain, dizziness, parasthesia and eye complaints. Secondary gain is often present. An apathetic attitude as well as feelings of hopelessness, insecurity, worry and fear are often characteristic. Similar patients have difficulty expressing affect in a modulated fashion, tend to overract and behave in an intropunitive fashion. They are characterized as immature, dependent, unoriginal, passive, evasive and resentful. Therapy outcome: small improvement (53%); decided improvement (12%) and no change (35%). Tranquilizers were used in the treatment of 40% of this sample.

8-3/3-8 Mean Discharge Profile (n=24)

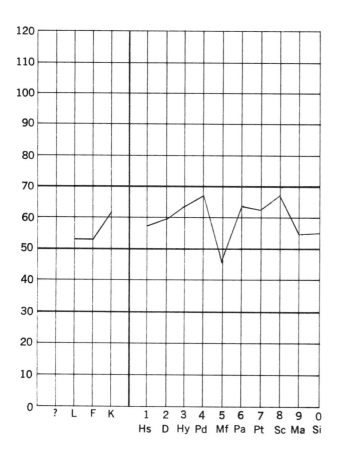

Automated Interpretation

See paragraph 54 (page 128).

High-point Scale 6

Scale 6 is profile high-point in 2.0% of males and 6.7% of females in a general psychiatric sample (Webb, 1971).

6 Spike

(GENERAL) When 6 is the only scale in the clinical range, especially if Scale 6 elevation exceeds 80 T, paranoia, paranoid schizophrenia or paranoid states are indicated. False positives are infrequent.

Automated Interpretation

See paragraph 30 (page 118).

6-8/8-6

This two-point code represented 2.02% of males and 3.91% of females in a sample of over 12,000 psychiatric outpatients (Webb, 1970).

(6-8/8-6 GENERAL) Paranoid Schizophrenia unless proved otherwise. This is the case with either Scale 6 and Scale 8 the only scales elevated in the clinical range or with Scale 6 and Scale 8 high-points in an elevated profile. When Scale 6 is 70-80 T and significantly greater than Scale 8, pre-psychotic adjustments in schizoid personality patterns are possible. High elevation (over 80 T) of the F Scale should be expected, and flat interpretation of F-K over 11 as malingering should be avoided.

(8-6 GENERAL: Stelmachers) This profile suggests a serious thinking disorder and paranoid mentation consistent with a paranoid schizophrenic reaction. The patient can be expected to suffer from the distress syndrome (nervousness, anxiety, depression), to be pervasively hostile and suspicious. A delusional system is likely to be present. General apathy is usually present and so is noticeable behavior regression and disorganization, as well as autistic and bizarre associations. Diagnostic Impression: Schizophrenic Reaction, Paranoid type.

(8-6/6-8 Profile Type; TEACHING HOSPITAL: Marks & Seeman, 1963)
Mean Female Profile (n=20)

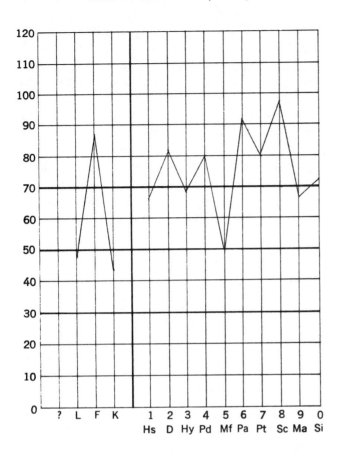

8-6/6-8 Profile Type Rules (Marks & Seeman, 1963):

1. Scales 8, 6, 4 and 2 over 70 T.
2. Scales 1 and 3 less than 2, 6, 7 and 8.
3. Scale 2 minus 1 more than 10 T.
4. Scale 6 minus 5 more than 25 T.
5. Scale 6 greater than 7.
6. Scale 8 minus 7 more than 10 T.
7. Scale 8 minus 9 more than 10 T.
8. Scale F greater than L and K, L and K less than 60 T.

A majority (68%) of patients who obtain this profile type are diagnosed psychotic (Schizophrenic, paranoid). Other diagnoses include personality disorder (18%—Paranoid) and brain syndrome (14%—Chronic). These patients think in unusual and unconventional ways, manifesting delusions, difficulty in concentration, grandiosity, autism and negativism. They spend much time in personal fantasy and daydreams, are suspicious, distrust people and keep them at a distance; these patients may be seen as shy, anxious and inhibited. Similar patients have difficulty expressing emotions in a modulated, adaptive way and are described as irritable, resentful, agitated, over-sensitive, moody, narcissistic and immature.

They are often unpredictable, emotionally inappropriate, ruminative and over-ideational. Fears or phobias and inner conflicts about sexuality are suggested. Onset of illness is often acute. Tranquilizers were used in 25% of this sample. Treatment outcome: no change (15%); small improvement (39%) and decided improvement (46%).

8-6/6-8 Mean Discharge Profile (n=30)

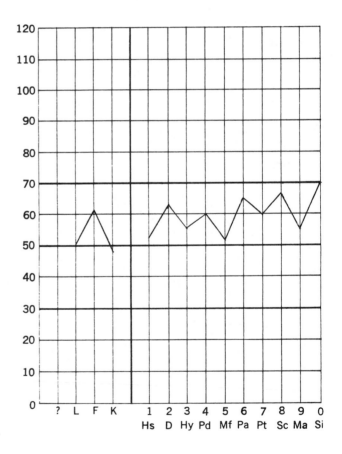

(8-6 (7-2) Profile Type; VA MALES: Gilberstadt & Duker, 1965)
Mean Profile (n = 10)

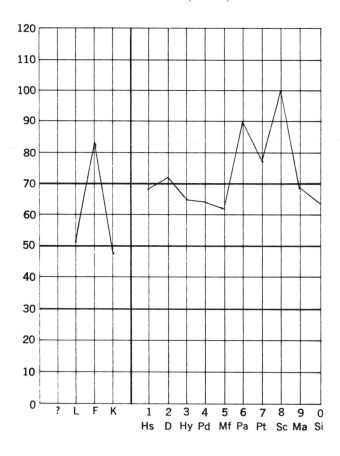

8-6 (7-2) Profile Type Rules (Gilberstadt & Duker, 1965):

1. Scales 8 and 6 over 70 T.
2. Scales 8 and 6 highest profile elevations.
3. Scale F may exceed 70 T.

Diagnosis: Schizophrenic Reaction, Paranoid type. Characteristics & rate of occurrence: Assaultive (30%), Auditory hallucinations (40%), Blunted inappropriate affect (60%), Paranoid delusions (bizarre) (90%) Suspicious (50%) and Withdrawn, introversive (50%).

These patients are described as shy, withdrawn and evidencing flat affect. Symptoms may include a florid schizophrenic thought disorder, confusion, poor memory and concentration, delusions and hallucinations. Their histories may include aggressive attacks following periods of drinking. They are usually single (70%); if married, their wives are likely to be seen as deviant. Social histories may include periods of reasonable vocational adjustment, though inefficiency and fatigue preceding psychotic reactions lead to marked decrease in ability to function.

(6-8/8-6 STATE HOSPITAL WHITES: Gynther et al., 1973)
Patients of this kind often seem unfriendly and angry for no apparent reason. They are apt to speak rapidly and jump from one topic to another. Evidence of thought disorder is not uncommon. Fragmentation, tangential thinking and circumstantiality are frequently displayed. (A high proportion of females obtain this code type.)

(6-8 STATE HOSPITAL WHITES: Gynther et al., 1973)
Paranoid delusions, especially delusions of grandeur, and hallucinations, especially of an auditory type, are often present. Poor judgment is typical. Patients are often unrealistic concerning how ill they are, feel no need for help, and do not know why they have been hospitalized.

Diagnostically, patients of this type are usually labeled psychotic, and more specifically, paranoid schizophrenic. They are less likely to be labeled alcoholic than patients in general.

(8-6 STATE HOSPITAL WHITES: Gynther et al., 1973)
Affect is apt to be blunted. Paranoid delusions and hallucinations, especially of an auditory type, are often present. Poor judgment is typical. Patients are often unrealistic concerning how ill they are, feel no need for help, and do not know why they have been hospitalized.

Diagnostically, patients of this type are usually labeled psychotic, and more specifically, paranoid schizophrenic. They are less likely to be labeled alcoholic than patients in general.

(6-8/8-6 STATE HOSPITAL: Lachar, 1968)
Mean Male (- -) & Female (—) Profiles

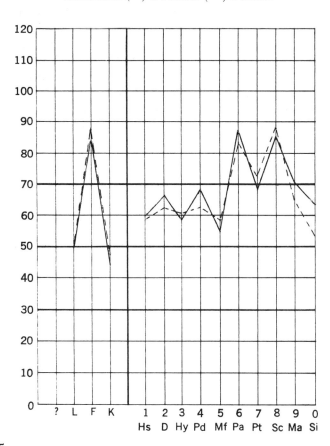

The 6-8/8-6 code was the most frequent (n=284) in this sample and was obtained by more female patients (64%) than male patients. The modal diagnosis was Paranoid Schizophrenia. Diagnostic frequencies: Schizophrenia—70%, Other psychotic—17% and Personality Disorder—10%.

Automated Interpretation

See paragraphs 61, 61A, 61B and 61C (pages 131-132).

6-9/9-6

This two-point code represented .96% of males and 1.63% of females in a sample of over 12,000 psychiatric outpatients (Webb, 1970).

(6-9/9-6 GENERAL) This is not a very common profile. The Scale 6 may reflect the paranoid aspects of grandiosity and self-aggrandizement of a fundamentally manic disorder. In general the role of Scale 6 seems to emphasize the amount of anger and aggression being directly expressed. This is especially true when Scale 4 shows some elevation, which is usually the case.

(9-6 GENERAL: Stelmachers) Patients with this kind of profile are characteristically tense and anxious, and typically react to even minor frustrations by irritability, jumpiness and ineffective excitability. They typically overreact to environmental stimuli in an emotional way and have difficulty thinking and concentrating. In their social contacts they manifest considerable hostility. They suffer from ideas of reference and pervasive suspiciousness which may, at times, take the form of outright paranoid mentation or even paranoid delusions. A great majority of patients with such profiles are found on the inpatient service with psychotic diagnoses. Diagnostic Impression: (1) Schizophrenic Reaction, Paranoid type; (2) Rule out Manic-depressive Psychosis, Manic type.

(9-6/6-9 Profile Type; TEACHING HOSPITAL: Marks & Seeman, 1963)

Mean Female Profile (n=20)

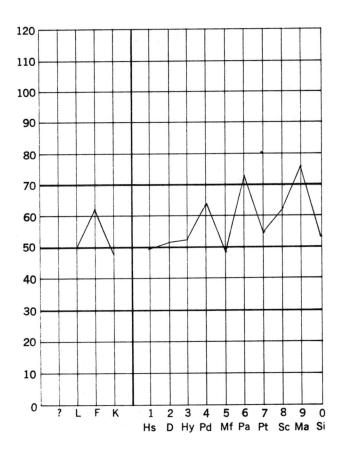

9-6/6-9 Profile Type Rules (Marks & Seeman, 1963):

1. Scales 9 and 6 over 70 T.
2. Scales 1, 2 and 3 less than 70 T.
3. Scale 4 cannot exceed 6 by more than 4 T.
4. Scale 9 minus 2 more than 15 T.
5. Scale 9 minus 4 more than 5 T.
6. Scale 9 minus 8 more than 10 T.
7. Scale 0 less than 70 T.
8. Scales L and K less than 70 T, F less than 80 T.

The majority (85%) of patients who obtain this profile type are diagnosed psychotic (Schizophrenic, paranoid) and a small number (10%) are diagnosed psychoneurotic (Mixed). Onset is often acute; symptomatology is often (40%) a repetition of previous episodes.

Similar patients distrust others, keep them at a distance and are afraid of emotional involvement. Poor concentration, delusional thinking, ideas of reference, hallucinations, thought disturbance, hostility, moodiness and excitability are characteristic. Thought is described as irrelevant, incoherent and retarded. They seem unable to express their emotions in any modulated, adaptive way. These individuals are overanxious, tense, nervous, emotionally labile and tend to be ruminative and over-ideational. Poor judgment and feelings of perplexity are noted. Projection is a characteristic defense mechanism. Inner conflicts about sexuality and an exaggerated need for affection are suggested. Treatment response: no change (31%); small improvement (38%) and decided improvement (31%). Tranquilizers (45%) and ECT (17%) were treatment approaches.

9-6/6-9 Mean Discharge Profile (n=18)

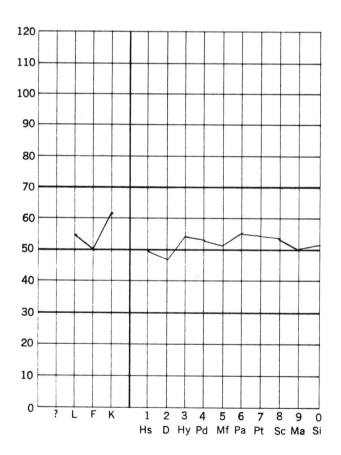

(*9-6/6-9 GENERAL*) Though Marks & Seeman label these patients paranoid schizophrenic, such a diagnosis is much less frequent in other settings. Manic reactions are often seen as modal. These manics have paranoid ideas; grandiosity and paranoid mentation often occur together. These individuals are anxious and tend to over-react with much social hostility.

(*6-9/9-6 STATE HOSPITAL WHITES: Gynther et al., 1973*) The symptoms that are most likely prominent in the clinical picture of this type of patient are those indicating excitement, specifically, flight of ideas, delusions of grandeur, loud voice and excessive amount of speech. There is typically a notable absence of depression or anxiety, but hostility is frequently present. Evidence of a thought disorder may be present, particularly circumstantiality. Organicity needs to be ruled out.

Automated Interpretation

See paragraph 62 (page 132).

7-8/8-7

This two-point code represented 6.91% of males and 4.48% of females in a sample of over 12,000 psychiatric outpatients (Webb, 1970).

(*7-8/8-7 GENERAL: Dahlstrom, Welsh & Dahlstrom, 1972*) Psychiatric cases with this code are rather evenly divided between neurotic and psychotic diagnoses. The neurotics were obsessive-compulsive, depressive, or showed mixed forms, but few somatization patterns were included. The psychotic cases also ranged widely, although the manic forms were not represented. Depression and introversion were the dominant clinical features, together with worrying, irritability, nervousness, apathy and social withdrawal.

(*7-8 GENERAL*) The relatively higher elevation on Scale 7 indicates a less fixed personality pattern. There is, in comparison with 8-7's, a great deal more anxiety, agitation and struggle in attempts to work through problems, even if ineffectively.

(7-8 (2-1-3-4 Profile Type; VA MALES: Gilberstadt & Duker, 1965)

Mean Profile (n = 9)

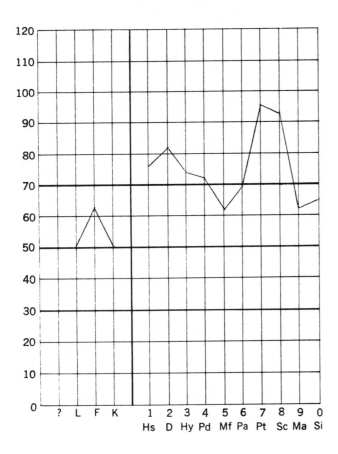

7-8 (2-1-3-4) Profile Type Rules (Gilberstadt & Duker, 1965):

1. Scales 7 and 8 over 70 T.
2. Scales 7 and 8 highest profile elevations.
3. Scales 7 and 8 separated by less than 10 T.

Most descriptive diagnosis: Psychoneurosis, Obsessive-compulsive Reaction.

Modal diagnoses: Psychoneurosis, Anxiety Reaction in a Schizoid Personality with somatization; Latent, or Chronic Boderline, Schizophrenia.

Characteristics & rate of occurrence: Difficult concentration (33%), Father strict (33%), Inferiority feelings (44%), Tension (56%), Worrying (44%), Depression (89%) and Nervousness (56%).

Such patients are described as shy, fearful, lacking confidence and as expressing feelings of inadequacy. They manifest somatic correlates of anxiety, especially GI complaints. They maintain a masculine identification but feel inferior. They manifest difficulties in interpersonal and heterosexual relations including guilt concerning sex and poor sexual performance. Marriages are frequently forced and lead to role and sexual problems.

Their social histories often include domination by fathers and older brothers which led to dependency-independency conflicts. Their assertive and stubborn behavior as early adults often covers up underlying weakness. They are conscientious but achieve poorly which results in feelings of guilt. Major conflicts over job conditions or with supervisors may result because of "adolescent idealism." They may drink to relax.

(8-7 GENERAL) Clear-cut, overt psychosis with great turmoil is often suggested. The addition of some Scale 2 elevation may indicate a schizo-affective reaction. These individuals are high suicide risks. The attempts are bizarre, in which attempts are for self-mutilation or punishment and often succeed. These individuals watch their own deterioration.

(8-7 GENERAL: Carson, 1969) When both scales are elevated above 75 T and when Scale 8 is relatively higher, this is often an established schizophrenic psychosis, especially if the neurotic triad is relatively low. Even in those cases in which psychosis can be ruled out, the problem is likely to be a very refractory one, such as a severe alienated character disorder.

(8-7 GENERAL: Stelmachers) The profile suggests chronic personality difficulties characterized by excessive worry, introspection and over-ideational rumination. The patient is likely to be passively dependent and to suffer from feelings of inadequacy, inferiority and insecurity. Patients with such profile types tend to be generally nervous and to lack established defense patterns. In relation to other people, they lack poise, assurance and dominance and characteristically have histories with few rewarding social experiences. Their actions and planning reveal a lack of common sense. They have rich fantasy lives, especially about sexual matters, and spend much time daydreaming. Diagnostic Impression: (1) Schizoid personality; (2) Rule out Schizophrenic Reaction.

Since patients in this group do not readily form stable and warm interpersonal relationships, they show typically poor response to psychotherapy. Probably a relatively long-term psychotherapy of a relationship type can be expected to produce gradual and at best moderate changes in the desirable direction.

(7-8/8-7 STATE HOSPITAL WHITES: Gynther et al., 1973) This type of patient may display some evidence of bizarre speech, such as perseveration, echolalia, clang associations or neologisms. Depersonalization may also be present.

(7-8/8-7 STATE HOSPITAL: Lachar, 1968)
Mean Male (--) & Female (—) Profiles

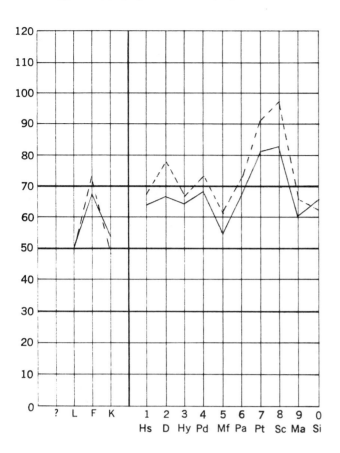

The 7-8/8-7 code was the 11th most frequent (n=123) in this sample. Half of this sample had not married. The modal diagnosis was Chronic Undifferentiated Schizophrenia. Diagnostic frequencies: Schizophrenic—57%, Other psychotic—13%, Personality Disorder—17% and Psychoneurotic—10%.

Automated Interpretation

See paragraphs 63, 63A, 63B and 63C (pages 132-133).

High-point Scale 8

Scale 8 is profile high-point in 17.9% of males and 15.4% of females in a general psychiatric sample (Webb, 1971).

8 Spike

(GENERAL) This pattern is pathognomonic of schizophrenia, if profile is valid.

Automated Interpretation

See paragraph 32 (pages 118-119).

8-9/9-8

This two-point code represented 2.59% of males and 2.35% of females in a sample of over 12,000 psychiatric outpatients (Webb, 1970).

(8-9/9-8 GENERAL: Carson, 1969) Such individuals handle their inability to relate, or fear of relating, by distractibility operations. This pattern is often associated with a highly malignant psychopathological process, and its occurrence should be viewed with extreme seriousness even where elevation is only moderate. These people cannot permit a focalization of issues and are therefore difficult to work with in psychotherapy.

(8-9 GENERAL: Stelmachers) A majority of patients with this type of profile show evidence of paranoid mentation and a thinking disorder. Onset is typically acute and accompanied by excitement, disorientation and general feelings of perplexity. They typically have well-established autistic trends and may manifest outright delusions and hallucinations. Regression is manifested by retarded and stereotyped thinking and by emotional inappropriateness. Besides exhibiting distress syndrome (depressed, anxious, nervous), these patients are often described as being hostile and irritable and as withdrawing from social contacts.

Most patients in this group are typically found on an inpatient service and are diagnosed as schizophrenic reactions. Diagnostic Impression: Schizophrenic Reaction.

(8-9/9-8 Profile Type; TEACHING HOSPITAL: Marks & Seeman, 1963)
Mean Female Profile (n=20)

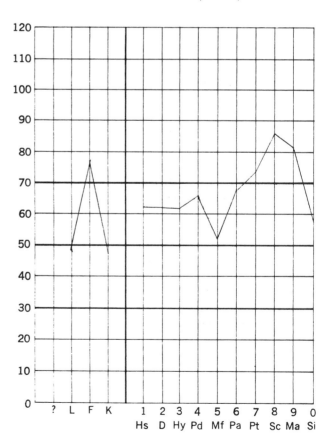

8-9/9-8 Profile Type Rules (Marks & Seeman, 1963):

1. Scales 8 and 9 over 70 T.
2. Scale 5 over 40 T.
3. Scale 8 minus 7 more than 5 T.
4. Scale 9 not to exceed 8 by more than 4 T.
5. Scale 0 less than 70 T.
6. Scale F greater than L and K.

The majority (70%) of patients who obtain this profile type are diagnosed psychotic (Schizophrenic/Mixed); a relatively small number (17%) were labeled psychoneurotic (Depressive). These patients display unusual and unconventional thought processes including delusions, gradiosity, autism, hallucinations, poor concentration and negativism. Clinically they are often seen as agitated, excitable, restless and display gestures. Thought is often described as irrelevant, retarded and incoherent. Emotion is often expressed in an unmodulated, nonadaptive fashion. Affect is often characterized as inappropriate, irritable, hostile and labile.

These patients spend a good deal of time in fantasy and daydreams, are suspicious and distrustful of others, afraid of emotional involvement and consequently keep people at a distance, avoiding close relations. They are often described as ruminative and over-ideational, disoriented, withdrawn and unpredictable. Projection, acting-out and regression are characteristic defense mechanisms. Feelings of perplexity and unreality and conflict about sexuality may be present. The above symptoms are usually associated with an acute onset. Tranquilizers were used the most with this profile type among the Marks & Seeman codes (60%). Response to treatment: no change (28%); small improvement (39%) and decided improvement (33%).

8-9/9-8 Mean Discharge Profile (n=24)

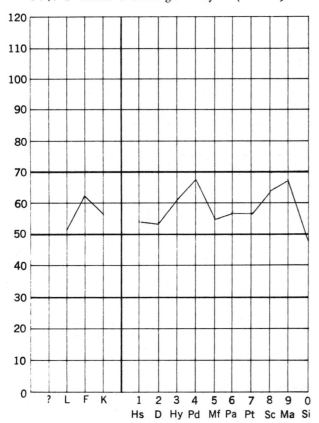

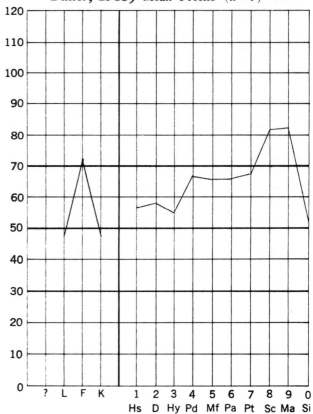

(8-9 Profile Type; VA MALES: Gilberstadt & Duker, 1965) Mean Profile (n=9)

8-9 Profile Type Rules (Gilberstadt & Duker, 1965):

1. Scales 8 and 9 over 70 T.
2. Scales 8 and 9 highest profile elevations.
3. Scales 8 and 9 separated by less than 16 T.

Most descriptive diagnosis: Schizophrenic Reaction, Catatonic type.

Modal Diagnoses: "Schizo-manic" Psychosis; Paranoid Schizophrenia.

Characteristics & rate of occurrence: Anxiety (56%), Circumstantial (33%), Compulsive (33%), Confusion (nonorganic) (56%), Father rejecting (22%), Father strict (33%), Financial status poor (44%), Hostile (44%), Hyperactive (56%), Paranoid delusions (bizarre) (44%), Paranoid trends (44%), Religious (78%), Restless (44%), Tension (56%), Depression (67%) and Poor work adjustment (67%).

The patients who obtain this code type are described as ambivalent, suspicious, vague, evasive, overtalkative, hyperactive, unmanageable, tense and panicky. Psychotic symptomatology includes disorganized thinking, delusions, hallucinations and excessive religiosity. They may become indecisive, withdrawn and catatonic. In an excited phase similar patients become hostile, demanding, pacing, dazed and disoriented.

They have high achievement needs which are rarely met. Vocational indecision and poor job role identification are suggested. Similar patients have obtained a poor sexual adjustment and are seldom married (33%). Marriages, when they occur, are characterized as unhappy. These patients are transference prone.

(8-9/9-8 STATE HOSPITAL WHITES: Gynther et al., 1973) Patients of this type often present a picture of hostile-paranoid excitement starting within a month of the time help was sought. Hostility tends to be unrealistic and paranoid ideation may reach delusional proportions.

(8-9 STATE HOSPITAL WHITES: Gynther et al., 1973) Excitement may be manifested by loud voice, flight of ideas, labile affect, or an increase in amount of speech or motor activity. Bizarre speech, such as clang associations, neologisms, echolalia, or perseveration, may also be present.

A history of school behavior problems is not uncommon.

These characteristics occur *less* frequently among 8-9's than among other state hospital patients: alcoholic and depressive symptoms and problems.

(9-8 STATE HOSPITAL WHITES: Gynther et al., 1973) Excitement may be manifested by loud voice, flight of ideas, labile affect, or over-talkativeness. Bizarre speech, such as clang associations, neologisms, echolalia, or perseveration, may also be present. They may not know why they are hospitalized.

A history of brain function difficulties and school behavior problems is not uncommon.

These characteristics occur *less* frequently among 9-8's than among other state hospital patients: alcoholic and depressive symptoms and problems.

(8-9/9-8 STATE HOSPITAL: Lachar, 1968)
Mean Male (- -) & Female (—) Profiles

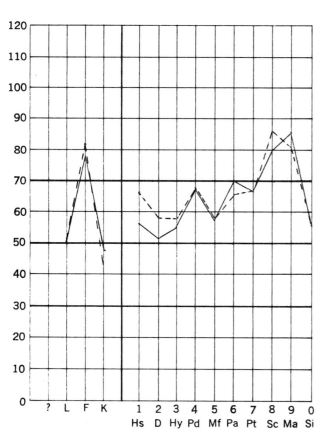

The 8-9/9-8 code was the 10th most frequent (n=127) in this sample. Over half (63%) of this sample had never married. The modal diagnosis was Schizo-affective Psychosis. Diagnostic frequencies: Schizophrenic—61%, Other psychotic—10% and Personality Disorder—20%.

Automated Interpretation

(8-9/9-8) See paragraph 65 (pages 133-134).

8-0/0-8

This two-point code represented .29% of males and .98% of females in a sample of over 12,000 psychiatric outpatients (Webb, 1970).

(8-0/0-8 GENERAL) The elevation of Scale 8 with Scale 0 points up the marked withdrawal and people-avoidance of these persons.

High-point Scale 9

Scale 9 is profile high-point in 8.0% of males and 8.5% of females in a general psychiatric sample (Webb, 1971).

9 Spike

(GENERAL) If Scale 9 is above 85 T with all other scales less than 70 T, the usual picture is one of hypomania. See interpretive statements above under single scale interpretive statements.

Automated Interpretation

See paragraphs 33, 34 and 35 (pages 119-120).

(9 Profile Type; VA MALES: Gilberstadt & Duker, 1965) Mean Profile (n=10)

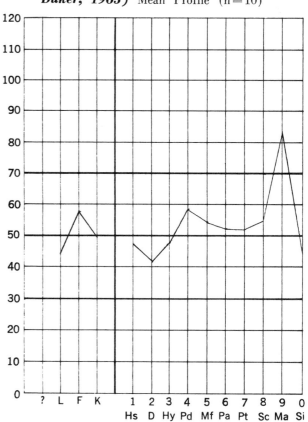

9 Profile Type Rules (Gilberstadt & Duker, 1965):

1. Scale 9 over 70 T.
2. No other scales over 70 T.
3. Scale 2 less than 50 T.

Diagnosis: Manic-depressive Reaction, Manic type.
Characteristics & rate of occurrence: Circumstantial (60%), Financial status poor (50%), Grandiose delusions (50%), Hostile (40%), Hyperactive (80%), Mother domineering (30%), Religious (30%), Talkative (70%), Depression (70%), Heavy drinking (50%) and Poor work adjustment (60%).

These patients present symptoms of hyperactivity, grandiosity and talkativeness. They are overactive and involved in a great number of projects. When acutely disturbed, these patients often display bizarre speech and thought patterns. They fear being slowed down as they anticipate impending depression. Irritability and belligerency are frequent responses to even minor frustration. They turn to religion strongly during an acute phase for control but simultaneously resent all controls.

Similar patients have had previous episodes of depression or mania. They are prone to having "anniversary reactions." Some evidence of genetic defect is likely present in the patient's family. Between phases or cycles of illness these patients maintain a normal job and life adjustment.

High-point Scale 0

Scale 0 is profile high-point in 1.2% of males and 5.8% of females in a general psychiatric sample (Webb, 1971).

0 Spike

(*GENERAL*) In rare cases, scores above 70 T in an otherwise low profile will pick up a schizoid factor which is missed by other scales in a relatively well put-together psychotic or schizoid personality types. Others disagree and feel that these rare types are mainly psychoneurotic. In any case, significant discomfort in social situations is indicated.

Automated Interpretation

See paragraph 36 (page 120).

"CHARACTEROLOGICAL" PROFILES

1-2-3-4

(1-2-3-4 Profile Type; VA MALES: Gilberstadt & Duker, 1965) Mean Profile (n=36)

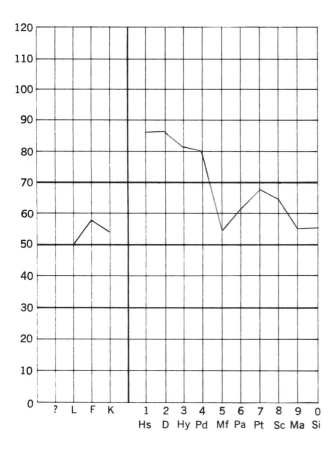

1-2-3-4 Profile Type Rules (Gilberstadt & Duker, 1965):

1. Scales 1, 2, 3 and 4 over 70 T and highest profile elevations.
2. Scale 0 less than 70 T.
3. Scales L, F and K less than 70 T, unless at least two clinical scales over 100 T, in which case F less than 80 T.

Most descriptive diagnosis: Personality Trait Disturbance with alcoholism, anxiety, depression and Psychophysiological Reaction.
Modal diagnoses: Anxiety Reaction; Depressive Reaction; Psychophysiological Reaction with Personality Trait Disturbance.
Characteristics & rate of occurrence: Anorexia, nausea, vomiting (47%), Assaultive (31%), Combative when drunk (17%), Conflict with wife (53%), Epigastric complaints (36%), Financial status poor (44%), Heavy drinking (78%), Hostile (53%), Insomnia (34%),

Irritable (42%), Mother domineering (14%), Nervousness (53%), Poor work adjustment (67%), Suicide attempt (20%), Suspicious (31%), Tension (39%), Weak, tired, fatigued (25%) and Depression (58%).

These patients often display somatic symptoms such as ulcers and other GI complaints, apparently in response to stress or frustration. Alcoholism is often a severe problem. They are often orally fixated, demanding and dependent to the extent that their needs are constantly being frustrated. A history of hostility and assaultiveness, particularly toward women such as wives or girlfriends, is often noted. These patients basically display a mixture of neurotic defenses and long-standing character defects which are hard to modify.

(1-2-3-4 Profile Type; VA MALES: Fowler & Athey, 1971) These descriptors were found significant for both the Gilberstadt & Duker (1965) study and the present sample (n=25): (1) Anorexia, nausea, vomiting, (2) Heavy drinking, (3) Hostile, (4) Insomnia, (5) Nervousness, (6) Tension, (7) Ulcer and (8) Depression. While the Gilberstadt & Duker study indicated direct expression of aggression, this sample showed instead a large variety of specific physical complaints. This pattern may represent control of hostility via somatization. Cardinal features noted were severe alcoholism, dependency and somatic symptoms. 64% had a primary diagnosis of Anxiety Reaction, 12% were diagnosed Passive-aggressive personality. 64% of the diagnoses included some reference to alcohol or drinking, and 20% some reference to depression.

1-4/4-1

This two-point code represented .84% of males and .51% of females in a sample of over 12,000 psychiatric outpatients (Webb, 1970).

(1-4/4-1 GENERAL) Elevations on Scale 1 accompanied by clear elevations on Scale 4, particularly if Scale 3 is relatively low, are usually obtained from individuals with clear hypochondriacal adjustment patterns. The role of Scale 4 seems to emphasize the pessimistic, grouchy, bitchy and dissatisfied aspects of the high Scale 1.

(1-4/4-1 STATE HOSPITAL WHITES: Gynther et al., 1973) Patients of this type may have a drinking problem. There may be an associated history of benders, jobs lost or arrests.

Automated Interpretation

See paragraph 39 (page 122).

2-4/4-2

This two-point code represented 5.97% of males and 7.51% of females in a sample of over 12,000 psychiatric outpatients (Webb, 1970).

(2-4/4-2 GENERAL) This code type is often obtained by a psychopathic personality who has in some sense been "caught," either by the law or a hospital. In any event these persons are reacting to situational (versus internal) stress. The depression abates when escape from stress is effective or manipulations promise to be effective. While the insight these persons show may be good and their verbal protestations of resolve to do better may seem genuine, long-range prognosis for behavior change is poor. Recurrences of acting out and subsequent exaggerated guilt are common.

2-4/4-2 Research

Alcoholism and/or addiction are possibilities. For example, a recent study of MMPIs obtained from various subclassifications of addicts treated during a four year period at Lexington (Berzins, Ross & Monroe, 1971) resulted in mean profiles with a primary 4-2/2-4 configuration and a secondary lesser Scale 8 elevation. (Note the 4-8-2/8-4-2/8-2-4 and the 8-2-4 (7) Code Types.)

Spiegel, Hadley & Hadley (1970) found that their alcoholic sample obtained Scales 2 and 4 as high points. This sample was described as displaying a strong sense of personal frustration and self-dissatisfaction which seemed to be related to an outlook on life which did little to constrain them from acting on impulse. These investigators speculated that drinking behavior provided for these alcoholics a temporary reduction in their sense of frustration and rewarded the individual with a momentary escape and a fleeting sense of euphoria and strength. The loss of social relations and employment which frequently accompanies alcoholism, however, likely leads to an expanding spiral of increasing frustration and increasing involvement with alcohol.

The cyclical nature of the 2-4/4-2 conduct disturbance is also suggested by the mean profile obtained by the habitual criminals studied by Panton (1962a).

On occasion these scales are grossly elevated together in prepsychotic individuals. These persons are angry at others and at themselves, which doesn't leave them much place to go. These individuals have a low frustration tolerance. When feeling guilty they become extropunitive, which leads to more guilt feelings, etc. In some cases Scale 2 represents a chronic depression and Scale 4 represents a characterological adjustment with depression and low frustration tolerance.

(2-4/4-2 STATE HOSPITAL WHITES: Gynther et al., 1973) Patients of this kind are often described as having a definite drinking problem and are more likely to be labeled as alcoholics than patients generally. They may be acutely intoxicated at admission. Their drinking history may include benders, arrests or previous hospitalization.

(2-4/4-2 MALE STATE HOSPITAL WHITES: Gynther et al., 1973) Another problem which may have arisen from their drinking is loss of their job.

These characteristics occur *less* frequently among 2-4/4-2 males than among other state hospital patients: delusions of persecution and grandeur, auditory hallucination, tangential thinking, fragmentation of thought, flight of ideas, poor remote memory, bodily concern, silliness and impaired insight and judgment.

(2-4/4-2 FEMALE STATE HOSPITAL WHITES: Gynther et al., 1973) Another problem which may have arisen from their drinking is family problems.

This type of patient is also more likely to be labeled diagnostically as depressive neurosis and to display depressive mood than the average patient. A recent history of crying episodes and, more important, of suicidal behavior may be present. The latter usually takes the form of attempts or gestures.

These characteristics occur *less* frequently among 2-4/4-2 females than among other state hospital patients: delusions of persecution and grandeur, auditory hallucination, tangential thinking, fragmentation of thought, flight of ideas, overtalkativeness, poor remote memory, bodily concern, silliness and impaired insight and judgment.

(2-4/4-2 STATE HOSPITAL: Lachar, 1968)
Mean Male (- -) & Female (—) Profiles

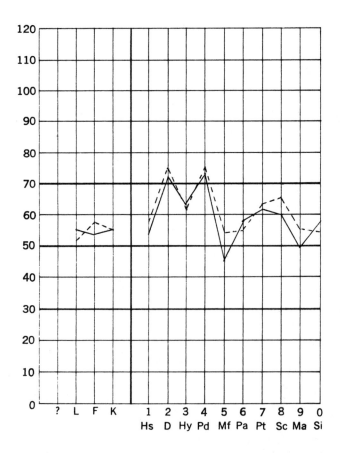

The 2-4/4-2 code was the 3rd most frequent (n=208) in this sample. The modal diagnosis was Personality Trait Disturbance. Diagnostic frequencies: Personality Disorder—43%, Psychoneurotic—17%, Brain Syndrome—10%, Schizophrenic—10% and Other psychotic—10%.

Automated Interpretation

See paragraph 45 (page 124).

2-7-4

(2-7-4 GENERAL: Carson, 1969) (This code type is accompanied by a high Scale 5 for males and a low Scale 5 for females.) Similar individuals present themselves to others as weak, inferior, guilty and submissive. They are markedly self-effacing and shun any outward appearance of strength or pride. They invite others to be patronizingly superior and deprecating and appear to feel at least uncomfortable in relationships when they are receiving such treatment. Ambivalence, immobility, and a sense of failure are characteristic. The clinical extreme of this form of behavior is the psychotic depressive reaction.

(2-7-4 GENERAL: Stelmachers) Persons with such profile types are characterized by the distress syndrome (depression, anxiety and nervousness) but the depressive features appear to be deeply integrated into their character structure and are of a chronic nature. More likely they would not be expressed affectively but rather as feelings of inadequacy and lack of self-confidence. Persons in this category seem to be basically oral-dependent and self-indulging characters who suffer from basic insecurity and need for attention and recognition. It is typical to find them in financial and marital difficulties and drinking problems are often found in their histories.

The majority of persons with such MMPIs receive a diagnosis of depressive reaction but a strong minority are labeled passive-aggressive personalities. Because the problems are deep-seated and chronic and because these patients are reluctant to expose themselves to anxiety, response to psychiatric treatment is rather poor. However, treatment can be aimed at reducing the depression to a more comfortable maintenance level which the patient has learned to tolerate without asking for psychiatric help.

(2-7-4/2-4-7/4-7-2 Profile Type; TEACHING HOSPITAL: Marks & Seeman, 1963)

Mean Male (- -) and Female (—) Profiles (n=20)

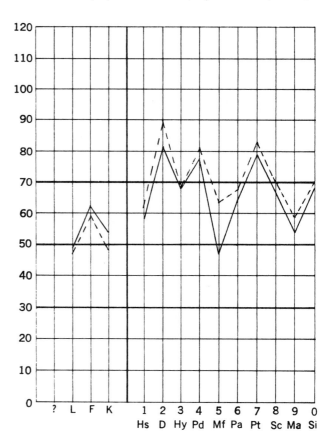

2-7-4/2-4-7/4-7-2 Profile Type Rules (Marks & Seeman, 1963):

1. Scales 2, 7 and 4 above 70 T.
2. Scale 2 minus 4 less than 15 T.
3. Scale 2 minus 7 less than 10 T.
4. Scale 7 greater than 1 and 3.
5. Scale 7 minus 4 less than 10 T.
6. Scale 7 at least 5 T more than 8.
7. Scale 8 greater than 9.
8. Scale 9 over 40 T.
9. Scales L and K less than 70 T, F less than 80 T.

Patients who obtain this profile type receive both psychoneurotic (43%—Depressive) and personality disorder (33%—Passive-aggressive) diagnoses. A small (19%) proportion are labeled psychotic (Mixed).

These patients often appear tearful, depressed, anxious, worrisome and emotionally labile. They become over-anxious about minor matters and express feelings of inferiority and guilt. Fears, phobias, obsessional tendencies and a ruminative over-ideational style may be present. They are described as insecure and as having an exaggerated need for affection. Conflicts about emotional dependency and sexuality may be suggested.

Somatic complaints, such as fatigue, ulcer and chest pain, often represent psychological conflicts. These symptoms often result in secondary gain. Some of these patients are described as impulsive, lacking in foresight and planning, and unable to express their emotions in a modulated, adaptive fashion. They may be seen as argumentative and excitable.

In treatment, these patients mainly (75%) received only psychotherapy. Treatment outcome: small improvement (38%); no change (31%) and decided improvement (31%).

2-7-4/2-4-7/4-7-2 Mean Discharge Profile (n=12)

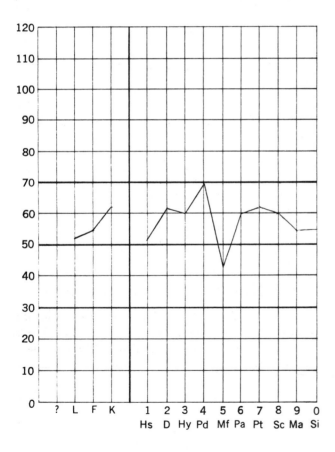

(2-7-4 (3) Profile Type; VA MALES: Gilberstadt & Duker, 1965) Mean Profile (n=27)

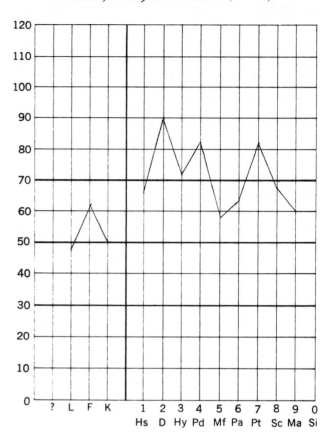

2-7-4 (3) Profile Type Rules (Gilberstadt & Duker, 1965):

1. Scales 2, 4 and 7 over 70 T.
2. Scale 7 at least 5 T more than 8.
3. Scale 7 does not exceed 2 by more than 10 T.
4. Scale 2 does not exceed 4 by more than 20 T.
5. Two of Scales 2, 4 and 7 do not exceed 99 T.
6. If Scale 4 is peak, include only if 4 does not exceed 2 or 7 by more than 10 T.
7. Scale 0 less than 70 T.
8. Scale 9 less than 8.
9. Scale 9 over 40 T.
10. If Scale 9 is less than 50 T, include only if 0 does not exceed 9 by more than 15 T.

Most descriptive diagnosis: Anxiety Reaction with alcoholism in a Passive-aggressive Personality.
Modal diagnoses: Depressive Reaction with alcoholism; Passive-aggressive Personality with alcoholism.
Characteristics & rate of occurrence: Anxiety (56%), Conflict with wife (56%), Financial status poor (26%), Heavy drinking (96%), Insomnia (30%), Tension (52%) and Depression (58%).

These patients are often described as anxious, tense and passive-aggressive, manifesting feelings of inferiority and guilt. They are often chronic alcoholics and may have histories which include delirium tremens and vocational instability. They are often significantly dependent on wives and mothers and display severe marital conflict. They characteristically obtain a poor response to therapeutic measures offered during hospitalization.

4-2-7 Research

Gilbert & Lombardi (1967) found that their young male addicts, in comparison to nonaddicted male controls of similar socioeconomic status, obtained a 4-2-7 mean profile. They interpreted these results to suggest that their addict sample could be described as tending to act out aggressively against authority or others, lacking in persistence, impatient, irritable, irresponsible and impulsive. They further suggested that the Scales 2 and 7 elevations represent feelings of guilt and depression which can only be alleviated by more drugs. Other traits suggested include apprehensiveness, insecurity, lack of self-confidence and difficulty in achieving a normal optimism with regard to the future.

3-4/4-3

This two-point code represented 5.21% of males and 7.83% of females in a sample of over 12,000 psychiatric outpatients (Webb, 1970).

(3-4/4-3 GENERAL) The elevation of Scales 3 and 4 above 70 T suggests conflicts which center around impulse control.

If Scales 3 and 4 are about equal in elevation above 70 T, there is often a great deal of experienced fear about impending loss of control.

If Scale 3 is higher than Scale 4, passive-aggressive personalities of the passive type are suggested. Such persons typically express a great deal of hostility in indirect and passive ways and have little or no insight into their behavior. The magnitude of Scale 4 seems to reflect the aggressive or hostile feelings and impulses that are present to a significant degree, while the Scale 3 elevation suggests that the repressive and suppressive controls are even stronger than the impulse. Consequently, the aggressiveness that these persons would otherwise express is kept from direct expression, appearing only obliquely, ineffectually or sporadically.

If Scale 4 is higher than Scale 3, but both show considerable elevation, then episodic acting out of impulses may occur, followed by periods of inhibition and restraint. If there is extreme elevation on both Scales 3 and 4 (above 85 T), dissociative, amnesic or fugue episodes involving acting out of sexual or aggressive impulses become increasingly likely. Where Scale 4 is greater than Scale 3, such persons are more likely to act out and exhibit less adequate self-control than if Scale 3 is greater than Scale 4.

(3-4/4-3 GENERAL: Carson, 1969) This pattern often identifies markedly immature persons who tend outwardly to be conformists and who discharge their hostile, rebellious feelings in indirect ways. Many of these people, for example, establish enduring relationships with marginal, acting-out individuals, thereby vicariously gratifying their own antisocial tendencies. The 3-4 pattern suggests fertile soil for dissociative phenomena.

(4-3 GENERAL: Stelmachers) This profile is indicative of a chronic and rather stable character disorder in which passive-aggressive elements dominate the clinical picture. The patient appears relatively well-defended and in little distress, the psychiatric disturbance and incapacitation being rather minimal in degree. Patients with such profiles tend to be chronically hostile, aggressive and extrapunitive in their reaction to stress and frustration. They typically handle their conflicts and anxieties by utilizing provocation and manipulation, as well as blame, projection and manifest attempts at domination. Women in this category tend to be sexually maladjusted and to have serious marital difficulties. Their children are prone to develop psychiatric difficulties. Their motivation for help is typically weak and often of questionable sincerity; they are apt to use psychotherapy for voicing complaints about their spouse instead of concentrating on their own problem areas. Diagnostic Impression: (1) Passive-aggressive Personality, aggressive type; (2) No psychiatric diagnosis.

(4-3 GENERAL MALE: Davis & Sines, 1971)
Prototypic Male Profile

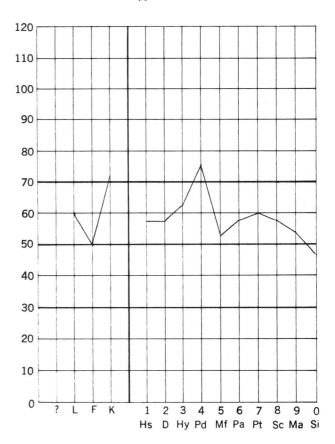

This pattern was obtained by 5% of a state hospital sample, 6.6% of a prison sample and 1.6% of a medical center sample. This code type suggests the following: (1) A consistent pattern of underachievement in school and work in spite of at least average intelligence. (2) A pattern of relating well but superficially to a small group of associates for only short periods of time (frequent moves, good first impression, well-liked). (3) Consistently poor marital adjustments both sexually and socially (wives frequently physically abused or threatened). (4) A significant need for social approval. Criticism from others often leading to anxiety, excessive drinking and other socially unacceptable behaviors. When feelings of social adequacy are threatened, questioned or criticized, intense hostility may result. (5) Histories which often involve fairly regular cycles of acute emotional upset severe enough to include grossly delusional thinking, hallucinatory experiences and assaultive responses. These periods of emotional upset are not very dependent on only objective environmental stress and represent the culmination of a 2-to 3-year cycle which is seemingly unalterable by any conventional therapeutic intervention. These individuals often appear seclusive between episodes. They are generally described as showing poor judgment and lack of social and financial responsibility which surprises acquaintances.

During periods of acute disturbance (less than 1 year) these men are felt to be a clear danger to society and authorities. They may become serious suicide risks following these acute periods.

If the patient remains institutionalized for a long period of time, a subsequent psychotic-like episode is likely. If released after an acute phase, they may make a marginal adjustment for 1-2 years. The pattern is then typically repeated: excessive drinking and a build-up of resentment, suspicion and hostility, especially toward women. The probability of assaultive behavior again becomes quite high.

(4-3 PRISON MALES: Persons & Marks, 1971)

A study of young male inmates of a maximum security institution suggested that of the 4-3's, 66.7% were currently incarcerated for violent crimes, while 85.4% had a history of committing violent offenses. These rates were significantly higher than for the inmates in general (33.3% & 39.6%). The other most frequent codes in this population (4-2, 4-9 & 4-8) did not differ from base rates on these historical factors.

Other testing suggested that the white 4-3's were more anxious, prone toward delinquent acting-out and more neurotic than other non-4-3 whites and, in addition, they felt more guilty than Negro inmates. In general, there was a trend for the Negro 4-3's to be less anxious, less inclined to delinquent acting out, less guilty morally and sexually, but more guilty over hostility than Ss in the other groups.

Guilt appears to be a prominent personality feature of the 4-3 group and may act to inhibit all but episodic overt aggression.

(4-3 Profile Type; VA MALES: Gilberstadt & Duker, 1965) Mean Profile (n=17)

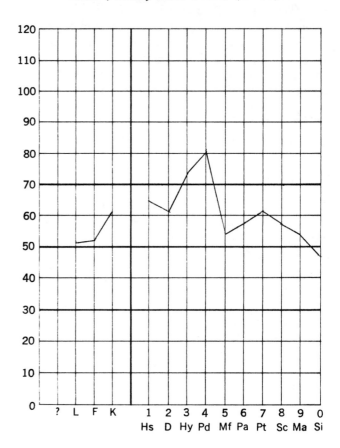

4-3 Profile Type Rules (Gilberstadt & Duker, 1965):

1. Scales 3 and 4 over 70 T.
2. No other scale over 70 T, Scale 1 excepted.

Most descriptive diagnosis: Personality Trait Disturbance, Emotionally Unstable Personality.
Modal diagnoses: Conversion Reaction; Passive-aggressive Personality, aggressive type.
Characteristics & rate of occurrence: Assaultive (29%), Father alcoholic (41%), Financial status poor (30%), Heavy drinking (76%), Headache (35%), Hostile (35%), Impulsive (29%), Moodiness (24%), Suicide attempt (41%), Conflict with wife (53%) and Depression (53%).

These patients are most often characterized by poorly controlled anger and resultant temper outbursts. Hostility turned outward results in homicidal threats or attempts to choke wives, children or others. Hostility turned inward results in a high rate of impulsive suicide attempts. In the hospital, they are likely to be described as excitable, sullen and moody.

They are seen as sensitive to rejection or frustration of their egocentric demands for attention and approval. This sensitivity may be the result of severe rejection in early childhood. Other characteristics include alcoholism, headache, blackout, eye complaints and symptoms of conversion reaction. Their social histories are likely to include poor educational and vocational adjustment, except as a salesman, as well as marked marital discord.

(3-4/4-3 STATE HOSPITAL: Lachar, 1968)
Mean Male (- -) & Female (—) Profiles

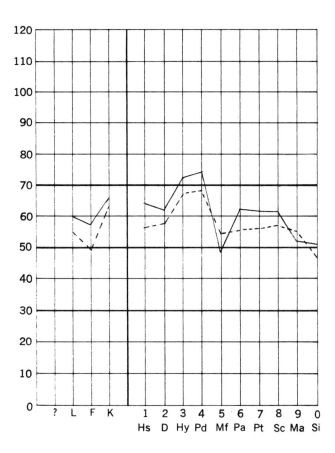

The 3-4/4-3 code was the 7th most frequent (n=156) in this sample. A majority of these patients (77%) were married or widowed. The modal diagnosis was Personality Trait Disturbance. Diagnostic frequencies: Personality Disorder—30%, Schizophrenic—23%, Other psychotic—17%, Psychoneurotic—17% and Brain Syndrome—10%.

Automated Interpretation

See paragraphs 51, 51A and 51B (page 127).

3-4-5/4-3-5

(3-4-5/4-3-5 GENERAL MALES) These men are seen as grossly immature and sexually inadequate. Exhibitionism, voyeurism and a need for more than usual sexual stimulation are suggested. Some court referrals fit this code type.

The relation between Scales 3 and 4 has a direct relation to the manifestation and personal acceptance of homoerotic sexual feelings stemming from personality in-version. Men who have elevated scores on Scale 5 and whose scores on Scale 3 are higher than their Scale 4 scores are likely to show fears of being homosexual but generally are less likely to act upon their sexual impulses than men with similar Scale 5 elevation, but with the relative elevations of Scales 3 and 4 reversed. The latter individuals are more likely to form a number of extended homosexual liaisons and may rather freely acknowledge homoerotic preferences and practices.

3-4-6

(3-4-6 GENERAL) Where Scale 3 is greater than Scale 4 and Scale 6 is also elevated, a picture is suggested of an individual who may show long periods of inhibited and moderate behavior punctuated by episodes of extreme acting out.

High-point Scale 4

Scale 4 is profile high-point in 19.2% of males and 26.1% of females in a general psychiatric sample (Webb, 1971).

(High-point Scale 4 GENERAL) The preponderance of Scale 4 elevations increases markedly in prison groups for both males and females. This code is associated with lack of social conformity or self-control and a persistent tendency to get into scrapes. Depending on socioeconomic status, such individuals may show psychopathic features, rebelliousness and poor adjustment to authority figures or ready superficial relations and a successful career as a salesman or junior executive. In general, this configuration suggests the presence of impulsivity and acting-out potential related to other significant scale elevations.

4 Spike

(GENERAL) When Scale 4 is elevated 5 to 10 T above all other scales, and especially if Scale 4 is above 70 T and all others are under 70 T, then the remarks contained in interpretive statements by single scale elevations (see above) are appropriate. Such individuals are likely to be seen as insightless, egocentric and shallow in their feelings for others. Asocial and antisocial behavior is frequent; these persons often seem unable to profit from experience and may have an unusually high threshold and tolerance for punishment. Scale 9 is usually the secondary elevation. If Scale 9 is low, then the Scale 4 elevation may be more an indicator of dissatisfaction with the people around him, suggesting a passively rebellious manner more than an overt attack on society.

(4 Profile Type: VA MALES: Gilberstadt & Duker, 1965) Mean Profile (n=17)

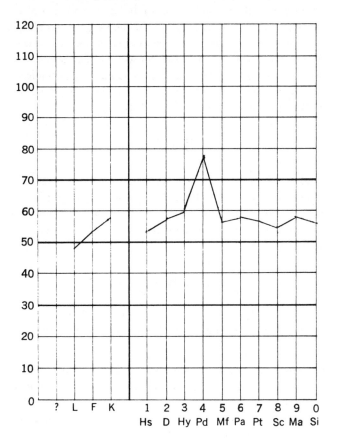

4 Profile Type Rules (Gilberstadt & Duker, 1965):

1. Scale 4 over 70 T.
2. No other scale over 69 T.

Most descriptive diagnosis: Personality Trait Disturbance, Passive-aggressive Personality, aggressive type.
Modal diagnoses: Emotionally Unstable Personality; Anxiety Reaction; Depressive Reaction with Personality Trait Disturbance.
Characteristics & rate of occurrence: Assaultive (53%), Emotional instability (35%), Financial status poor (29%), Guilt (41%), Heavy drinking (65%), Immature (41%), Depression (59%) and Poor work adjustment (53%).

These patients are often described as impulsive, irresponsible, careless, immature and childish. They are often demanding, restless and emotionally unstable. Their low frustration tolerance often leads to periods of tension, moodiness and depression. Similar patients precipitate hospitalization by suicide attempts, aggressive outbursts directed toward wives, and the problems associated with alcoholism.

Social histories include overprotection and overindulgence, especially by mothers, poor family conditions and poor relations with siblings. Sexual maladjustment and a relatively high frequency of perverse sexual activity and extramarital behavior is often noted. Though these patients obtain a poor marital adjustment they are usually married. Their wives' nurturant, succorant, motherly attitude of sympathy and forbearance may be responsible for this stability.

Automated Interpretation

See paragraph 29 (page 118).

4-5/5-4

This two-point code represented 5.69% of males and .61% of females in a sample of over 12,000 psychiatric outpatients (Webb, 1970).

(4-5/5-4 GENERAL: Carson, 1969) Females: This pattern is often found among women who are rebelling against the female role. Generally speaking, the high 5 female's behavior becomes more clearly deviant with increasing elevation on Scale 4.

Males: Elevation on Scales 4 and 5 is a not uncommon configuration and indicates a Bohemian type of character who leaves little doubt as to his nonconformity. Such people delight in defying and challenging convention and by their general behavior and appearance so indicate. Many overt homosexuals exhibit this pattern and are often not in the least reticent about discussing their sexual behavior with anyone who seems interested. The foregoing comments may not apply where the profile shows other peaks, as well as where the profile is generally elevated.

(4-5 MALE GENERAL: Stelmachers) This profile suggests a chronic character disorder. The patient does not appear either depressed or anxious and, if he appears clinically upset, this disturbance is likely to be rather short-lived and followed by acting out. The patient can be expected to have nonconformist and defiant attitudes and values as well as aggressive and antisocial tendencies. He is likely to exhibit emotional passivity and poorly recognized desires for dependency. Dependency conflicts may be acted out and create masculine protest type of behavior as well as a variety of conduct disturbances. The guilt feelings and remorse about the acting-out may temporarily prevent further antisocial behavior but, in the long run, the strong tendency to narcissistically indulge themselves and their lack of frustration tolerance will probably determine their actions. The patient has an excessively feminine interest pattern and orientation typically found in males who are preoccupied with and worried about their masculinity. The patient may be even

obsessed with and bothered by the idea of being a homosexual and he actually may be practicing homosexuality. Diagnostic Impression: Conduct Disturbance and masculine protest, in a Passive-dependent male. (R/O homosexuality as a source of conflict.)

Relatively brief re-educational psychotherapy may be quite productive in cases where the clinical history is favorable, regardless of the low distress level. This code suggests pseudo-masculine behavior in effeminate men who display anger and hostility. Severe marital conflict is common. They fear being dominated by women and are very sensitive to any demands made by their wives.

(high 4, low 5 FEMALE GENERAL: Carson, 1969)
These are often hostile, angry women who are unable to express such feelings directly. Instead they resort to various masochistic operations that provoke other people to anger and rage, often taking satisfaction in pitying themselves because they have been mistreated; there is often an accompanying elevation on Scale 6 that reflects the degree to which the transfer of blame elements in this pattern become involved in a generalized paranoid posture. (See 4-6/6-4 females below.) These women are often extremely adroit in eliciting rage, and this is likely to create special problems in therapeutic management.

(high 4, low 5 MALE GENERAL: Carson, 1969)
This pattern suggests a tendency toward flamboyant masculinity; in teenagers this tendency is often manifested as delinquency.

4-6/6-4

This two-point code represented 1.71% of males and 5.12% of females in a sample of over 12,000 psychiatric outpatients (Webb, 1970).

(4-6/6-4 GENERAL: Carson, 1969)
Peaks on Scales 4 and 6 identify angry, sullen people who utilize excessively a transfer of blame mechanism. Typically they are rigidly argumentative and difficult in social relations and are frequently seen as obnoxious. They are poor candidates for treatment.

(4-6/6-4 FEMALE GENERAL: Stelmachers)
This syndrome is usually seen in females who obtain considerable elevations on Scales 4 and 6 with an accompanying Scale 5 that is 10 or more T-scores below the 50 T line (the "passive-aggressive V"). These women are very passive and dependent and excessively identified with the traditional feminine role. They usually have an inordinate demand for affection which can hardly ever be satisfied. Their dependency on men is usually of a rather hostile type and can become quite demanding, provocative and manipulative in order to get what they want. These maneuvers are usually self-defeating as men typically become more irritated and give less affection. Here Scale 6 does not represent paranoid mentation but chronic feelings of resentment and bitterness as well as a tendency to project blame to other persons and outside circumstances for one's deficiencies and failures.

These women are suspicious of men and don't get along with other women. They are generally hostile, irritable, easily hurt, extrapunitive and do not give up anger. They are very demanding in therapy and very narcissistic, demanding attention. Conflicts about sexuality are frequent and poor marital adjustment easily results. Psychotherapy is not very helpful; it is usually depreciated and resentment of demands and authority are prominent. Countertransference difficulties may occur. This profile pattern usually reflects a passive-aggressive or demanding dependency orientation.

A high proportion of women in this 4-6 low Scale 5 group were found by Sines (1966) to have a history that includes two to four of these characteristics: (1) difficulty in accepting the feminine role, (2) history of abrupt weight gain or loss, (3) menstrual irregularity, (4) dysmenorrhea, or (5) hirsutism.

(4-6/6-4 MALE GENERAL)
In men this code appears less frequently and is suggestive of a more malignant picture than it is for women. This pattern is often suggestive of prepsychotic or borderline states. At best these are sullen, angry men with histories of severe social maladjustment.

Where anger and hostility are not being already directly expressed, there is a likelihood of indirect expression in allergies, hypertension, etc.

If Scale 4 is greater than 70 T, alcoholic personalities with a record of familial conflicts and poor work histories are common. If Scale 6 is greater than 70 T, the likelihood of distinctly paranoid features in prepsychotic states may be further emphasized. These men are generally controlled but exhibit occasional outbursts of violence. These are controlled, suspicious individuals whose control is dependent upon external limits. When external threat of retaliation is removed they can be quite vicious and hostile to the surprise of the people around them.

(4-6 (8)/6-4 (8) Profile Type; TEACHING HOSPITAL: (Marks & Seeman, 1963)
Mean Female Profile (n=20)

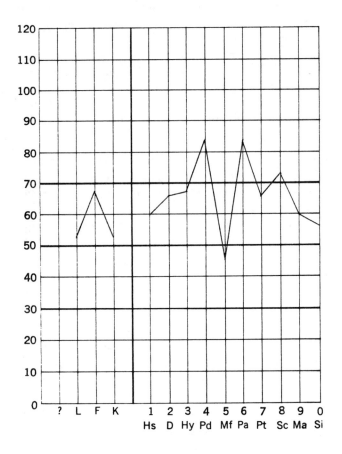

These patients are often seen as impulsive and manipulative; they resent, and are often in conflict with, authority figures. Poor sexual and marital adjustment is often noted. Suicide attempts (39%) and drug usage/addiction (28%) are noted in this sample. Physical complaints, when present, may include blackout spells, headache, chest pain and neurasthenia. This profile type represents a relatively chronic, stable adjustment. Response to treatment: decided improvement (21%); small improvement (36%) and no change (43%).

4-6 (8)/6-4 (8) Mean Discharge Profile (n=14)

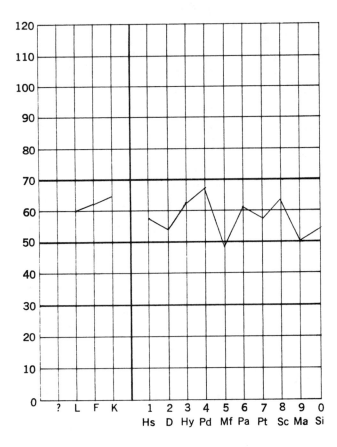

4-6 (8)/6-4 (8) Profile Type Rules (Marks & Seeman, 1963):

1. Scales 4 and 6 over 70 T.
2. Scale 4 minus 2 more than 15 T.
3. Scales 4 and/or 6 exceed 5 by more than 25 T.
4. Scales 4 and 6 greater than 8.
5. Scale 6 minus 2 more than 10 T.
6. Scale 8 greater than 7 and 9.
7. Scales 9 and 0 less than 70 T.
8. Scales L, F and K less than 70 T.

The patients who obtain this profile type are fairly evenly divided into psychotic (55%—Schizophrenic, paranoid) and personality disorder (45%—Mixed) diagnoses. The psychotic diagnoses reflect in part the Scale 8 elevation shown in the mean profile; this profile type would be better classified as 4-6-8/6-4-8.

Similar patients are seen as evasive, defensive about admitting to problems, and as handling anxieties and conflicts by refusing to recognize their presence. They are described as hostile, irritable, demanding, argumentative, resentful, suspicious, immature, narcissistic, egocentric and self-indulgent. Rationalization and projection are noted defense mechanisms. Other symptoms may include ideas of reference, delusions, emotional lability, tension and anxiety.

(4-6-8 GENERAL: Stelmachers) This profile suggests a chronic emotional disturbance, most likely a character disorder or paranoid type of schizophrenia. Patients with such profile types are described as being evasive and defensive about admitting psychological conflicts and as being generally hostile, irritable and suspicious in their relationships with other people. They are easily hurt by criticism and tend to suffer from ideas of reference. However, their typically extrapunitive ways of dealing with frustration do not prevent them from being quite tense, nervous and anxious. They can be very demanding, in a narcissistic and egocentric way, for attention, affection and sympathy from others. Inner conflicts about sexuality are often present and are likely to be responsible, among others, for their characteristically poor marital adjustment.

Psychiatric treatment of any kind does not seem to help these patients very much and the interviews are

made difficult by the patient's tendency to rationalize and to be argumentative, and by their deepseated resentfulness to authority and to anything that can be construed as a demand. Their range of response to disagreeable therapeutic measures goes from passive resistance to aggressive dependency and open defiance and hostility.

(4-6/6-4 STATE HOSPITAL: Lachar, 1968)
Mean Male (- -) & Female (—) Profiles

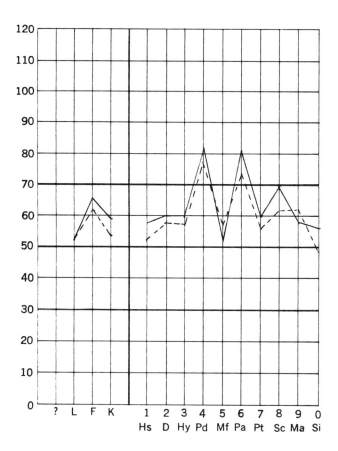

The 4-6/6-4 code was the 4th most frequent (n=171) in this sample. Three-fourths of this sample were female and half of this sample had never married. (Note the similarity between the female profile and the Marks & Seeman 4-6/6-4 mean profile above.) The modal diagnosis was Paranoid Schizophrenia. Diagnostic frequencies: Schizophrenic—50% and Personality Disorder—40%.

Automated Interpretation

See paragraphs 56A, 56B and 88 (pages 128-129, 140).

4-6-2

(4-6-2 GENERAL: Stelmachers) This profile suggests the distress syndrome (anxiety, depression, nervousness), but this patient is likely to accentuate the complaints by a tendency to be self-dramatic and histrionic. The patient can be expected to be chronically hostile and resentful and to use projection and acting-out as preferred defense mechanisms. Impulse control is likely to be deficient and ineffective. Expression of hostility and depression (Scales 4 & 2) often form a cyclic pattern: expression of hostility often leads to feelings of guilt. Anger then recurs more intensely because they begin to resent their guilt feelings, etc.

It is characteristic of individuals with such profile types to be self-centered and dependent and to have an exaggerated need for affection. They tend to have inner conflicts about their emotional dependency. They feel uncomfortable when they are with other people, lack poise and social assurance, and tend to withdraw from social contacts. In their work, they are apathetic and lack interest and involvement. Serious sexual and marital maladjustment is often found among their difficulties. Diagnostic Impression: (1) Passive-aggressive Personality; (2) Psychoneurosis, mixed. Prognosis is rather fair for small improvement with psychotherapy.

(4-6-2/6-4-2 Profile Type; TEACHING HOSPITAL: Marks & Seeman, 1963)
Mean Female Profile (n=20)

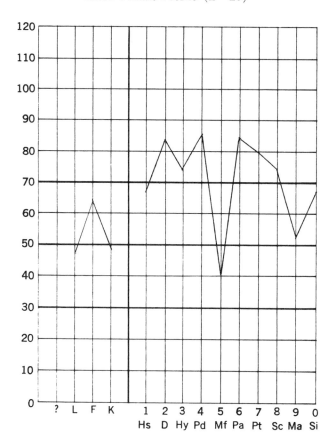

4-6-2/6-4-2 Profile Type Rules (Marks & Seeman, 1963):

1. Scales 4, 6 and 2 over 70 T.
2. Scale 4 minus 2 less than 15 T.
3. Scales 4 and 6 greater than 8.
4. Scale 7 not more than 4 T greater than 4.
5. Scale 6 minus 2 less than 10 T.
6. Scale 8 not more than 4 T greater than 7.
7. Scale 9 less than 70 T.
8. Scales L and K less than F, F less than 80 T.

The majority (60%) of patients who obtained this profile type received a diagnosis of personality disorder (Passive-aggressive). Others were labeled psychoneurotic (30%—Mixed) or psychotic (10%—Mixed). Similar patients were described as impulsive, lacking in self-control and resentful of authority figures. They were seen as demanding, manipulative, resentful, critical, skeptical and not easily impressed. Other descriptors include excitable, irritable, argumentative, provocative and oversensitive. They are distrustful of people and question their motives.

Clinically they appeared agitated, tearful, depressed, anxious and tense upon examination. Sexual difficulties and suicide attempts and threats were noted. They were seen as self-dramatizing, histrionic, self-centered and self-indulgent. Frequent defense mechanisms include acting-out, projection and rationalization. This profile type represents, as the discharge profile suggests, a chronic, stable personality pattern. Response to treatment: small improvement (57%); decided improvement (14%) and no change (29%).

4-6-2/6-4-2 Mean Discharge Profile (n=26)

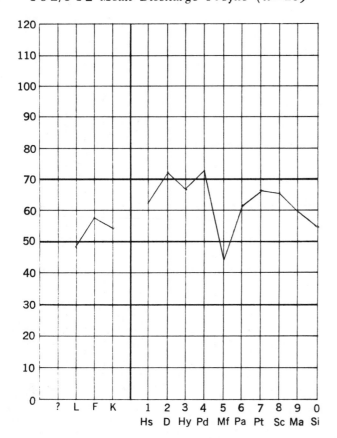

4-7/7-4

This two-point code represented 2.71% of males and 2.29% of females in a sample of over 12,000 psychiatric outpatients (Webb, 1970).

(4-7/7-4 GENERAL: Dahlstrom, Welsh & Dahlstrom, 1972) This configuration suggests both excessive insensitivity (Scale 4) and excessive concern about one's actions (Scale 7). This psychological contradiction frequently appears behaviorally as an alternation of phases or cyclical variations. For a period these persons may act with little control or forethought, violating social and legal restrictions and trampling on the feelings and wishes of others heedlessly. Following this, however, guilt, remorse and deep regret over their actions may appear and for a while they may seem overly controlled and contrite. Excessive alcoholic indulgence or stepping out/promiscuity may be a part of these activity swings. While their conscience pangs may be severe, even out of proportion to the actual behavior deviations, the controls of these individuals do not appear to be effective in preventing further episodes.

At the end of an acting-out spree these individuals appear in the clinic or are admitted to the hospital, often against their will. Scale 2 is frequently elevated along with Scales 4 and 7 when these individuals are hospitalized. The Scale 2 elevation emphasizes temporary guilt and feelings of self-condemnation.

Automated Interpretation

See paragraph 57 (pages 129-130).

4-8/8-4

This two-point code represented 5.21% of males and 8.70% of females in a sample of over 12,000 psychiatric outpatients (Webb, 1970).

(4-8/8-4 GENERAL: Stelmachers/Dahlstrom, Welsh & Dahlstrom, 1972) These individuals are unpredictable, peculiar in action and in thought. They straddle the fence between character disorder and psychosis. Schizoid is usually the most descriptive label. Nonconforming and uneven educational and vocational adjustment is often associated with this code. Poor social intelligence, subtle communication problems, impaired empathy and difficulty in becoming emotionally involved are characteristic. In young patients delinquency is fairly common and suggests a poor prognosis.

In females this configuration suggests a schizoid, unstable, acting-out individual. Pregnancies out-of-wedlock are common. They are seen as high suicide risks. Their core problem is that they cannot communicate, have a low self-concept and over- or underreact to social situations. Their relationship to their mothers has dynamic importance. In therapy it is important to evaluate their relationship to men; they characteristically pick losers,

men inferior to them. If a relationship is formed with an adequate man, they become worse and wreck the relationship. They are the most comfortable with those who they feel are as no good as they are. They fear emotional involvement and prefer to relate to others only sexually.

Males are seen as delinquent and as acting-out in self-defeating ways. These individuals are often labeled pseudo-psychopathic schizophrenics in those instances in which they have not been allowed to act-out. Their best level of adjustment often then includes a thinking disorder and an introverted, nomadic existence. Older 4-8 males are often sexual deviates. Bizarre, self-defeating crimes are noted. These individuals often do things that seem designed so they will get caught; the crimes are stupid and sometimes vicious and assaultive. These individuals are often seen as classical "psychopaths."

(4-8/8-4 GENERAL: Carson, 1969) Typically such a person's problems stem from the early establishment of an attitude of distrust toward the world. These are people who, as children, acquired a set to perceive other people as hostile, rejecting and dangerous. They also learned, however, that they could protect themselves and alleviate to some degree their painful anticipations of hurt by striking out in anger and rebellion. This pattern is continued into adulthood, the person being so rebellious and angry that his social behavior continually reinforces his alienation from the group. Intervention into this vicious circle by way of psychotherapy is an extremely difficult operation.

(4-8/8-4(F)-low 2 GENERAL: Carson, 1969) This is usually an aggressive, punitive individual who is most comfortable when inspiring anxiety and guilt in others. Often such individuals drift into roles in which such behavior is socially sanctioned, or at least not manifestly condemned. The behaviors expected here range all the way from stern, punitive, cold disapproval to clinical sadism. When these individuals find themselves in situations in which their guilt- and fear-provoking operations are blocked, they are likely to feel unprotected, anxious and uncomfortable. Many individuals diagnosed as sociopaths obtain this configuration.

(4-8 GENERAL) These are clearly odd and peculiar individuals who are impulsive and unpredictable in behavior. They typically show a schizoid-like adjustment which may be quite marginal. The simultaneous elevation of Scales 4 and 8 points toward a great deal of dissatisfaction with, and anger toward, others, plus an inability to handle or express such feelings.

(8-4 GENERAL) Such persons are typically angry, rebellious and often show psychotic and/or psychopathic features. Intense familial conflict and early problems in self-identification are often observed as part of the dynamics. These patients tend to see the world as hostile and punitive. They often show a great deal of anger toward others and tend to make others angry at them. In effect, their social behavior often sets up the conditions of a self-fulfilling prophecy which reinforces their alienation from others.

(8-4 VA MALES: Gilberstadt & Duker, 1965) Look for immaturity, alcoholism, sexual deviation and paranoid trends.

4-8/8-4 Research

The 4-8/8-4 pattern has been found among self-mutilators in a state prison population (Panton, 1962b) and among solitary male delinquents (Randolph, Richardson & Johnson, 1961).

(4-8/8-4 MALE STATE HOSPITAL WHITES: Gynther et al., 1973) A history of antisocial behavior may be encountered for patients of this type, particularly promiscuity or family desertion.

(4-8/8-4 FEMALE STATE HOSPITAL WHITES: Gynther et al., 1973) A history of promiscuity or family desertion may be encountered for patients of this type.

(4-8/8-4 STATE HOSPITAL: Lachar, 1968)
Mean Male (- -) & Female (—) Profiles

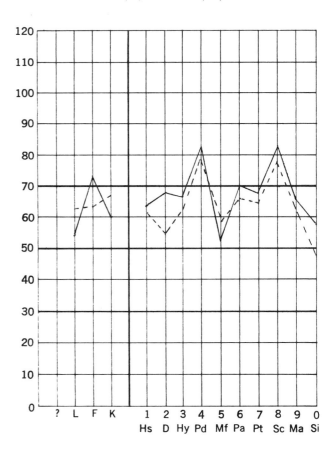

The 4-8/8-4 code was the 2nd most frequent (n=223) in this sample. Half had never married. The modal diagnosis was Paranoid Schizophrenia. Diagnostic frequencies: Schizophrenic—60%, Other psychotic—10% and Personality Disorder—27%.

Automated Interpretation

See paragraph 58 (page 130).

4-8-2

(4-8-2 GENERAL: Stelmachers) This profile suggests a distress syndrome of moderate proportions (depression, anxiety, nervousness). In addition, the patient appears to be irritable, hostile and suspicious, tends to distrust people in general and may suffer from ideas of reference. Projection is likely to be a prominent defense mechanism. This personality type is basically schizoid and the patient is probably socially isolated, keeps people at a distance and avoids close relationships because of fear of emotional involvement. Social intelligence is likely to be poor and serious difficulties can be expected in the areas of empathy and communication ability. Persons with such profiles are often moody and emotionally inappropriate and cannot express emotions in a modulated, adaptive way. In their behavior, they are characteristically unpredictable, changeable, and nonconforming. Their educational and occupational histories are noted by underachievement, marginal adjustment and uneven performance. These individuals suffer from a basic insecurity and have an excessive craving for attention and affection. Sexual difficulties and inner conflicts about them, as well as marital difficulties, are often found in this group. Suicide attempts are relatively common. Diagnostic Impression: (1) Schizoid Personality with Depressive Reaction; (2) R/O Schizophrenic Reaction. If schizophrenic, the decompensation shows only primary signs, i.e., manifests little if any regression, disorganization, bizarreness or hallucinations. Autistic thinking, a sense of unreality and poor self-concept of schizophrenic dimensions are usually present.

These individuals are often young unmarried females who are dependent, unstable and relatively symptom-free except when under stress. Elevated Scale 0 here is a good indicator of a schizoid process. When Scale 0 is low, a characterological adjustment and an alcoholic father are good possibilities.

These individuals are seen differently at different settings. At Minnesota (unlike Marks & Seeman below) most of these patients are schizoid, have chronic depressive trends and also, surprisingly, have distinctly hysterical features. They also have histories of some form of acting-out or, at least, definite nonconforming qualities. Very few of them were judged to be schizophrenic.

(4-8-2/8-4-2/8-2-4 Profile Type; TEACHING HOSPITAL: Marks & Seeman, 1963)
Mean Male (- -) and Female (—) Profiles (n=20)

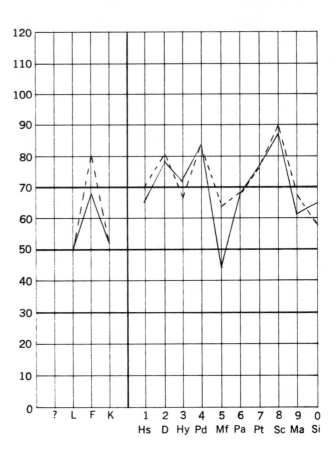

4-8-2/8-4-2/8-2-4 Profile Type Rules (Marks & Seeman, 1963):

1. Scales 4, 8 and 2 over 70 T.
2. Scale 4 minus 2 less than 15 T.
3. Scale 7 not to exceed 4 by more than 4 T.
4. Scale 8 minus 2 less than 15 T.
5. Scale 8 minus 7 more than 5 T.
6. Scale 8 minus 9 more than 10 T.
7. Scale 9 less than 70 T.
8. Scales L and K less than F, F less than 80 T.

Patients who obtained this profile type were mainly diagnosed psychotic (71%—Schizophrenic, paranoid) though others were seen as personality disorders (21%—Sociopathic). They are described as resentful, argumentative, irritable, moody, worrisome, hostile and oversensitive to demands from others. Similar patients often are seen as schizoid in that they distrust people, keep them at a distance and, in general, fear emotional involvement with others. They may have inner conflicts about sexuality, often admit to sexual difficulty and usually obtain a poor marital adjustment.

Clinically they may appear withdrawn, emotionally labile and admit to feelings of guilt, inferiority and hopelessness. These patients are often unpredictable and are unable to express their emotions in a modulated, adaptive way. Frequent defense mechanisms include projection, rationalization and acting-out. They may be described as insecure, evidencing an exaggerated need for attention and affection along with an inner conflict over emotional dependency.

This profile type represents a chronic, stable personality pattern. Response to treatment: no change (22%); small improvement (39%) and decided improvement (39%). A significant subset of these patients (30%) terminated their treatment by commitment to another hospital.

4-8-2/8-4-2/8-2-4 Mean Discharge Profile (n=20)

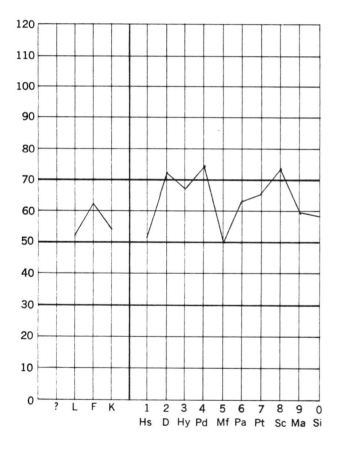

(8-2-4 (7) Profile Type; VA MALES: Gilberstadt & Duker, 1965) Mean Profile (n=9)

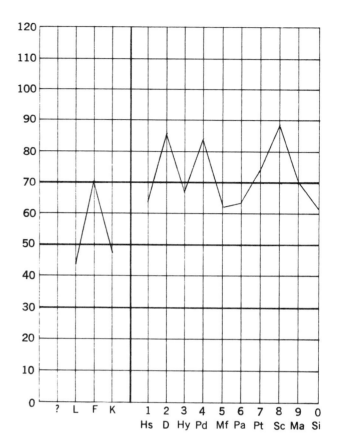

8-2-4 (7) Profile Type Rules (Gilberstadt & Duker, 1965):

1. Scales 2, 4 and 8 over 70 T.
2. Scale 2 or 8 greater than 4.
3. Scale 0 less than 70 T.
4. Scale 6 less than 70 T.
5. Scales L and K less than 70 T.
6. Scale 4 at least 10 T greater than 3.
7. Scale 8 not more than 13 T greater than 2.

Most descriptive diagnosis: Personality Pattern Disturbance, Paranoid Type.
Modal diagnosis: Schizophrenic Reaction, Paranoid Type.
Characteristics & rate of occurrence: Heavy drinking

(67%), Hostile (44%), Immature (36%), Inferiority feelings (33%), Paranoid trends (44%), Restless (44%), Anxiety (56%), Depression (56%) and Poor work adjustment (67%).

These patients are characterized by extreme irritability, hostility and tension. Though concerned about acting-out in others, they frequently presented similar behavior such as alcoholism and fighting. Though a characterological impression was quickly formed, further evaluation suggested pervasive and apparently deep-seated guilt as well as tendencies to deteriorate into frank psychosis over time which indicated the malignancy of the underlying psychopathology.

The majority (67%) of these patients were unmarried. When married, a deviant sexual orientation appeared to be a major problem leading to severe maladjustment. Their social histories often included overly close relationships with their mothers and vocational maladjustment which resulted from a lack of drive and responsibility.

(4-8-2 SANITY EVALUATION: Cooke, 1969)
Cooke (1969) presents data on male patients referred by the courts who were subsequently evaluated as competent (n=122) or incompetent (n=93) to stand trial. These mean profiles are presented below. The incompetent group (- -) produced a mean profile with peaks on Scales 2, 4 and 8 while the competent group (—) produced essentially a 4 spike profile (see page 79):

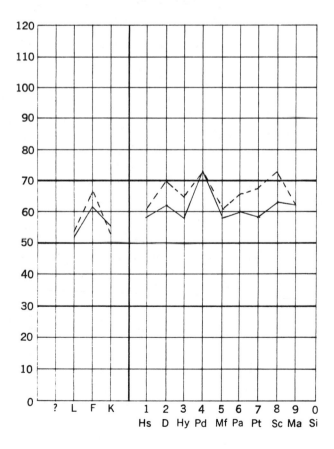

IQ appeared to have little to do with the determination of competency in this sample. In general the 4-8-2 pattern was associated with psychotic diagnostic classifications

while the 4 pattern was associated with personality disorders of the antisocial and dyssocial types. Patients diagnosed drug and/or alcohol addiction did not produce MMPI profiles which related in any systematic fashion to their judged competency.

4-9/9-4

This two-point code represented 5.79% of males and 6.69% of females in a sample of over 12,000 psychiatric outpatients (Webb, 1970).

(4-9/9-4 GENERAL: Carson, 1969) This pattern is frequent in the behavior disorders. Such a pattern is nearly always associated with some form of acting-out behavior. The individual exhibits an enduring tendency to get into trouble with his environment, usually only in a way that damages his own or his family's reputation; antisocial and criminal acts are not uncommon, however. Arousal seeking and an inordinate need for excitement and stimulation characterize the 4-9 groups as a whole.

(4-9 GENERAL: Stelmachers) Persons with such profiles are generally impulsive and irresponsible in their behavior, and are untrustworthy, shallow and superficial in their relationship to others. They typically have easy morals; they are selfish and pleasure-seeking.

Many temporarily create a favorable impression because they are internally comfortable and free from inhibiting anxiety, worry and guilt but are actually quite deficient in their role-taking ability. Their judgment is notably poor and they do not seem to learn from past experiences. They lack the ability to postpone gratification of their desires and therefore have difficulty in any enterprise requiring sustained effort.

Nonconforming, antisocial and unlawful conduct is frequently associated with this profile type, and it is likely that this patient has a history of acting-out and conduct disturbance of one type or another.

A high percentage of patients in this group engage in extramarital relationships and have very poor marital adjustment, as well as considerable sexual difficulties. Diagnostic Impression: (1) Sociopathic Personality; (2) Emotionally Unstable Personality. The great majority of patients with this profile type show no change with any type of treatment, and they tend to drop out from therapy.

(9-4 GENERAL) Where Scale 9 is greater than Scale 4 by at least 10 T, tension, fatigue and possibly physical problems following a frankly hypomanic episode are common.

(4-9/9-4 GENERAL) Other scales modify the basic psychopathic 4-9/9-4 picture. Scales 1, 7 and especially 2, 3 and 5 (male) seem to serve to inhibit or suppress the acting-out potential represented by the Scale 4 elevation. Suppression of acting-out by Scales 2 and 7 is likely due to external limits and will be short-lived. Scale 3 and/or 5 (male) elevation, on the other hand, represents

a more pervasive characterological suppression of acting-out, and episodes are likely to be less frequent and of a more subdued nature. Elevations on Scales 6 and 8 and increased Scale 9 elevation increase the probability and intensity of the acting-out episodes.

(4-9 Profile Type; TEACHING HOSPITAL: Marks & Seeman, 1963)

Mean Male (- -) and Female (—) Profiles (n = 20)

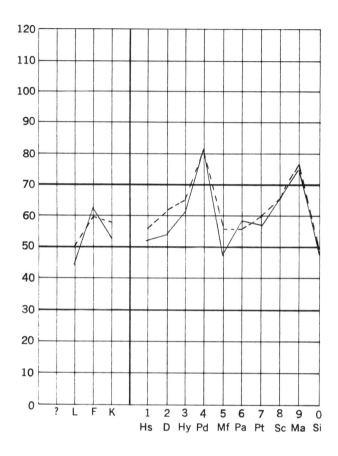

4-9 Profile Type Rules (Marks & Seeman, 1963):

1. Scales 4 and 9 over 70 T.
2. Scale 4 greater than 8.
3. Scale 9 greater than 4 by less than 5 T.
4. Scale 6 less than 8.
5. Scale 9 minus 8 more than 5 T.
6. Scales 2 and 7 less than 70 T.
7. Scale 0 less than 60 T.
8. Scale F greater than L and K, F below 70 T.

The great majority (80%) of patients who obtain this profile type evidence a personality disorder (Sociopathic/Emotionally Unstable). A small proportion (15%) were diagnosed psychotic (Mixed). These patients are described as impulsive, acting with insufficient thinking and deliberation, egocentric, narcissistic and self-indul-

gent. They are seen as having an exaggerated need for affection and attention though experiencing conflict over dependency and keeping people at a distance, avoiding close relationships.

Clinically, they are seen as hostile, irritable, immature and manipulative. Affect is likely expressed in a non-adaptive fashion. They resent authority figures and are sensitive to anything than can be construed as a demand. A rapid personal tempo is often manifest in fast talking, moving and thinking. Characteristic defense mechanisms include acting-out and rationalization.

Social histories frequently note behavior problems in childhood, including delinquency. Poor marital adjustment, extramarital relations and sexual difficulty are noted. Their behavior is often suggestive of poor social judgment and amoral trends: alcoholism, drug usage and homicidal and homosexual behavior.

This profile type represents a very stable personality pattern and a poor prognosis for behavior change or even participation in therapy, as 38% terminated treatment against therapist advice. Response to treatment: no change (80%) and small improvement (20%). Psychotherapy was the only treatment modality for the majority (80%) of these patients.

4-9 Mean Discharge Profile (n = 18)

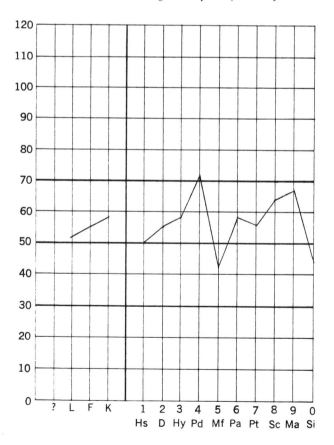

(4-9 Profile Type; VA MALES: Gilberstadt & Duker, 1965) Mean Profile (n=10)

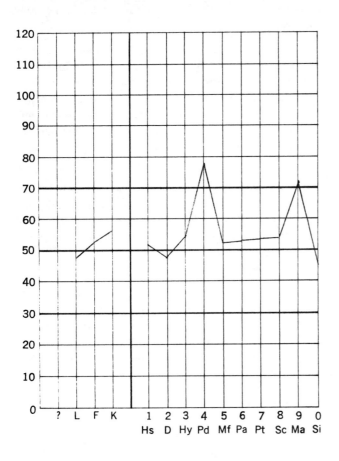

4-9 Profile Type Rules (Gilberstadt & Duker, 1965):

1. Scales 4 and 9 over 70 T.
2. No other scale over 70 T.
3. Scale L less than 60 T.
4. Scale 9 at least 15 T more than 8.
5. Scale 4 at least 7 T more than 5.

Most descriptive diagnosis: Sociopathic Personality Disturbance, Antisocial Reaction.
Modal diagnosis: Emotionally Unstable Personality.
Characteristics & rate of occurrence: Financial status poor (30%), Heavy drinking (70%), Hostile (90%), Irritable (40%), Conflict with wife (60%), Poor work adjustment (70%) and Tension (50%).

These patients are described as impulsive, restless, irritable, immature, moody, hostile and rebellious. Their low frustration tolerance leads to frequent acting-out and/or psychosomatic reactions (e.g., ulcers). They often lack respect for authority, are poorly socialized and display poor morals and standards. Their social relations are superficially friendly, outgoing and likeable but others often see them as self-centered, grandiose, haughty and hostile. They show no affection for adults but like children.

Presenting symptoms may include drinking, which results in paranoid psychotic episodes, and impulsive suicidal attempts. At times they appear to become lonely and perplexed to the point of panic when they consider their inability to relate meaningfully to others. Their social histories often include indulgent mothers, poor work and marital adjustment and "psychopathic" occupations.

(4-9/9-4 STATE HOSPITAL WHITES: Gynther et al., 1973)
Antisocial behavior tends to distinguish this type of patient from others. A history of excessive fighting and attempts to harm others, resulting in arrests and convictions, may be present.

(4-9/9-4 MALE STATE HOSPITAL WHITES: Gynther et al., 1973)
A history of alcoholic benders is encountered more frequently than for the average patient.

These characteristics occur *less* frequently among 4-9/9-4 males than among other state hospital patients: suicide attempts and history of brain function difficulties.

(4-9/9-4 FEMALE STATE HOSPITAL WHITES: Gynther et al., 1973)
This characteristic occurs *less* frequently among 4-9/9-4 females than among other state hospital patients; history of brain function difficulties.

(4-9/9-4 STATE HOSPITAL: Lachar, 1968)
Mean Male (- -) & Female (—) Profiles:

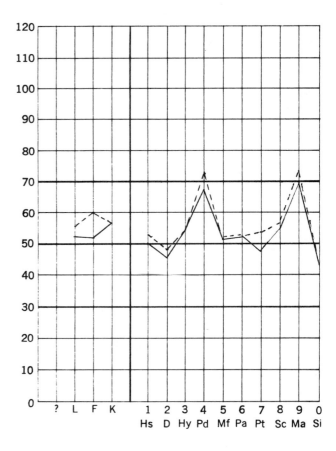

The 4-9/9-4 code was the 8th most frequent (n=152) in this sample. The modal diagnosis was Personality Trait Disturbance. Diagnostic frequencies: Personality Disorder—33%, Schizophrenic—23%, Other psychotic—17%, Psychoneurotic—10% and Brain Syndrome—10%.

Automated Interpretation

See paragraph 59 (pages 130-131).

4-9-6

(4-9-6 GENERAL: Carson, 1969) A 4-9-6 code indicates the probability of explosive outbursts of aggression; this is especially true if Scale 8 is also elevated. These individuals do not trust you, and it would be to your best interest to exercise caution in dealing with them.

High-point Scale 5

Scale 5 is profile high-point in 12.2% of males and .59% of females in a general psychiatric sample (Webb, 1971).

(High-point Scale 5 GENERAL) Developmentally, Scale 5 elevation decreases throughout adolescence in females and increases over time with males. In general, elevations toward the feminine end of this scale produce the kinds of problems for both men and women which lead them to seek psychological assistance.

(High 5, low 4 MALES GENERAL) Such individuals may project themselves as weak, inferior and overly deferent to others. They in effect establish self-effacing behavior as a way of life and appear more comfortable when treated by others in an arbitrary and depreciating manner.

"INDETERMINATE" PROFILES

1-3-9

(1-3-9 Profile Type; VA MALES: Gilberstadt & Duker, 1965) Mean Profile (n=9)

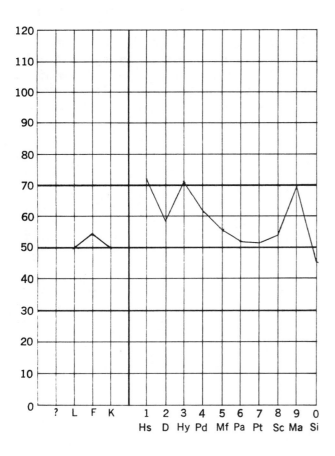

1-3-9 Profile Type Rules (Gilberstadt & Duker, 1965):

1. Scales 1, 3 and 9 highest elevations.
2. Either 1, 3 or 9 over 70 T.
3. Scale 3 exceeds 2 by at least 8 T.
4. Scale 0 less than 60 T.
5. If Scale 9 over 70 T, 8 at least 18 T less than 9.
6. If Scale 9 less than 70 T, 8 at least 7 T less than 9.

Most descriptive diagnosis: Chronic Brain Syndrome associated with brain trauma.
Modal diagnoses: Conversion Reaction (with additional organic diagnosis); Anxiety Reaction.
Characteristics & rate of occurrence: Abdominal pain (33%), Anorexia, nausea, vomiting (33%), Back pain (33%), Blindness, eye complaint (33%), Conflict with wife (67%), Headache (56%), Hostile (67%), Irritable (56%), Loss of consciousness (44%), Numbness (33%), Tremor and trembling (44%) and Nervousness (56%).

These patients often evidence signs of cerebral dysfunction which frequently are seen as posttraumatic syndromes. Somatic symptoms include hearing difficulties, eye complaints, tremor and shaking and multiple somatic complaints; these symptoms often are of a hysteroid variety (e.g., back pain). Associated phenomena include abnormal EEGs, stormy interpersonal relations and temper outbursts. Lowered frustration tolerance may lead to impulsivity and cumulative irritation, and eventually to episodes of perhaps combative and destructive behavior.

Their premorbid histories were often described as suggesting much ambition and overcompensation for feelings of inferiority.

1-9/9-1

This two-point code represented .65% of male and .34% of females in a sample of over 12,000 psychiatric outpatients (Webb, 1970).

(1-9/9-1 GENERAL) This configuration suggests the picture of acute distress in a tense, restless individual who has been frustrated by his inability to attain high goals. The 1 elevation may be considered an indicator of basic passivity and strong needs for dependency, which are being struggled against in counterphobic denial fashion by hyperactivity and tremendous efforts to produce. Somatic complaints such as spastic bowels and headache syndromes are associated.

The 1-9/9-1 code may be associated with neurological trauma producing organic brain injury. Physical complaints and an overconcern with physical integrity are suggested. Attempts to deny lowered abilities through overactivity and overproduction are indicated.

In general, this profile is the result of a counterphobic denial of passivity or weakness, whether the result of functional or organic etiologies.

Automated Interpretation

See paragraph 43 (page 123).

2-6/6-2

This two-point code represented .72% of males and 1.74% of females in a sample of over 12,000 psychiatric outpatients (Webb, 1970).

(2-6/6-2 GENERAL) Depending on the elevation of Scale 6, paranoid trends are likely. If Scale 6 is markedly elevated, the possibility of an early stage of psychosis is indicated. In any event, there is a great deal of other-directed anger present, which is probably not entirely masked by depressed feelings. Resentfulness, hostility and aggressiveness may be present, along with fatigue and depression. Sensitivity is probably marked.

It should be noted that many high Scale 2 patients seem rather unable to use projection and correspondingly obtain rather low Scale 6 scores. Were such people more able to express anger toward others, they would not be so angry and upset with themselves. The 2-6/6-2 configuration, then, suggests a vast amount of anger that is channeling into both self-blame and other-blame.

Automated Interpretation

See paragraph 46 (pages 124-125).

2-9/9-2

This two-point code represented .77% of males and .39% of females in a sample of over 12,000 psychiatric out-patients (Webb, 1970).

(2-9/9-2 GENERAL) This code represents an interesting contradiction. Simultaneous elevation of Scales 2 and 9 is statistically rare and clinically paradoxical. This configuration, especially in older populations, may make up to 8% of the clinic population. Such profiles occur in three distinct populations:

(1) Where Scales 9 and 2 are greater than 70 T, an organic brain lesion or deterioration is possible. Such patients are similar to 1-9/9-1's, but are showing more depression and recognition of their losses than those who express their depression in somatic equivalents. These patients seem to be in actual confrontation with organic losses. The Scale 9 seems to reflect a loss of control and/or compensatory coping.

(2) Another possibility is a manic-depressive patient in the manic phase. Such persons may fit into the classic picture of mania as a "flight from depression."

(3) This configuration may reflect a state of rumination and self-absorption. This is most common in the "identity crisis" of adolescence, but may occur in older persons who are narcissistically absorbed in themselves and the problems of the world as they center in on them.

Automated Interpretation

See paragraph 49 (page 126).

3-5/5-3

This two-point code represented 2.62% of males and .31% of females in a sample of over 12,000 psychiatric out-patients (Webb, 1970).

(3-5/5-3 MALES GENERAL) The simultaneous elevation of Scales 3 and 5 in the absence of other significant elevations points toward the likelihood of a very passive individual who projects a cultured, well-bred, well-

socialized and perhaps affected image. If such patterns appear in voluntary patients, they are often subordinate to the distress scales (2 & 7).

(3-5/5-3 VA MALES: Gilberstadt & Duker, 1965) Look for deep-seated psychosexual passivity.

3-6/6-3

This two-point code represented .67% of males and 1.93% of females in a sample of over 12,000 psychiatric out-patients (Webb, 1970).

(3-6/6-3 GENERAL: Carson, 1969) Such individuals may be seen as blandly repressive in regard to hostile and aggressive impulses. They often deny suspicious and competitive attitudes and comfort themselves by consciously perceiving the world in naïvely positive and accepting terms. Others may find them hard to get along with on more than a casual basis, since their underlying hostility, egocentricity and ruthless power operations are likely to be apparent to a degree that is inversely proportional to social distance.

(3-6 GENERAL) If Scale 3 is at least 10 T greater than Scale 6, overt paranoid features are rather unlikely. What is likely is a great deal of anger which is not being recognized by the individual. In the clinic such persons most often present some kind of pain, typically in the head or gut. In behavior they tend to be rather as people who smile sweetly, but say in their indirect way, "you give me a pain." If the anger is recognized by the patient, it is most probably highly rationalized and presented in what the patient perceives as an acceptable social form. The staff is likely to disagree about this perception.

(6-3 GENERAL) When Scale 6 is higher than Scale 3, a hostile, egocentric individual engaged in a struggle for social power and prestige is suggested. Such persons are likely to be blandly repressive concerning any hostility or aggression on their part. They are often presenting some kind of psychosomatic reaction when seen in a hospital setting. They are rigid, uncooperative, uncommonly defensive and resent the slightest hint that there are psychological implications to their difficulties. They may show more markedly paranoid or prepsychotic features. The prognosis is not good.

Automated Interpretation

See paragraph 52 (page 127).

3-7/7-3

This two-point code represented .67% males and 1.13% of females in a sample of over 12,000 psychiatric outpatients (Webb, 1970).

Automated Interpretation

See paragraph 53 (page 128).

3-9/9-3

This two-point code represented 1.29% of males and 1.92% of females in a sample of over 12,000 psychiatric outpatients (Webb, 1970).

(3-9/9-3 GENERAL) Although an uncommon profile type, persons showing such a pattern have probably been caught in the midst of an episodic attack of acute distress. Anxiety, tachycardia and, infrequently, conversion phenomenon are part of the clinical picture. Hostility toward a domineering mother may be present. The prognosis is reported to be good, although periods of acute distress may be recurrent.

Automated Interpretation

See paragraph 55 (page 128).

6-7/7-6

This two-point code represented .38% of males and .66% of females in a sample of over 12,000 psychiatric outpatients (Webb, 1970).

Automated Interpretation

See paragraph 60 (page 131).

7-9/9-7

This two-point code represented .69% of males and .56% of females in a sample over 12,000 psychiatric outpatients (Webb, 1970).

Automated Interpretation

See paragraph 64 (page 133).

OTHER CODES

F > 16

Blumberg (1967) found that within a medical school inpatient service, patients who obtain these profiles, regardless of age, are more often diagnosed psychotic (55.7% to 31.4%), spent more days in the hospital (70.8 to 47.4) and were more often discharged to a state hospital (28.6% to 8%). The F > 16 occurred more frequently among younger patients.

Gynther (1961) found that F > 16 in a sample of court referrals admitted to a state hospital suggested a characterological impression associated with aggressive and sadistic behavior. In a further study Gynther (1965) replicated this finding for court referrals while finding that the majority of hospitalized psychiatric patients (69%) who obtain this profile are diagnosed as psychotic.

These three studies, as well as that of Gauron, Severson and Engelhart (1962) clearly indicate that patients who obtain F > 16 are very seldom (0-7.5%) diagnosed as neurotic.

F > 25

(F > 25 STATE HOSPITAL WHITES: Gynther et al., 1972) The patient has responded to the MMPI items in an unusual or inconsistent manner, and it is therefore possible that the patient has answered carelessly, arbitrarily or antagonistically. Usually, however, this type of patient would be described in terms that suggest confusion. The capacity to think abstractly is often poor. Orientation is more likely to be impaired for the average patient. There is a tendency for attention span to be short. There may be some indication of impaired judgment and the patient may not understand the need for hospitalization.

In an interview situation, patients of this type tend to be withdrawn and verbally unproductive. Verbalizations elicited may indicate tangential and/or fragmented thinking. Delusions of reference and hallucinations, particularly auditory hallucinations, may be present.

Diagnostically, this type of patient is usually labeled as psychotic and, within this general category, usually as schizophrenic. Despite the frequency of symptoms of confusion, organic diagnoses are not more common than for other patients. A diagnosis of alcoholism is relatively infrequent.

High F-K

(High F-K GENERAL: Stelmachers) This is an invalid profile because the patient checked an unlikely collection of very deviant items. Nevertheless, it is not the result of a random performance and probably expresses the patient's subjective perception of himself, however distorted it may be. Such distortion can be viewed as part of the patient's illness. Here are some likely reasons for this type of invalidity: (1) Patient is psychotic, or in acute turmoil. (2) Patient is deliberately faking illness, exaggerating symptoms, etc., in order to achieve some personal gain. (3) Patient is an emotionally unstable, narcissistic and self-indulging person who habitually exaggerates and dramatizes complaints, has a tendency to feel very unfortunate and sorry for himself, expecting immediate attention, help and pity. This type of patient may be genuinely miserable, upset or at a loss, but the clinical picture is strongly colored by the style and intensity of expression of these symptoms.

Normal K+ Profile Type

(Normal K+ Profile Type; INPATIENT TEACHING HOSPITAL: Marks & Seeman, 1963)

Normal K+ Profile Type Rules (Marks & Seeman, 1963):

1. Psychiatric inpatients only.
2. All clinical scales less than 70 T.
3. Six or more clinical scales less than 60 T.
4. Scales L and K greater than F.
5. Scale K minus F more than 5 T.
6. Scale F less than 60 T.

These profiles are, in the classical psychometric sense, "test misses."

Patients who obtained these low profiles were most often labeled psychotic (48%—Schizophrenic, Mixed). Other diagnoses included brain syndrome (24%—Chronic), personality disorder (14%—Sociopathic) and psychoneurotic (14%—Obsessive-compulsive). These patients were seen as uncooperative, defensive about admitting to psychological difficulties, passively resistant, and as avoiding situations where their performance would be inferior to others.

They were described as suspicious, shy, anxious, worried, overcontrolled, withdrawn and inhibited, afraid of emotional involvement with others and as avoiding close interpersonal relations. These patients were submissive, suggestible and overly responsive to others and evidenced conflict about emotional dependency. They tended to spend considerable time in fantasy and daydreams and seemed unable to express their emotions in a modulated, adaptive fashion. Therapy outcome: no change (25%); small improvement (56%) and decided improvement (19%).

K+ Discharge

(K+ Discharge: Stelmachers) (If this profile occurs in a repeat or discharge MMPI, following an admission MMPI which is indicative of more psychiatric disturbance and little defensiveness, the following interpretation may be used.)

The MMPI indicates a significant reduction in psychiatric symptomatology but this reduction appears to be mostly due to an increased defensiveness and unwillingness to communicate psychopathology. The increased capacity to recognize deviant mentation and to withhold its expression, of course, is a sign of better reality contact and mental control and, hence, symptomatic improvement. The patient is probably no longer willing to discuss his/her emotional problems and seems to have profited maximally from the treatment program.

"Floating" Profiles

("Floating" Profiles: INPATIENT TEACHING HOSPITAL: Newmark & Sines, 1972)

Mean Admission (—) & Discharge (- -) Profiles (n=24)

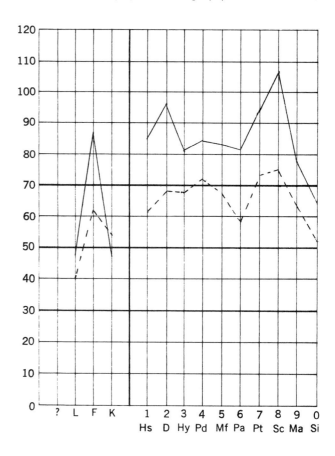

Inclusion Criteria: Scales 1-9 all over 69 T, regardless of validity configuration.

This profile was typically obtained by a young male college student. Social history characteristics included absence of one or both natural parents in the home, ambiguous sex role identification, considerable interpersonal difficulties and an intense fear and hostility toward women. Academic histories often included disciplinary problems or underachievement.

Upon admission these patients were described as rather passive and dependent, moderately anxious and depressed, and as manifesting a tendency to be self-analytical and ruminatively introspective. Loss of efficiency and initiative, inability to concentrate, excessive indecision, doubting and social withdrawal, and oversensitivity were noted characteristics. They possessed an extremely poor self-concept and did not demonstrate a decisively masculine interest pattern.

A history of psychiatric illness and/or previous hospitalization was often present. Current treatment frequently included major tranquillizers and perhaps anti-depressants. Hospitalization was relatively longer than with other patients, and group therapy appeared more effective than individual psychotherapy. Though mild to moderate improvement was noted to treatment, considerable residual psychopathology was evident at the time of discharge.

III AUTOMATED INTERPRETATION

INTRODUCTION

This section provides an interpretive approach to personality assessment which is capable of producing a general personality description in narrative form based entirely on MMPI data. This approach, implemented in the form of a computer program, generates fairly comprehensive blind interpretations with all of the limitations of other blind interpretations as well as the positive features of systematic approach and high reliability.

The resulting interpretations are applicable to samples of adults who have been identified in some manner as psychiatric patients and take the MMPI as a part of the evaluative process. This system of interpretive statements and rules attempts to simulate the steps taken in clinical interpretation of MMPI profiles. It is unique in that the organization of statements and specification of rules reflects the author's experience. The similarities which do exist between this and other systems reflect commonalities in approach to clinical interpretation and sources of interpretive data.

There are two problems inherent in all computer-generated test interpretations. Any information presented in the format of a computer print-out has spurious face validity. Additionally, blind interpretations have relatively more potential for misapplication than conventional test interpretations. In an attempt to minimize the effects of these two problems, a conservative interpretive system was developed. Narrative paragraphs and the rules which determine their selection were carefully constructed to interpret the most relevant portion of any given MMPI profile's variance. This conservative approach is also exemplified by only defining highpoint codes as scales which exceed 69 T and by the construction and elaboration of interpretive statements which will be applicable to many populations.

A parsimonious approach was used in designing the interpretive system. The number of paragraphs were reduced by making them appropriate for males and females whenever possible. Also, complex branching rules were used only where profile slope could not be accounted for in any other manner. This approach will facilitate any future program modification and allow application of rules and statements to construct narratives without computer support.

The individual clinician will be able to use this system and reduce the limitations of blind interpretation. In a manner similar to that proposed by Hovey & Lewis (1967), this system will direct the clinician to specific paragraphs which are likely to be most appropriate. Clinical judgment, base rates, moderator variables, etc., may then be used by the clinician to form the decision as to whether a given paragraph, or portion of a paragraph, is included.

INITIAL STUDY OF PROGRAM APPLICATION

Eichman (1972) raises several issues in his review of current commercial automated MMPI systems. He notes that the user of most present systems can only hypothesize the relationship between test data and interpretive output because such documentation is unavailable for the user's evaluation. The user is also unable to differentiate frequent from infrequent statements and has no estimate of the accuracy of independent statements. System acceptance and use is therefore essentially based on faith in the individual or organization which offers the service and the apparent face validity of the interpretations offered.

Several steps have been taken to avoid these difficulties with the present system. This volume presents all rules and interpretive statements needed to apply this interpretive system and therefore clearly documents the relationship between test scores and test interpretation. This material is presented with the expressed hope that other investigators interested in computer applications and objective personality assessment will conduct their own studies of this material. Such efforts would, hopefully, modify and improve this system as well as provide additional data concerning its generalizability.

The interpretive statements of this system were individually evaluated using a direct assessment design. Each patient's MMPI narrative was read by the responsible clinician (psychiatrist, psychologist, social worker) after at least one hour's contact with the patient. His responsibility was to rate each paragraph as accurate or inaccurate, following the outline presented in Appendix D. This dichotomous rating was used rather than a more complex rating instrument as Lushene & Gilberstadt (1972) found in a similar study that clinicians used two of eight rating categories ("correct," "incorrect") ninety percent of the time to describe interpretive statements.

Eighteen different psychiatric services, including five inpatient, eleven outpatient and two general medical services, cooperated in this initial six month study. The characteristics of these settings varied, as did their geographic location. Altogether the MMPI narratives from 1472 patients were evaluated. The nature of these patients' presenting complaints varied from minor personal problems expressed at a college counseling center to symptoms of an acute psychotic decompensation presented at a private psychiatric facility. This sample is predominantly young, male (75%) and obtained from military medical facilities (85%). These characteristics do not present significant limitations, however, as a significant number of female (366), civilian-evaluated (216) and older (35+ years-362) patients have been included in this sample. The military-evaluated component of this sample has the advantage of comprising a very heterogeneous group of active duty members and their dependents in terms of personality characteristics, and demographic variables such as geographic origin, education and life style. The distribution of age, education and source in this sample is presented below.

AGE

	male	female	total %
18-24	638	162	54%
25-34	210	100	21%
35-44	179	64	17%
45-54	65	30	6%
> 54	14	10	2%
total	1106	366	

EDUCATION

	male	female	total %
0-8	17	20	3%
9-11	99	54	10%
12	629	171	54%
13-15	210	81	20%
16	102	24	9%
> 16	49	16	4%

PATIENT SOURCE

	male	female	total %
Inpatient	430	137	39%
Outpatient	565	176	50%
General medical	111	53	11%

The numerical notation at the end of each paragraph gives the reader a summary of these clinician ratings as well as an indication of the frequency of each paragraph in this large sample. For example, the notation (5/104) indicates that this paragraph appeared in 104 of 1472 narratives and was judged inaccurate five times. In considering paragraphs which occur with only males or only females, the reduced sample size should be used to calculate the frequency of occurrence.

Some paragraphs do not present substantive material which can be evaluated as accurate or inaccurate by a clinician; in these instances the first member of the notation has been left blank. In a few instances the data suggested rule changes which could be easily made (e.g., paragraphs 9, 9A, 10, 10A). In these cases the data has been regrouped for this presentation according to the revised rule. Here the accuracy notation can not be presented, though the frequency estimate is given.

An arbitrary decision was made to exclude inaccuracy data on paragraphs which occurred less than fifteen times, as this number did not represent a sufficient sample for analysis. It should be noted that even within this large sample several statements did not appear at least fifteen times — certainly other studies reported in the literature with much smaller sample sizes suffer to a greater extent from this limitation.

When mean profiles are presented to illustrate the types of data which generate specific paragraphs, an attempt was made to exclude those mean profiles based on less than five subjects.

PROGRAM DESIGN

The present program separates profiles initially into three types:

A Type I Narrative is constructed when the clinical profile has one or more clinical scales (1-4, 6-0) above 69 T.

A Type II Narrative results from a profile which, though not containing clinical scales which exceed 69 T, possesses certain characteristics (usually scale elevations 60-69 T) which may have clinical import.

Type III Narratives form the remainder of possible interpretations and basically suggest "normal" personality characteristics.

The following diagrams illustrate the basic design of each of these narrative types.

TYPE I NARRATIVE

REQUIRED: One or more of the clinical scales (1-4, 6-0) exceed 69 T.

Subroutines Used

Validity	1.	Use one major paragraph and appropriate extensions from paragraphs 1-14. If paragraph 1 or 2 is printed, discontinue remainder of narrative, using only critical items, profile and scale scores.
Code	2.	If only one clinical scale exceeds 69 T, use one major paragraph and appropriate extensions from paragraphs 24-36. If more than one clinical scale exceeds 69 T use the two-point paragraph available (Note Scale 0 is used in this determination only if combined with Scale 2). If two or more scales are tied for T-value, take in numerical order. Use appropriate extensions. Paragraphs 37-65 are considered.
Significant Elevations	3.	Excluding Code Scales [i.e., HP (high point) scales], use up to three scale statements and appropriate extensions in *descending* elevation, on Scales 1-4, 6-9. Paragraphs 24A, 26A, 33A, 34A, 66-83 are considered.
Configuration	4.	Consider paragraphs 85-97. Use all appropriate paragraphs. (Excludes paragraph 94.)

TYPE II NARRATIVE

REQUIRED: No clinical scales exceed 69 T, but rules met for using at least one Significant Elevations statement (1, 3, 4, 8 or 9 exceeds 64 T; 2, 6, 7 or 0 exceeds 59 T).

Subroutines Used

Validity	1.	Use one major paragraph and appropriate extensions from paragraphs 1-14. If paragraph 1 or 2 is used, discontinue remainder of narrative, using only critical items, profile and scale scores.
Introductory Statements	2.	Use paragraph 15.
Significant Elevations	3.	Use up to three scale statements, in order of *descending* elevation, on Scales 1-4, 6-9. Consider paragraphs 24A, 33A, 66-82.
Configuration	4.	Consider paragraphs 85-97. Use all appropriate paragraphs. (Exclude paragraphs 94, 96 and 97.)

TYPE III NARRATIVE

REQUIRED: No rules met for Code or for Significant Elevations.

Subroutines Used

Validity	1.	Use one major paragraph and appropriate extensions from paragraphs 1-14. If paragraph 1 or 2 is used, discontinue remainder of narrative, using only critical items, profile and scale scores.
Introductory Statements	2.	Use paragraph 16.
Normal Variance	3.	Use in *ascending* order up to 3 statements, when appropriate, on 3 lowest clinical scales (1-4, 6-8). Consider paragraphs 17-23.
Configuration	4.	Consider paragraphs 89-94. Use all appropriate paragraphs.

An explanation of each subroutine will be found preceding the narrative paragraphs for that subroutine. Narrative paragraphs are numbered in the sequence in which they are used by the program. An alphabetic addition to these numbers indicates a sex-linked statement, a possible extension of the basic paragraph which has the same number, or tags the same paragraph used in a different

subroutine. Paragraphs with numbers ending in -1 as well as statement 97 are found in the concluding section of the narrative under the heading COMMENTS.

If two or more scales are tied in elevation, the scales are used by the program in numerical sequence (Scale 1 before Scale 2, etc.).

All scale scores are K-corrected, where appropriate.

INTERPRETIVE SYSTEM UPDATES
WPS TEST REPORT SERVICES

The MMPI interpretive system presented in this monograph has been incorporated into a comprehensive computer service which provides an adjunct for clinical evaluation and research. The computer printout includes, in addition to an interpretive narrative, 45 scale values, clinical profile, extended critical item list and application of adolescent norms. Interested mental health professionals are invited to write to Western Psychological Services, 12031 Wilshire Boulevard, Los Angeles, CA 90025 to obtain additional information about this computer service.

System-Relevant References

Adams, K.M., and Shore, D.L. The accuracy of an automated MMPI interpretation system in a psychiatric setting. *Journal of Clinical Psychology*, 1976, *32*, 80–82.

Klinge, V., Lachar, D., Grisell, J.L., and Berman, W. Effects of scoring norms on adolescent psychiatric drug users' and nonusers' MMPI profiles. *Adolescence*, 1978, *49*, 1–11. (Reprint)

Lachar, D. Accuracy and generalizability of an automated MMPI interpretation system. *Journal of Consulting and Clinical Psychology*, 1974, *42*, 267–273.

Lachar, D., and Alexander, R.S. Veridicality of self-report: Replicated correlates of the Wiggins MMPI content scales. *Journal of Consulting and Clinical Psychology*, 1978, *46*, 1349–1356.

Lachar, D., Berman, W., Grisell, J.L., and Schooff, K. The MacAndrew alcoholism scale as a general measure of substance misuse. *Journal of Studies on Alcohol*, 1976, *37*, 1609–1615.

Lachar, D., Klinge, V., and Grisell, J.L. Relative accuracy of automated MMPI narratives generated from adult norm and adolescent norm profiles. *Journal of Consulting and Clinical Psychology*, 1976, *44*, 20–24.

Lachar, D., and Wrobel, T.A. Validating clinicians' hunches: Construction of a new MMPI critical item set. *Journal of Consulting and Clinical Psychology*, 1979, *47*, 277–284.

Lane, J.B., and Lachar, D. Correlates of broad MMPI categories. *Journal of Clinical Psychology*, 1979, *35*, 560–566.

Newmark, C.S., Gentry, L., and Whitt, J.K. Interpretive accuracy of two MMPI short forms with geriatric patients. *Journal of Clinical Psychology*, 1982, *38*, 573–576.

Newmark, C.S., and Thibodeau, J.R. Interpretive accuracy and empirical validity of abbreviated forms of the MMPI with hospitalized adolescents. In C.S. Newmark (Ed.), *MMPI: Clinical and research trends* (pp. 248–275). New York: Praeger, 1979.

Wrobel, T.A., and Lachar, D. Validity of the Wiener subtle and obvious scales for the MMPI: Another example of the importance of inventory-item content. *Journal of Consulting and Clinical Psychology*, 1982, *50*, 469–470.

SUBROUTINE VALIDITY

This subroutine evaluates the absolute elevation of Scales L, F & K and their relationship to each other. It selects the most appropriate narrative paragraph from 15 alternatives and then considers possible extension paragraphs where indicated.

Two general conditions are felt to raise sufficient question as to profile validity to support a decision to exclude the remainder of the interpretation. First the F-K ratio is evaluated. If it exceeds +16 raw it has been my experience that inattention to test items or a deliberate attempt to fake bad are often suggested. The presence of a highly elevated clinical profile, especially when Scale 8 is a high point, supports these interpretations. An F-K value of 12-16 results in a highly cautionary statement (1A). The second general condition which excludes the remainder of the narrative is when more than 30 items are left unanswered. This choice of 30 items as a cutoff point is an extremely conservative one, and may be increased in some instances.

Sometimes a high F-K accompanies a moderate 8 spike which has been produced by an individual with a history of previous hospitalization and sometimes a protocol with 50 items missing generates a classical 4-9/9-4 profile. When this type of profile is obtained it should be the psychologist's role to determine the validity which can be placed on the resultant profile. Inferences such as possible suppression of clinical elevations or a partial random sort approach cannot be made in these situations without extra-protocol data.

SUBROUTINE VALIDITY STATEMENT SELECTION RULES

Select only the *first* acceptable statement.

I.
1. **F-K exceeds +16 and F exceeds 99 T, use paragraph 1 and exclude remainder of narrative.**

2. More than 30 omissions, use paragraph 2 and exclude the remainder of the narrative.

3. **F-K is +12-16, or F-K exceeds +16 and F is less than 100 T, use paragraph 1A.**

II. If F less than 70 T continue, otherwise turn to section III.

4. F exceeds 59 T and L exceeds F by more than 5 T and K exceeds F by less than 10 T, use paragraph 3.
OR
F less than 60 T and K less than 59 T and L more than 55 T, use paragraph 3.
AND
L exceeds 63 T, use in addition paragraph 3A.

5. F less than 60 T and L more than 55 T and K 59-64 T, use paragraph 4.

6. F exceeds 59 T and is 10-14 T less than K, use paragraph 5.
OR

F less than 60 T and K 65-69 T, use paragraph 5.
AND
L exceeds 59 T and K and L both at least 10 T greater than F, use in addition paragraph 5A.

7. F exceeds 59 T and is at least 15 T less than K, use paragraph 6.
OR
F less than 60 T and K more than 69 T, use paragraph 6.
AND
L exceeds 59 T and K and L both at least 10 T greater than F, use in addition paragraph 5A.

8. F exceeds 64 T and L less than 55 T and K less than 45 T, use paragraph 7.

9. F less than 70 T, paragraphs 3-7 not used, use paragraph 14.

III. If L and K less than 66 T continue, otherwise turn to rule 13.

10. F less than 80 T, use paragraph 8.
AND
F-K is +8-11, use in addition paragraph 8A.

11. F less than 100 T, use paragraph 9.
AND
F-K is +8-11, use in addition paragraph 9A.

12. F exceeds 99 T, use paragraph 10.
AND
F-K is +8-11, use in addition paragraph 10A.

13. F exceeds 69 T and K more than 65 T and L less than 66 T, use paragraph 11.

14. F exceeds 69 T and L more than 65 T and K less than 66 T, use paragraph 12.

15. F exceeds 69 T and L and K more than 65 T, use paragraph 13.

SUBROUTINE VALIDITY (Use only the *first* acceptable paragraph.)

Paragraph 1

Mean Female (−) (n=9) and Male (--)
(n=53) Profiles

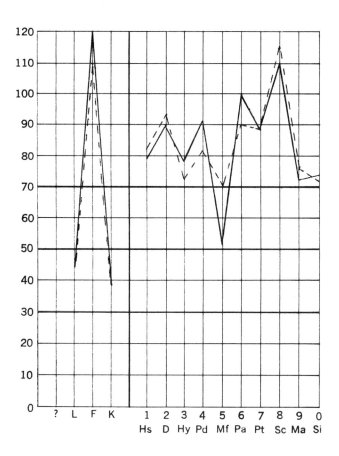

RULE
F-K Index: exceeds +16 and F exceeds 99T, use paragraph 1 and exclude remainder of narrative.

(1) The validity configuration suggests that great care should be taken in evaluating this patient's test results. It is likely that a standard interpretation of this data would result in a description which does not reflect this patient's current status. Possible explanations for these results include:

This patient may be acutely disturbed and unable at present to correctly complete this task. If so, a subsequent administration is suggested after some positive clinical change is noted.

This patient may be consciously exaggerating or malingering in an attempt to obtain some goal. If so, a subsequent administration following discussion of response set, validity scale interpretation and critical items with the patient may lead to a more accurate self-description.

Other explanations for these results include limited comprehension, exaggeration of complaints as a "cry for

help," lack of cooperation in testing, some atypical response set or test error.

The report which may be generated from the clinical profile is not presented. A qualified psychologist may be able to provide additional explanation of these results.

[NOTE: The decision rule that generated paragraph 1 in the first evaluation study was F-K Index: exceeds +16. (/62)]

Paragraph 2
RULE
More than 30 omissions: use paragraph 2 and exclude the remainder of narrative.

(2) This profile has doubtful validity. This patient omitted more than 30 items. As the interpretation of the resulting profile based on partial data may lead to incorrect interpretation, this report is not presented. This MMPI should be returned to the patient for completion.

Paragraph 1A

Mean Profile

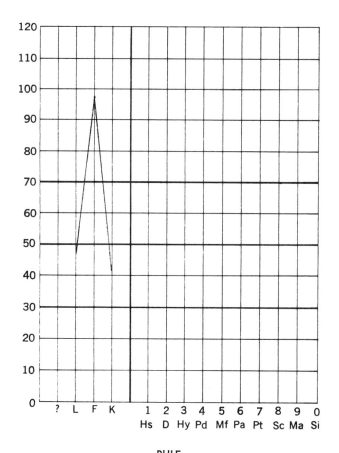

RULE
F-K Index: is +12 through +16, or F-K exceeds +16 and F is less than 100 T, use paragraph 1A.

(1A) Great care should be taken to confirm the accuracy of this report from other sources. The F-K Index suggests the possible effect of a response set which may have led to exaggeration or distortion of the patient's current status. Such a response set may be due to a "cry for help," an acute disturbance or malingering. This hypothesis is most likely accurate among outpatients. Hospitalized patients with acute, often psychotic, reactions often obtain F-K Index values in this range, though their test results are often quite accurate.

[NOTE: The decision rule that generated paragraph 1A in the first evaluation study was F-K Index: +12 through +16. (/60)]

Paragraph 3

Mean Profile (n=82)

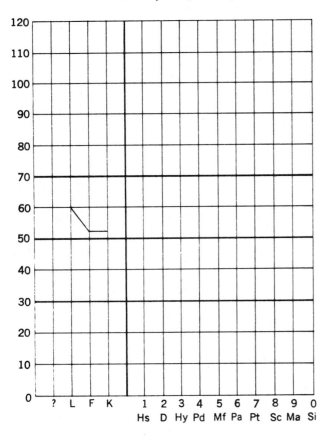

RULES
Scale F: exceeds 59 T.
Scale L: exceeds Scale F by more than 5 T.
Scale K: exceeds Scale F by less than 10 T.
        OR
Scale F: less than 60 T.
Scale K: less than 59 T.
Scale L: more than 55 T, use paragraph 3.

(3) This is a valid profile. Persons who obtain similar scores are often seen as naively defensive individuals who have a strong need to present an image of virtuousness and perhaps strong moral character. They tend to have little insight or awareness of their own stimulus value. (2/105)

Paragraph 3 + 3A

Mean Profile (n=23)

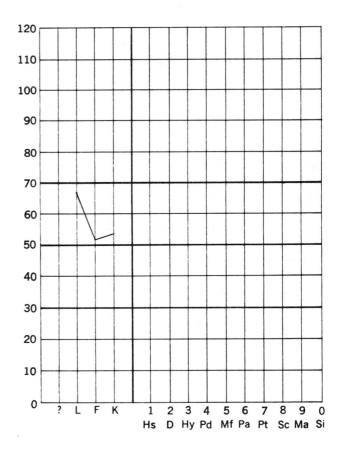

RULES
Use paragraph 3.

Scale L: exceeds 63 T, use in addition paragraph 3A.

(3A) The excessive use of repression and denial is suggested. These individuals lack flexibility and have a poor tolerance for stress and pressure. A naive, hysterical view of the world and self is common in such people. (0/23)

Paragraph 4

Mean Profile (n=65)

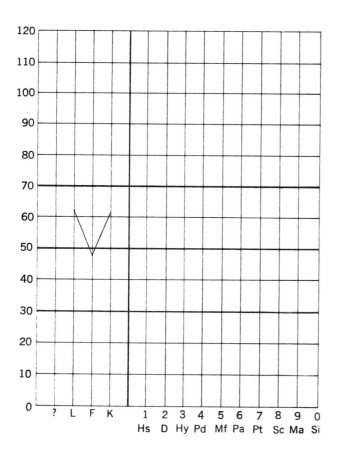

Paragraph 5

Mean Profile (n=70)

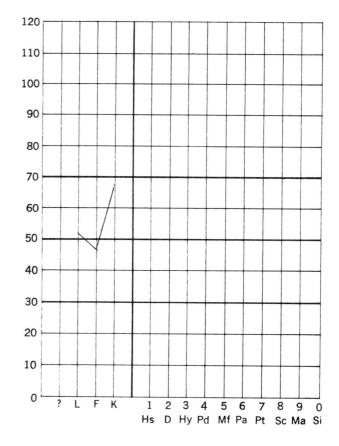

RULES

Scale F: less than 60 T.
Scale L: more than 55 T.
Scale K: 59-64 T, use paragraph 4.

(4) This is a valid profile. The validity configuration suggests a strong need to see oneself and to be seen by others as an extremely virtuous individual. These individuals often present themselves in an improbably favorable light concerning self-control, moral values and freedom from commonplace human frailties. Look for psychological naivete. (3/65)

RULES

Scale F: exceeds 59 T   AND
          10-14 T less than K.
                OR
Scale L: less than 60 T.
Scale K: 65-69 T, use paragraph 5.

(5) This is a valid profile. This patient responded to the test items in a defensive fashion. Similar individuals tend to present themselves in a good light and minimize or overlook socially acceptable limitations. Though this configuration suggests good social skills and ego functioning, especially in well educated individuals, it is likely to predict resistance to treatment for those individuals who are referred or "voluntarily" request treatment. (6/100)

Paragraph 5 + 5A			*Paragraph 6*	
Mean Profile (n=30)			*Mean Profile (n=28)*	

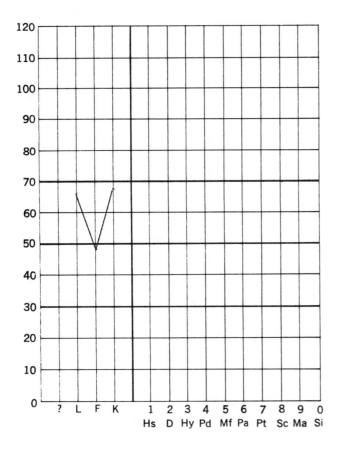

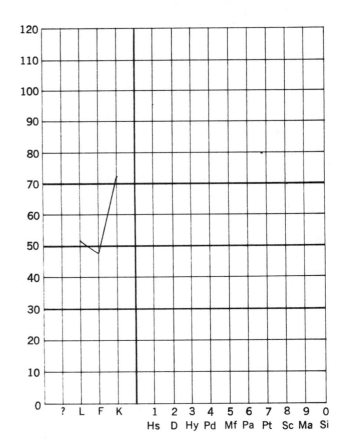

RULES

Use paragraph 5.

Scale L: exceeds 59 T AND
at least 10 T greater than Scale F.
Scale K: at least 10 T greater than Scale F, use in
addition paragraph 5A.

(5A) The "V" configuration adds support to these statements and further suggests marked evasiveness. Look for pronounced use of repression and denial. A neurotic picture is likely. Generalized lack of flexibility, poor insight and over-evaluation of moral worth may be present. (8/52)

RULES

Scale F: exceeds 59 T AND
at least 15 T less than Scale K.
OR
Scale L: less than 60 T.
Scale K: more than 69 T, use paragraph 6.

(6) The validity of this profile may have been affected by a response set characterized by a marked tendency to be defensive and to present oneself in a very favorable light. The clinical profile may, therefore, be unduly lowered in some way. Individuals who obtain similar test results attempt to minimize and overlook faults in themselves, their family and their circumstances. Lack of insight, unwillingness to accept psychological interpretations and poor acceptance of the role of a patient are common characteristics. Though this pattern is less deviant in well educated individuals, it does suggest defensive rigidity and overcompensation for feelings of inadequacy. (1/50)

Paragraph 6 + 5A	*Paragraph 7*
Mean Profile (n=22)	*Mean Profile (n=38)*

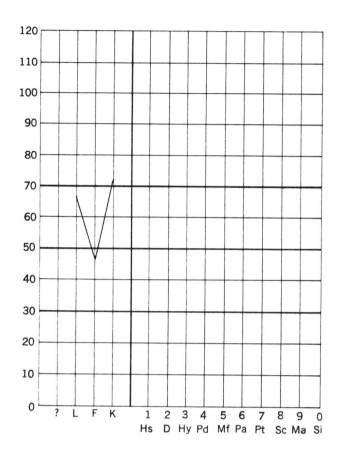

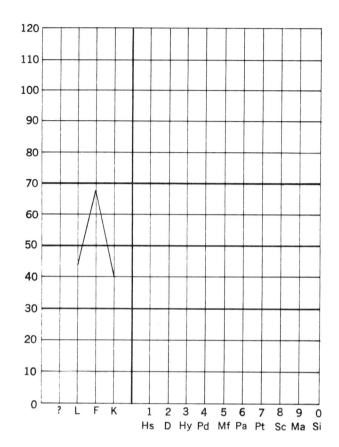

RULES	**RULES**

<table>
<tr><td>

RULES

Use paragraph 6.

Scale L: exceeds 59 T AND
at least 10 T greater than Scale F.

Scale K: at least 10 T greater than Scale F, use in addition pargraph 5A.

(5A) (See above.)

</td><td>

RULES

Scale F: exceeds 64 T.

Scale L: less than 55 T.

Scale K: less than 45 T, use paragraph 7.

(7) This is a valid profile. Individuals who obtain similar profiles tend to be rather open and blunt in speech and manner. Low ego strength and inadequate defense mechanisms are characteristic of all but adolescents. These individuals are seen as somewhat unusual in some way. If a significant psychological disorder is present, a neurotic adjustment is very unlikely. (0/38)

</td></tr>
</table>

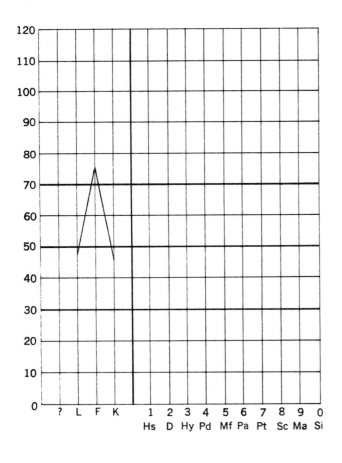

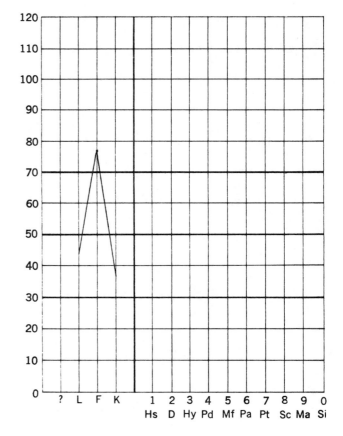

RULES

Scale F: less than 80 T.
Scale L: less than 66 T.
Scale K: less than 66 T, use paragraph 8.

(8) This profile is valid. Individuals who obtain similar validity configurations are often seen as displaying deficits in ego functions. A general negative self-image and realization of need for psychological assistance are common characteristics. Significant psychological problems are likely present and delineation of their characteristics will be described below from the clinical scales. A clearcut neurotic picture is, however, very unlikely. (2/160)

RULES

Use paragraph 8.

F-K Index: is 8-11, use in addition paragraph 8A.

(8A) Self-depreciation and exaggeration of symptoms may be characteristic. Similar individuals are often seen as very unguarded and do not possess normal social defensiveness and concern about the opinion of others. (2/23)

<table>
<tr><td align="center">**Paragraph 9**</td><td align="center">**Paragraph 9 + 9A**</td></tr>
<tr><td align="center">*Mean Profile (n=58)*</td><td align="center">*Mean Profile (n=63)*</td></tr>
</table>

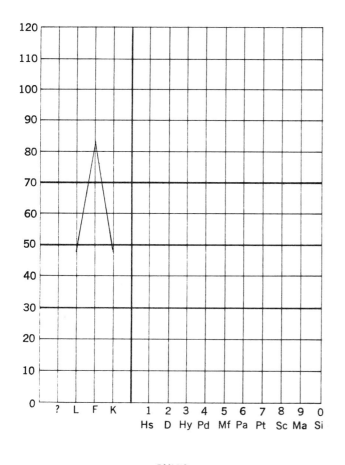

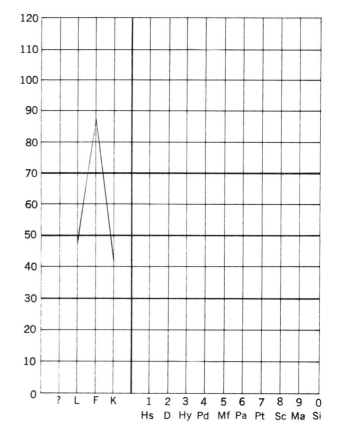

<table>
<tr><td align="center">RULES</td><td align="center">RULES</td></tr>
</table>

Scale F: less than 100 T.
Scale L: less than 66 T.
Scale K: less than 66 T, use pargraph 9.

Use paragraph 9.

F-K Index: is 8-11, use in addition paragraph 9A.

(9) This profile is valid. The validity configuration suggests that this patient has significant psychological problems which the patient would like to discuss. Individuals obtaining similar results are often described as somewhat moody and opinionated, unstable and rebellious. They tend to be overly critical of themselves and readily admit to psychological problems. It is likely that characteristic defense mechanisms are ineffective in dealing with current difficulties. This patient may feel vulnerable and defenseless. (/121)

(9A) Although these results reflect the problems of this patient, their intensity may be exaggerated. It is unlikely that this reflects intentional distortion, but rather, it indicates a request for assistance and an openness to psychotherapeutic intervention. This patient may currently be experiencing unusually high levels of stress. (/63)

Mean Profile (n=2)

Mean Profile (n=8)

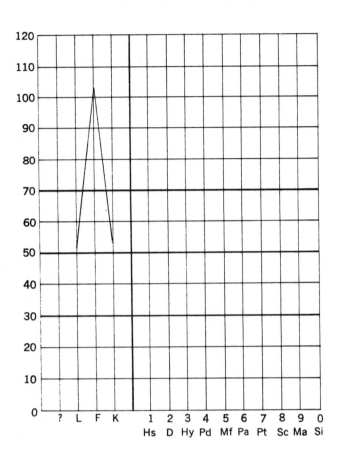

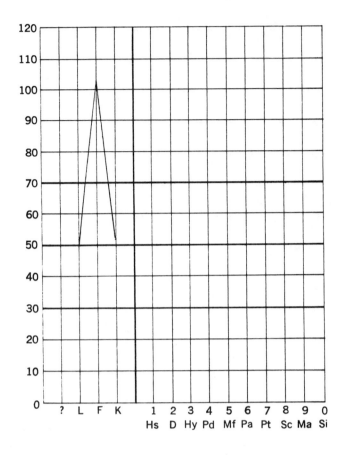

RULES
Scale F: exceeds 99 T.
Scale L: less than 66 T.
Scale K: less than 66 T, use paragraph 10.

(10) This profile is probably invalid. Because this patient produced a large number of extremely rare responses it is unlikely that the test items were understood adequately or that the test instructions were followed. Such a response tendency is likely to reflect lack of motivation or negativism (a random sort usually gives a raw F score 25-35), reading limitations, or receptor deficits. Severe psychopathology should be ruled out. The following report should not be considered valid, though useful clinical information may be presented. Additional interviews or further testing may clarify these findings. (/10)

RULES
Use paragraph 10.

F-K Index: is 8-11, use in addition paragraph 10A.

(10A) It is quite likely that this patient has greatly exaggerated existing problems or is malingering in an attempt to obtain some sort of assistance. Evaluation for secondary gain possibilities is strongly suggested. (/8)

Paragraph 11

Mean Profile (n=2)

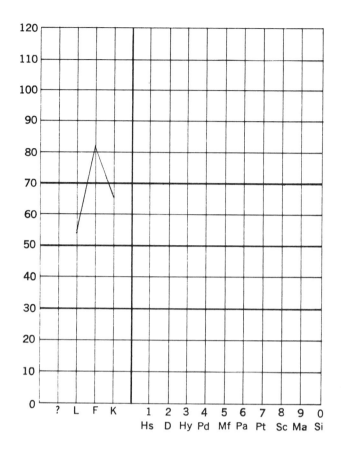

Paragraph 12

Mean Profile (n=7)

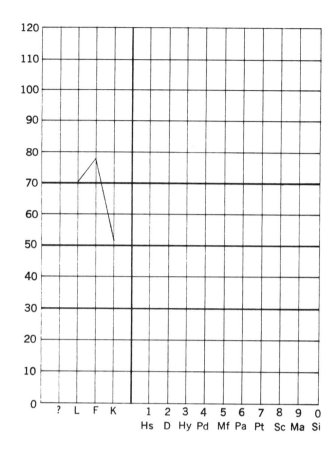

RULES

Scale F: exceeds 69 T.
Scale K: more than 65 T.
Scale L: less than 66 T, use paragraph 11.

(11) Though this appears to be a valid profile, the validity configuration suggests an unusual response set. This patient is both admitting to significant psychological problems and trying to appear psychologically sound. This pattern sometimes suggests the presence of an acute disturbance in an individual with rather intact defenses. On the other hand, these results may suggest a severely disturbed individual who is trying to be defensive but is not very successful. The equilibrium between open expression of pathology and defensive control in these individuals is both unstable and unpredictable. (/2)

RULES

Scale F: exceeds 69 T.
Scale L: more than 65 T.
Scale K: less than 66 T, use paragraph 12.

(12) This appears to be a valid profile, though a deviant response set is suggested. This patient is both admitting to serious psychological problems and naively attempting to appear well-adjusted. Such approaches to this inventory are characteristic of individuals from lower socio-economic backgrounds who are being quite defensive about their problems. If several clinical scales are elevated, however, this response set is often characteristic of psychotic states. (/7)

111

Mean Profile (n=6)

Mean Profile (n=686)

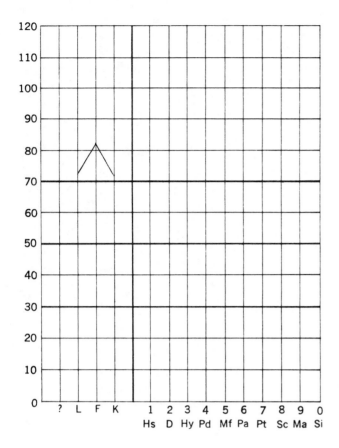

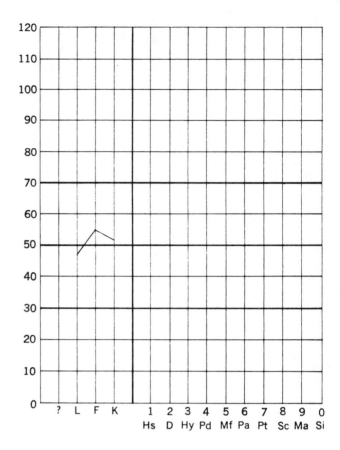

RULES
Scale F: exceeds 69 T.
Scale L: more than 65 T.
Scale K: more than 65 T, use paragraph 13.

(13) This profile has doubtful validity. These test results suggest a highly unusual response set. An all-false response set may be indicated. It appears that this patient has admitted to certain significant problems and at the same time has attempted to appear extremely well-adjusted. Such contradictions, in valid profiles, suggest either a decompensation of past status or, in a psychotic picture, may represent an attempt at reintegration or at least a realization of socially desirable behaviors. (/6)

RULE
Scale F: less than 70 T, paragraphs 3-7 not used.
Use paragraph 14.

(14) This is a valid profile. It appears that this patient has made an attempt to follow instructions and read the items carefully. The responses appear to be realistically truthful and are likely to reflect this individual's current status. (3/686)

INTRODUCTORY STATEMENTS

Paragraphs 15 and 16 follow a validity paragraph in Type II and Type III Narratives, respectively. They are meant to convey an impression of "within normal limits." Paragraph 15 is essentially a lead-in, as it is always followed by at least one interpretive paragraph. Paragraph 16 may stand alone as the body of the narrative, though this possibility occurs very infrequently.

Paragraph 15

RULES
One Significant Elevation statement presented (i.e., at least one of Scales 2-4, 6, 7 more than **59 T** or one of Scales 1, 8, 9 more than **64 T**).

(15) This profile is essentially within normal limits. There are, however, certain scale elevations which suggest personality characteristics which may be of clinical interest. (/263)

Paragraph 16

RULES
Scales 2, 3, 4, 6, 7, 0: less than 60 T.
Scales 1, 8, 9: less than 65 T, use paragraph 16.

(16) This profile is within normal limits. Although this is a profile often associated with individuals whose personalities are without significant pathology, it is essential that this individual be evaluated carefully to rule out deviant behavior and experiences. (/66)

SUBROUTINE NORMAL VARIANCE

This segment of the program is only used in Type III Narratives and only appears after paragraph 16. This subroutine includes paragraphs 17-23 and 94. These paragraphs, in essence, present hypotheses associated with submerged clinical scales.

Here elevation determines selection. Of those scales below 45 T (1-4, 6-8) up to three paragraphs may be printed in order of increasing elevation. Statement 94 is then considered and, when appropriate, becomes a fourth stated hypothesis.

Initial clinical use of this subroutine on hospitalized patients (medical and psychiatric) suggests that this subroutine is not very effective. In fact, most submerged profiles produced by psychiatric patients are test "misses." Statement 16 implies this possibility. Considering, however, that this was meant to be an "all purpose" program, these items were added. They may serve a role in psychiatric screening functions and may occasionally identify inappropriate requests for consultation or hospitalization.

These statements are not grounded in the substantial empirical research and clinical lore which is available for the majority of Code and Significant Elevations statements. For this reason, and to avoid contradictions in interparagraph content, these statements have been assigned a distinctly secondary role.

SUBROUTINE NORMAL VARIANCE (Use in ascending order up to 3 statements.)

Paragraph 17
RULES
Use paragraph 16.

Scale 1: less than 45 T, use paragraph 17.

(17) Similar individuals are described as having few body complaints and little concern about their own health. They are often alert, optimistic and capable individuals who are seen as effective in living. (4/15)

Paragraph 18
RULES
Use paragraph 16.

Scale 2: less than 45 T, use paragraph 18.

(18) This individual is probably cheerful, enthusiastic, optimistic and outgoing. Some individuals who obtain similar results tend to arouse hostility in others and may be seen as exhibitionistic and ostentatious. (/10)

Paragraph 19
RULES
Use paragraph 16.

Scale 3: less than 45 T, use paragraph 19.

(19) There are suggestions of a rather tough minded and hard headed approach to social interaction. This person may be rather nonadventurous and conventional and have narrow interests. Similar individuals have difficulty becoming acquainted with others and seldom give much attention to matters not of personal concern to themselves. (/6)

Paragraph 20
RULES
Use paragraph 16.

Scale 4: less than 45 T, use paragraph 20.

(20) This individual is likely to be seen as quite conventional and conforming. A passive, nonassertive orientation is suggested. Such individuals often lack heterosexual aggressiveness and tend to possess a narrow range of interests. (/9)

Paragraph 21
RULES
Use paragraph 16.

Scale 6: less than 45 T, use paragraph 21.

(21) Similar individuals may be rather distrustful of others and tend to present only socially acceptable behavior. They may be seen as cautious, stubborn and touchy. Interpersonal antagonism may be present. (/9)

Paragraph 22
RULES
Use paragraph 16.

Scale 7: less than 45 T, use paragraph 22.

(22) A relaxed attitude toward responsibilities and self-confidence are suggested. Such individuals are usually efficient and tend not to worry. (1/17)

Paragraph 23
RULES
Use paragraph 16.

Scale 8: less than 45 T, use paragraph 23.

(23) Strong interest in people and practical matters is suggested. Similar individuals are often described as compliant, controlled, concrete and unimaginative. (2/19)

SUBROUTINE CODE

This subroutine is used in every Type I Narrative. It selects a one-point HP code if only one scale (1-4, 6-0) exceeds 69 T, or selects a two-point HP code when at least two of these scales exceed 69 T. In general, the highest two scales determine paragraph selection. Scale 0, however, is only considered if it is a one-point code or is coupled with Scale 2 to form a two-point HP code.

These code paragraphs were available during this study:

One-point codes: Scales 1-4, 6-8, Scale 9 70-74 T, Scale 9 75-79 T, Scale 9 > 79 T, Scale 0.

Two-point codes: 1-2/2-1, 1-3/3-1, 1-4/4-1, 1-6/6-1, 1-7/7-1, 1-8/8-1, 1-9/9-1, 2-3/3-2, 2-4/4-2, 2-6/6-2, 2-7/7-2, 2-8/8-2, 2-9/9-2, 2-0/0-2, 3-4/4-3, 3-6/6-3, 3-7/7-3, 3-8/8-3, 3-9/9-3, 4-6/6-4, 4-7/7-4, 4-8/8-4, 4-9/9-4, 6-7/7-6, 6-8/8-6, 6-9/9-6, 7-8/8-7, 7-9/9-7, 8-9/9-8.

The rules for the appropriate code will indicate possible extension paragraphs or other effects on the remainder of the narrative. For example, if paragraph 38A is used, Scale 2 statements (67-69 & 97) are not used. Another example is the 6-8/8-6 code which may run in length from one to four paragraphs, depending on the presence of a paranoid valley and the absolute elevation of Scales 6 and 8. Also, it is very important to note that paragraph notations ending in "-1" indicate that these statements appear in the COMMENTS section if the rules are met for the paragraph whose number preceeds the "-1".

Though the inaccuracy notations suggest that this subroutine functions quite well, a few possible weaknesses are suggested. As only a two-point code is used, misinterpretations are likely to occur in some cases. For example, in the case of a 2-7-8 profile, if Scale 2 is the highest, a one T-point difference between Scale 7 and 8 will determine whether a predominantly psychotic or neurotic description is given. The addition of three-point narrative paragraphs may improve the accuracy of this subroutine, though the two-point classification scheme is well-accepted by contemporary investigators such as Gynther et al. (1973) and Graham (1973).

SUBROUTINE CODE (Use, when applicable, the one appropriate statement.)

ONE-POINT ELEVATION STATEMENTS

Paragraph 24 (1')

RULES
Scale 1: exceeds 69 T.
Scales 2, 3, 4, 6-9: less than 70 T, use paragraph 24.

(24) This patient is expressing a greater than normal concern about body functioning. Though the exaggeration of symptoms based on actual ailments may be present, the control of unacceptable impulses through somatization defenses is suggested. Diffuse, nonspecific physical complaints are likely. (/5)

Paragraph 27 (2')

Mean Female (—) (n=7) and Male (- -) (n=32) Profiles

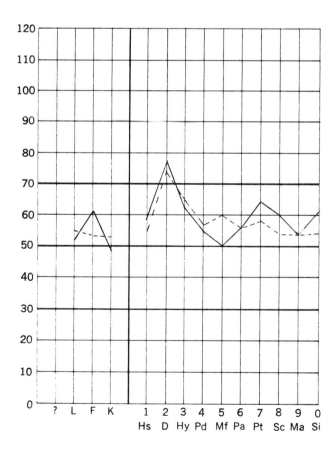

RULES
Scale 2: exceeds 69 T.
Scales 1, 3, 4, 6-0: less than 70 T, use paragraph 27 and 27-1.

(27) Individuals who obtain similar profiles are often seen as significantly depressed, worried and pessimistic. Feelings of inadequacy and self-depreciation are likely present. These people internalize stress and usually withdraw when put under pressure. An acute reactive depression is suggested. If depression is denied by this patient, its effects should still be carefully evaluated. Response to chemotherapy, psychotherapy and environmental manipulation is often good. (2/39)

(27-1) Reactive depression is suggested.

Paragraph 28 (3')

Mean Female (—) (n=7) and Male (- -) (n=11) Profiles

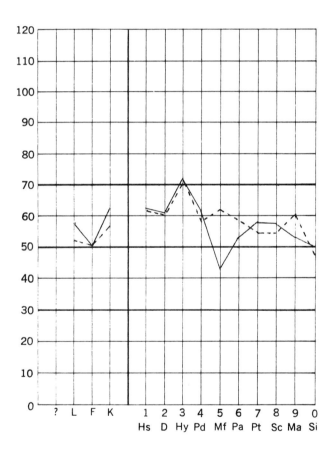

RULES
Scale 3: exceeds 69 T.
Scales 1, 2, 4, 6-9: less than 70 T, use paragraph 28.

(28) Individuals who obtain similar profiles are often made extremely uncomfortable in situations demanding the expression of feelings of hostility or anger. They often have difficulty taking a position of strength in regard to principles in which they believe. They are generally immature, egocentric, suggestible and demanding individuals with hysteroid characteristics. Physical

symptoms, when present, tend to have obvious functional components. These patients need to see themselves in a favorable way and are often able to maintain a calm and relaxed facade in the face of significant failure. Strong demands for affection, support and attention are expressed by unconscious stratagems. Characteristic use of repression and denial often leads to an inability to accept psychological interpretation of current problems. (2/18)

form quick, superficial relationships but have difficulty responding to intimacy and forming close personal ties. They are usually referred for evaluation by societal agents and do not see any problems in themselves. This patient is unlikely to attend regularly or cooperate in therapy. (6/57)

(29-1) Character disorder quite likely.

Paragraph 29 (4')

Mean Female (—) (n=13) and Male (--) (n=44) Profiles

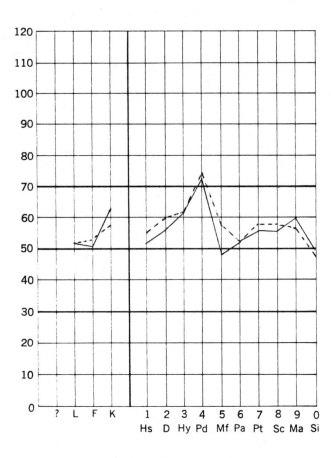

RULES

Scale 4: exceeds 69 T.
Scales 1, 2, 3, 6-9: less than 70 T, use paragraphs 29 and 29-1.

(29) Individuals who obtain similar profiles often have difficulty expressing hostility in a modulated fashion. Weak internal controls may result in impulsive behavior and poor self-control, depending upon social and intellectual characteristics. These patients usually resent authority, have limited frustration tolerance, and often have a history of conflicts with society. They are often adventurous, sociable and energetic. Such individuals

Paragraph 30 (6')

RULES

Scale 6: exceeds 69 T.
Scales 1-4, 7, 8, 9: less than 70 T, use paragraphs 30 and 30-1.

(30) Patients who obtain similar profiles are often described as oversensitive and rigid. They often feel pressed by social and vocational aspects of their life space. Suspiciousness, distrust, brooding and resentment are likely. This patient may utilize a projection of blame mechanism to an excess. Poor social relations are expected. (/10)

(30-1) Differentiate characterological features from fixed belief patterns which are reality-based or delusional in nature.

Paragraph 31 (7')

RULES

Scale 7: exceeds 69 T.
Scales 1-4, 6, 8, 9: less than 70 T, use paragraph 31.

(31) Patients who obtain similar profiles are seen as tense and anxious. They possess a low threshold for anxiety and tend to over-react to problems. Such individuals are orderly, self-critical and rigid. Rationalization and intellectualization are common defense mechanisms. Phobias, compulsions, and obsessive rumination may be present. (/6)

Paragraph 32 (8')

RULES

Scale 8: exceeds 69 T.
Scales 1-4, 6, 7, 9: less than 70 T, use paragraph 32.

(32) Patients who obtain similar profiles often relate poorly and tend to escape from reality pressures and their own unacceptable impulses into need-fulfillment fantasies. Some original, unusual, or eccentric qualities may be present in this patient's thinking. These characteristics may represent a schizoid adjustment or reflect limited reality testing. A thorough evaluation to rule out a thought disorder is suggested. (/5)

Paragraph 33 (9')

Mean Female (−) (n=5) and Male (--) (n=30) Profiles

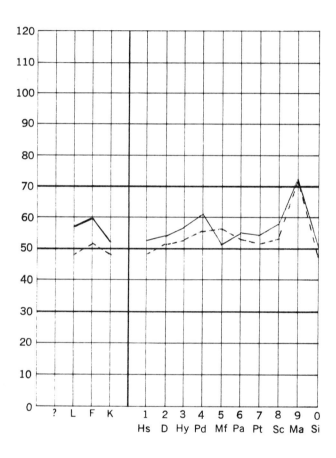

RULES

Scale 9: 70-74 T.
Scales 1-4, 6, 7, 8: less than 70 T, use paragraph 33.

(33) An individual who is full of plans and tends to be somewhat restless and impulsive is suggested. In psychiatric populations these individuals often display low frustration tolerance and perhaps ineffective hyperactivity of thought and action. (7/35)

Paragraph 34 (9')

Mean Female (−) (n=8) and Male (--) (n=11) Profiles

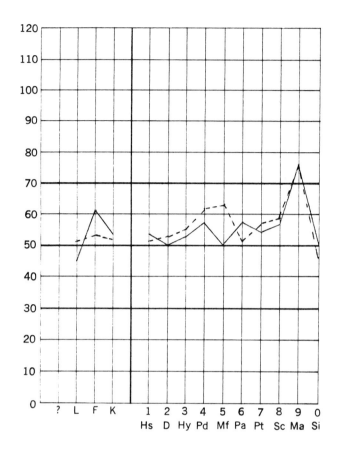

RULES

Scale 9: 75-79 T.
Scales 1-4, 6, 7, 8: less than 70 T, use paragraph 34.

(34) Similar individuals are often seen as talkative, distractible and restless. A low frustration tolerance and an insufficient capacity for delay is often accompanied by irritability and maladaptive hyperactivity of thought and action. (1/19)

119

Paragraph 35 (9')

RULES

Scale 9: exceeds 79 T.
Scales 1-4, 6, 7, 8: less than 70 T, use paragraphs 35 and 35-1.

(35) Individuals who obtain similar profiles are often described as extremely energetic, active and ambitious. Maladaptive hyperactivity, irritability, an insufficient capacity for delay, and ready anger at minor obstacles and frustrations are often characteristic. Similar psychiatric patients often display manic features, including grandiosity and a flight of ideas. (/11)

(35-1) Evaluate history for similar episodes or periods of depression. Rule out affective disorder. Consider chemotherapy.

Paragraph 36 (0')

Mean Female (—) (n=6) and Male (--) (n=5) Profiles

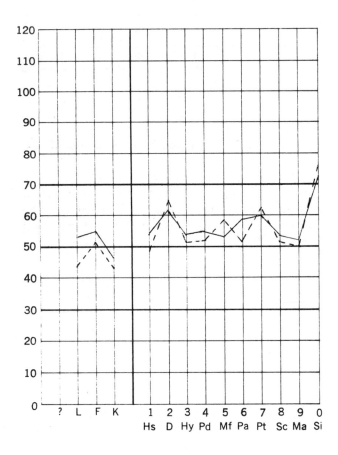

RULES

Scale 0: exceeds 69 T.
Scales 1-4, 6-9: less than 70 T, use paragraph 36.

(36) Individuals who obtain similar profiles experience significant discomfort in social situations. They are socially introverted, shy and tend to be socially inept. Such persons tend to be rather withdrawn and aloof. These patients are seen as being either chronically schizoid or as presenting a neurotic adjustment. The latter individuals are characterized by worry, lack of confidence and moodiness. (/11)

TWO-POINT ELEVATION STATEMENTS

Paragraph 37 (1-2/2-1)

Mean Female (—) (n=6) and Male (--) (n=24) Profiles

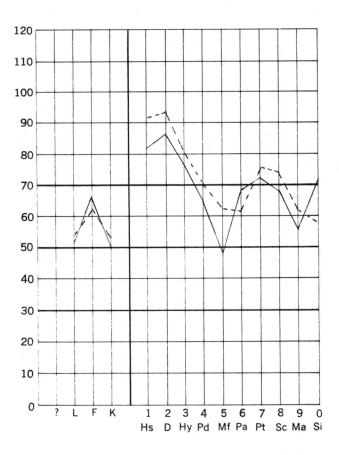

RULES

Scale 1: exceeds 69 T AND
    is higher than Scales 3, 4, 6-9.
Scale 2: exceeds 69 T AND
    is higher than Scales 3, 4, 6-9, use paragraphs 37 and 37-1.
NOTE: If Scale 2 is greater than Scale 1, then Scale 1 must equal or exceed Scale 0.

(37) Individuals who obtain similar profiles often present themselves as physically ill, but their chronic com-

plaints are not usually substantiated upon examination. Pain is often a presenting symptom and complaints may center around the viscera. Fatigability and irritability are characteristic. Prominent features suggested are depression, generalized anxiety and somatic concern. These patients are unwilling to accept that their physical symptoms are the result of emotional conflicts. A chronic adjustment utilizing repression, denial, somatization and a passive-dependent orientation make any psychological intervention, save temporary supportive measures, extremely difficult. (0/30)

(37-1) Rule out psychophysiological reaction. Poor prognosis. Conservative treatment is suggested.

(38) Individuals who obtain similar profiles often present themselves as being physically ill. Pain is a frequent complaint, and is often localized in the extremities. Headache, neck discomfort and back pain are common symptoms. These individuals characteristically develop physical symptoms as reactions to mental stress. Repression and denial make psychiatric intervention difficult. (7/63)

(38-1) Rule out hysterical neurosis, hysterical personality and psychophysiological reaction. Conservative treatment is suggested.

Paragraph 38 (1-3/3-1)

Mean Female (—) (n=7) and Male (--) (n=20) Profiles

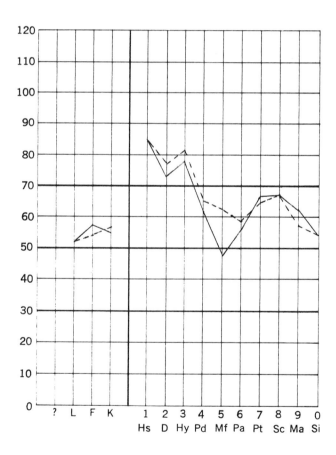

RULES

Scale 1: exceeds 69 T AND
        is higher than Scales 2, 4, 6-9.
Scale 3: exceeds 69 T AND
        is higher than Scales 2, 4, 6-9, use paragraphs 38 and 38-1.

Paragraph 38 + 38A

Mean Female (—) (n=9) and Male (--) (n=27) Profiles

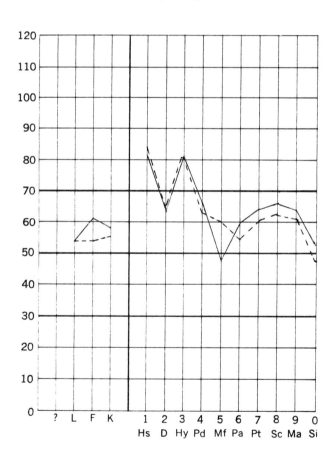

RULES

Use paragraph 38.

Scale 1: exceeds Scale 2 by at least 5 T.
Scale 3: exceeds Scale 2 by at least 10 T, use in addition paragraphs 38A and 38A-1.

NOTE: Do not use paragraphs 67, 68, 69, 97.

(38A) Such individuals may emphasize, but fail to show any real concern about their somatic symptoms. Ego-

121

centricity, immaturity, dependency, and a passive-aggressive orientation are often characteristic. The conspicuous absence of psychological distress and conflict and the presence of an "everything's right with the world" attitude are often maintained at some considerable effort and cost in emotional control and repression. (4/36)

(38A-1) Rule out secondary gain and conversion symptomatology.

Paragraph 39 (1-4/4-1)

RULES
Scale 1: exceeds 69 T AND
      is higher than Scales 2, 3, 6-9.
Scale 4: exceeds 69 T AND
      is higher than Scales 2, 3, 6-9, use paragraphs 39 and 39-1.

(39) Individuals who obtain similar profiles are often seen as egocentric, demanding and very concerned with physical complaints. Though a history of asocial behavior or poor impulse control is unlikely, a predisposition toward these dimensions often leads to an adjustment characterized by pessimism, dissatisfaction and bitterness. Hypochondriacal adjustment patterns are usually chronic and quite resistant to change. (/12)

(39-1) Characterological elements are suggested.

Paragraph 40 (1-6/6-1)

RULES
Scale 1: exceeds 69 T AND
      is higher than Scales 2, 3, 4, 7, 8, 9.
Scale 6: exceeds 69 T AND
      is higher than Scales 2, 3, 4, 7, 8, 9, use paragraphs 40 and 40-1.

(40) Individuals who obtain similar profiles are often described as rigid, stubborn, touchy, difficult and over sensitive to the requests of others. Hostility and projection of blame are often prominent features. Resentment may be expressed toward relatives. Physical symptoms, when present, are usually the result of accumulated stress. Insight is poor. (/0)

(40-1) Rule out paranoid trends and evidence of thought disorder.

Paragraph 41 (1-7/7-1)

RULES
Scale 1: exceeds 69 T AND
      is higher than Scales 2, 3, 4, 6, 8, 9.
Scale 7: exceeds 69 T AND
      is higher than Scales 2, 3, 4, 6, 9, use paragraph 41.

(41) Individuals who obtain similar profiles are often described as chronically tense and anxious. Physical symptoms, when manifested, are usually related to this tension and anxiety. Defenses may appear as over concern with bodily complaints, intellectualization or obsessive-compulsive behavior patterns. Though these people often demand continual medical care, this behavior pattern is quite resistant to change. (/6)

Paragraph 42 (1-8/8-1)

Mean Female (−) (n=5) and Male (- -) (n=23) Profiles

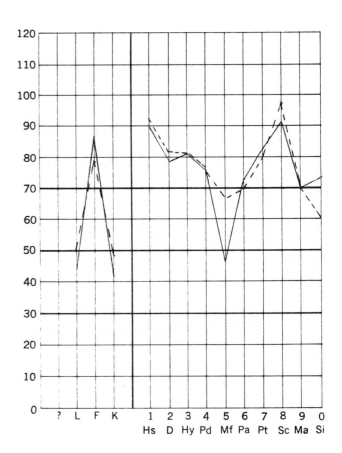

RULES
Scale 1: exceeds 69 T AND
      is higher than Scales 2, 3, 4, 6, 7, 9.
Scale 8: exceeds 69 T AND
      is higher than Scales 2, 3, 4, 6, 7, 9, use paragraph 42 and 42-1.

(42) Individuals who obtain similar profiles often manifest a history of vague physical complaints, which may seem rather odd or peculiar. Such people tend to maintain social distance and feel socially inadequate. Lack of interpersonal trust and inability to express anger in a modulated fashion may be characteristic. Prognosis is poor. (2/28)

(42-1) A history of confusion/disorientation, when present, suggests a borderline or prepsychotic state. Rule out somatic delusions.

Paragraph 43 (1-9/9-1)

RULES
Scale 1: exceeds 69 T AND
    is higher than Scales 2, 3, 4, 6, 7, 8.
Scale 9: exceeds 69 T AND
    is higher than Scales 2, 3, 4, 6, 7, 8, use paragraphs 43 and 43-1.

(43) Individuals who obtain similar profiles often present the picture of acute distress in a tense, restless individual who has been frustrated by an inability to attain high goals. Hyperactivity and tremendous efforts to produce, when present, may be seen as counterphobic denial of characteristic basic passivity and strong dependency needs. Physical complaints and an over concern with physical integrity are indicated. The presence of neurological trauma, in these cases, would suggest that these individuals are attempting to deny lowered abilities through over activity and over production. (/7)

(43-1) Rule out OBS.

Paragraph 44 (2-3/3-2)

Mean Female (—) (n=10) and Male (--)
(n=42) Profiles

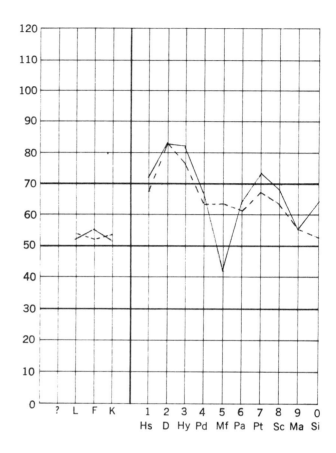

RULES
Scale 2: exceeds 69 T AND
    is higher than Scales 1, 4, 6-9.
Scale 3: exceeds 69 T AND
    is higher than Scales 1, 4, 6-9, use paragraphs 44A and 44-1 if patient female, use paragraphs 44B and 44-1 if patient male.

NOTE: If Scale 2 is greater than Scale 3, then Scale 3 must equal or exceed Scale 0.

(44A) Individuals who obtain similar profiles are characterized by the ineffective use of repressive defenses and hysteroid mechanisms. Such individuals may show symptoms of apathy, dizziness, and lowered efficiency as well as symptomatic depression. Chronic tension, feelings of inadequacy and self-doubt, bottled-up emotion and general over control are frequently characteristic. She may present physical complaints which often have a hysterical quality. Sexual maladjustment, immaturity and dependency are often characteristic. In general, these individuals have little insight, are resistant to psychodynamic formulations of their problems and have little genuine motivation to seek help. (/10)

(44B) Individuals who obtain similar profiles are characterized by the ineffective use of repressive defenses and hysteroid mechanisms. Such individuals may show symp-

toms of apathy, dizziness and lowered efficiency as well as symptomatic depression. Chronic tension, feelings of inadequacy and self-doubt, bottled-up emotion and general over control are frequently characteristic. He may present complaints which are the physical effects of prolonged tension and worry, such as ulcers. In general, these individuals have little insight, are resistant to psychodynamic formulations of their problems and have little genuine motivation to seek help. (0/42)

(44-1) Neuroses are common and characterological impressions are rare. Prognosis is poor.

Paragraph 45 (2-4/4-2)

Mean Female (−) (n=18) and Male (--) (n=47) Profiles

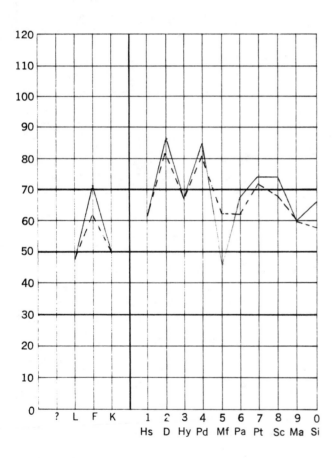

RULES

Scale 2: exceeds 69 T AND
      is higher than Scales 1, 3, 6-9.

Scale 4: exceeds 69 T AND
      is higher than Scales 1, 3, 6-9, use paragraphs 45 and 45-1.

NOTE: If Scale 2 is greater than Scale 4, then Scale 4 must equal or exceed Scale 0.

(45) Individuals who obtain similar profiles often display depression, restlessness and agitation to situational stress. This reaction is characteristic of a long-standing cyclic pattern of poor behavioral control which is followed by exaggerated feelings of guilt. This distress is often relieved after environmental manipulation or the beginning of another period of acting-out. The behavioral patterns of these individuals suggest a self-defeating and self-punitive tendency. Low frustration tolerance and a tendency toward addictive states may be present. While the insight these persons show may be good and their protestations of resolve to do better seem genuine, long range prognosis for behavior change is poor. Recurrence of acting-out and subsequent exaggerated guilt are common. (1/65)

(45-1) Assess suicide potential. A careful review of history may reveal similar episodes. These individuals are most often seen as character disorders, though prepsychotic states may occur.

Paragraph 46 (2-6/6-2)

Mean Female (−) (n=8) and Male (--) (n=8) Profiles

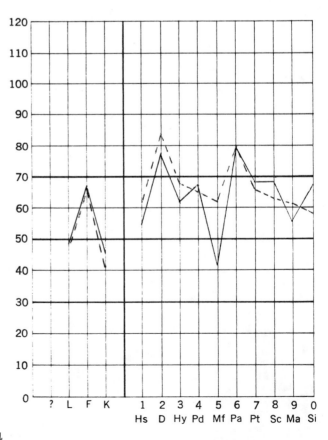

Scale 2: exceeds 69 T AND
is higher than Scales 1, 3, 4, 7, 8, 9.

Scale 6: exceeds 69 T AND
is higher than Scales 1, 3, 4, 7, 8, 9, use
paragraphs 46 and 46-1.

NOTE: If Scale 2 is greater than Scale 6, then Scale
6 must equal or exceed Scale 0.

(46) Individuals who obtain similar profiles are often
seen as depressed, oversensitive, hostile and aggressive.
Resentfulness and anger tend to induce rejection by others
and lead to a poor general social adjustment. The simultaneous presence of anger and depression suggests a vast
amount of anger which can only be controlled by both
internalization and externalization. This is usually a
chronic adjustment pattern. (1/16)

(46-1) Rule out prepsychotic state. Paranoid trends
likely.

Paragraph 47 (2-7/7-2)

*Mean Female (−) (n=15) and Male (- -)
(n=76) Profiles*

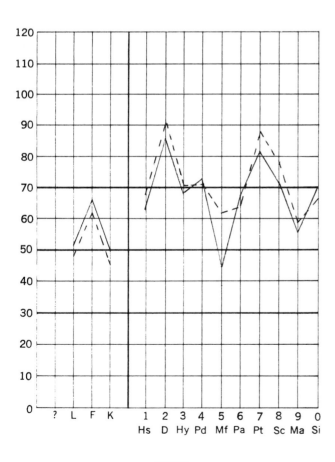

Scale 2: exceeds 69 T AND
is higher than Scales 1, 3, 4, 6, 8, 9.

Scale 7: exceeds 69 T AND
is higher than Scales 1, 3, 4, 6, 8, 9, use
paragraphs 47 and 47-1.

NOTE: If Scale 2 is greater than Scale 7, then Scale
7 must equal or exceed Scale 0.

(47) Individuals who obtain similar profiles are seen as
manifesting multiple neurotic symptoms which include
depression, nervousness, anxiety, weakness, fatigue, lack
of initiative and a pervasive lack of self-esteem and self-
confidence. Insomnia and decreased appetite may accompany psychic conflicts which are represented in hypochondriacal tendencies and somatic complaints. Sexual
adjustment may be poor. These patients are likely to be
pessimistic worriers, guilt ridden and intropunitive, generally fearful and obsessively preoccupied with their personal deficiencies. When their need for achievement is
frustrated, they usually respond by self-blame and neurotic guilt feelings. (3/91)

(47-1) Consider psychotherapy and chemotherapy. Diagnostic possibilities include anxiety reaction, depressive
reaction and obsessive-compulsive neurosis. Rule out suicidal ideation.

Paragraph 48 (2-8/8-2)

*Mean Female (−) (n=16) and Male (- -)
(n=62) Profiles*

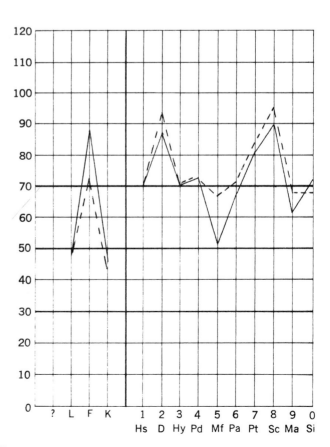

RULES

Scale 2: exceeds 69 T AND
is higher than Scales 1, 3, 4, 6, 7, 9.

Scale 8: exceeds 69 T AND
is higher than Scale 1, 3, 4, 6, 7, 9, use
paragraphs 48 and 48-1.

NOTE: If Scale 2 is greater than Scale 8, then Scale
8 must equal or exceed Scale 0.

(48) Individuals who obtain similar profiles are seen as unsociable and afraid of emotional involvement. Depressive and hysterical features are likely. Complaints often include loss of efficiency, periods of confusion and inability to concentrate. Unusual physical complaints and pervasive apathy may be present. This profile pattern often suggests a prepsychotic state or major affective disorder. This adjustment is likely to be chronic and resistant to change. Withdrawal, unrealistic feelings of guilt, anxiety and agitation may be present. (6/78)

(48-1) Rule out suicidal preoccupation. Evaluate reality testing. Affect disorder suspected. Consider anti-psychotic/anti-depressive medication.

Paragraph 49 (2-9/9-2)

RULES

Scale 2: exceeds 69 T AND
is higher than Scales 1, 3, 4, 6, 7, 8.

Scale 9: exceeds 69 T AND
is higher than Scales 1, 3, 4, 6, 7, 8, use
paragraphs 49 and 49-1.

NOTE: If Scale 2 is greater than Scale 9, then Scale 9
must equal or exceed Scale 0.

(49) Individuals who obtain similar profiles are often seen as attempting to compensate for feelings of depression and/or loss of ability. Such patients are seen as tense, agitated, ruminative and preoccupied with self-absorption. An increase in activity level is suggested. This change may reflect a fight against underlying depression or an attempt to compensate for recognized organic deterioration. An egocentric orientation may be present. (/10)

(49-1) Rule out OBS. Rule out cyclic affective disorder. Evaluate history for ethanol use.

Paragraph 50 (2-0/0-2)

Mean Female (—) (n=7) and Male (--) (n=5) Profiles

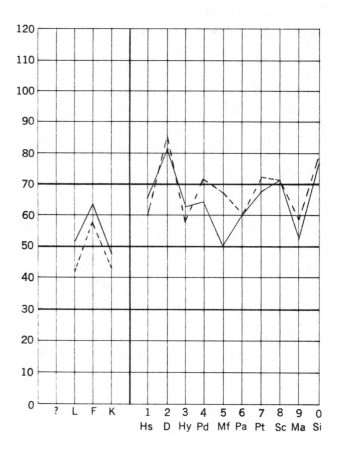

RULES

Scale 2: exceeds 69 T AND
is higher than Scales 1, 3, 4, 6-9.

Scale 0: exceeds 69 T AND
is higher than Scales 1, 3, 4, 6-9, use paragraphs 50 and 50-1.

(50) Individuals who obtain similar profiles are often seen as depressed and socially withdrawn. Feelings of inadequacy and insecurity in social situations and a real ineptitude and lack of skill in social interaction often accompany their introverted attitudes. Insomnia, worry and tension may be present. (/12)

(50-1) Consider chemotherapy for depression. Rule out schizoid adaptation.

Paragraph 51 + 51A (4-3)
Mean Female (—) (n=2) and Male (- -) (n=4) Profiles

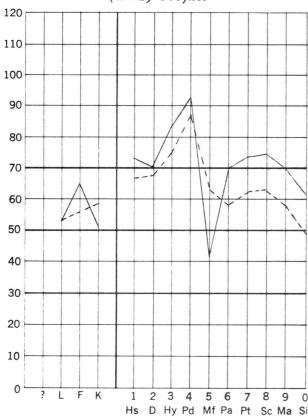

Paragraph 51 + 51B (3-4/4-3)
Mean Female (—) (n=12) and Male (- -) (n=6) Profiles

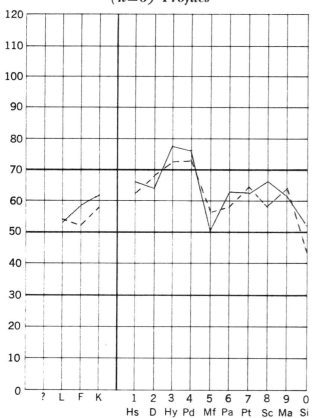

RULES

Scale 3: exceeds 69 T AND
is higher than Scales 1, 2, 6-9.

Scale 4: exceeds 69 T AND
is higher than Scales 1, 2, 6-9, use paragraphs 51 and 51-1.

NOTE: If Scale 4 exceeds Scale 3 by at least 6 T, use paragraph 51A.
If Scale 4 does not exceed Scale 3 by at least 6 T, use paragraph 51B.

(51) Individuals who obtain similar profiles are often seen as evidencing conflicts which center around impulse control and social conformity. These difficulties are likely chronic and may be seen as more of a problem by others than by the patient. (2/24)

(51-1) Consider character disorder.

(51A) This patient is seen as emotionally unstable and is likely to have a history of episodic acting-out of impulses which are followed by periods of inhibition and restraint. Self-control is tenuous and periods of aggressive behavior, promiscuity or excessive drinking are likely. These episodes of acting-out are likely to conflict with other people's general expectations of this patient. (/6)

(51B) This patient appears to be a passive-aggressive individual who maintains impulse control with some difficulty. Hostility is characteristically expressed in indirect and passive ways and insight into sporadic aggressive behavior is unlikely. Marital and family problems occur frequently. Inconsistency and unpredictability are characteristic. These individuals often appear demanding and resistant in therapy. (2/18)

Paragraph 52 (3-6/6-3)

RULES

Scale 3: exceeds 69 T AND
is higher than Scales 1, 2, 4, 7, 8, 9.

Scale 6: exceeds 69 T AND
is higher than Scale 1, 2, 4, 7, 8, 9, use paragraphs 52 and 52-1.

(52) Individuals who obtain similar profiles are seen as displaying a great deal of unrecognized anger which is often directed toward family members. If the anger is recognized and presented in what is perceived by the patient as an acceptable social form, others are likely to disagree with this judgment. Psychosomatic reactions are common. In general, these patients are usually rigid, uncooperative, uncommonly defensive and resent the suggestion that there are psychological implications to their difficulties. (/4)

(52-1) Rule out paranoid trends. Look for prepsychotic features.

Paragraph 53 (3-7/7-3)

RULES

Scale 3: exceeds 69 T AND
is higher than Scales 1, 2, 4, 6, 8, 9.
Scale 7: exceeds 69 T AND
is higher than Scales 1, 2, 4, 6, 8, 9, use
paragraph 53.

(53) This is a statistically rare profile. Individuals with similar profiles often present physical symptoms which appear to be the result of accumulated psychological stress. Though they may display indications in behavior and history of tension and discomfort, they are likely to deny any problems. Repressive defenses make psychological intervention difficult.. (/6)

Paragraph 54 (3-8/8-3)

RULES

Scale 3: exceeds 69 T AND
is higher than Scales 1, 2, 4, 6, 7, 9.
Scale 8: exceeds 69 T AND
is higher than Scales 1, 2, 4, 6, 7, 9, use
paragraphs 54 and 54-1.

(54) Individuals who obtain similar profiles are often seen as rather unusual and peculiar. Though they may present vague physical symptoms, unusual thought processes and social withdrawal are often significant characteristics. These patients frequently have a history of family disruption. When they are evaluated they often appear tense, depressed and nervous and are seen as hostile, dependent and immature. Supportive measures may prove most effective. (/8)

(54-1) Schizoid adaptation is likely. Rule out a thought disorder.

Paragraph 55 (3-9/9-3)

RULES

Scale 3: exceeds 69 T AND
is higher than Scales 1, 2, 4, 6, 7, 8.
Scale 9: exceeds 69 T AND
is higher than Scales 1, 2, 4, 6, 7, 8, use
paragraph 55.

(55) Individuals who obtain similar profiles often present periods of acute, intense physical complaints which readily improve with superficial treatment. Symptoms may include chest pain, anxiety, headache and intestinal cramps. Conversion phenomenon are a possibility. These patients are often emotionally labile and dramatic. Hostility and irritability may be important characteristics. (/7)

Paragraph 56 (4-6/6-4)

Mean Female (−) (n=10) and Male (--) (n=13) Profiles

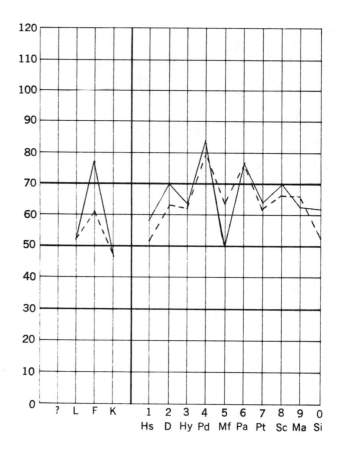

RULES

Scale 4: exceeds 69 T AND
is higher than Scales 1, 2, 3, 7, 8, 9.
Scale 6: exceeds 69 T AND
is higher than Scales 1, 2, 3, 7, 8, 9, use
paragraphs 56A and 56A-1 if patient female,
use paragraphs 56B and 56B-1 if patient
male.

128

(56A) Individuals who obtain similar profiles are generally seen as hostile, irritable, easily hurt, extrapunitive and do not resolve anger. Anger is usually expressed in subtle, indirect ways. An excessive identification with the feminine role is a common characteristic. These women are passive and dependent and unconsciously angry about this orientation. They are suspicious concerning men and don't get along with other women. They are very demanding in therapy and appear very narcissistic. They often enter therapy as a manipulative ploy. Conflicts about sexuality are frequent and poor marital adjustment easily results. Psychotherapy is not very helpful. This intervention is depreciated, and resentment of demands and authority may be present. (/10)

(56A-1) Passive-aggressive personality is likely. Watch out for counter-transference.

(56B) Individuals who obtain similar profiles are often angry, sullen, demanding people who utilize excessively a transfer of blame mechanism. Typically they are rigidly argumentative and are difficult in social relations, especially with women. Where anger and hostility are not being directly expressed, there is a likelihood of indirect expression. Depression, irritability, suspiciousness and judgment defects may be characteristic. When this profile is obtained by men within psychiatric populations, a malignant picture is often presented. Alcoholic personalities with a record of familial conflicts and poor work histories are common. These men are generally controlled but exhibit occasional periods of impulsivity. When external controls are removed, they can become quite hostile to the surprise of people around them. (/13)

(56B-1) Rule out borderline or prepsychotic state. Sociopathy is a possibility.

Paragraph 57 (4-7/7-4)

Mean Female (—) (n=6) and Male (- -) (n=17) Profiles

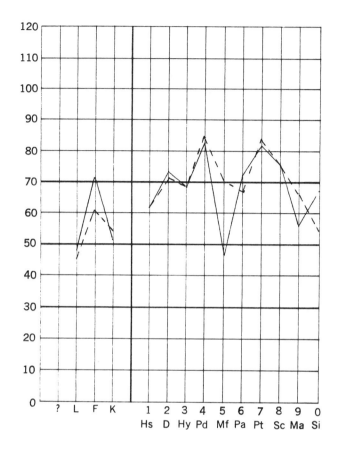

RULES

Scale 4: exceeds 69 T AND
    is higher than Scales 1, 2, 3, 6, 8, 9.
Scale 7: exceeds 69 T AND
    is higher than Scales 1, 2, 3, 6, 8, 9, use
    paragraphs 57 and 57-1.

(57) Individuals who obtain similar profiles often show contradictions in their behavior and perceptions. This contradiction frequently appears as an alternation of phases or cyclical variations. For a period these persons may act impulsively, violating social limits and showing little care for others. These periods are characteristically followed by guilt, remorse and deep regret for their actions. For a time they may seem over controlled and contrite. While their self-condemnation and depression may be severe and out of proportion to their actions, they are unable to prevent further episodes. (5/23)

(57-1) A history of periods of alcoholic indulgence or other forms of acting out may be characteristic. Character disorder is likely.

(58) Individuals who obtain similar profiles are often seen as introverted, unpredictable and peculiar in action and thought. Psychiatric patients who obtain this pattern usually display clearly deviant behavior. These individuals experience subtle communication problems; they have impaired empathy and find becoming emotionally involved with others difficult. Similar individuals often act-out in self-defeating ways and have difficulty evaluating social situations. They are often angry with others but are unable to handle or express such feelings. These patients should be carefully evaluated. They may have the potential for antisocial or schizotypic behavior. (1/46)

(58-1) A history of schizoid adaptation is likely. Rule out paranoid trends and thought disorder. Characterological and psychotic syndromes possible.

Paragraph 58 (4-8/8-4)

Mean Female (−) (n=15) and Male (··) (n=31) Profiles

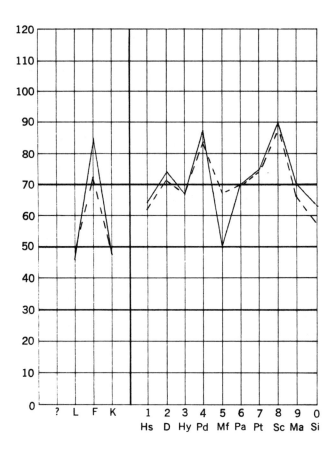

Paragraph 59 (4-9/9-4)

Mean Female (−) (n=7) and Male (··) (n=43) Profiles

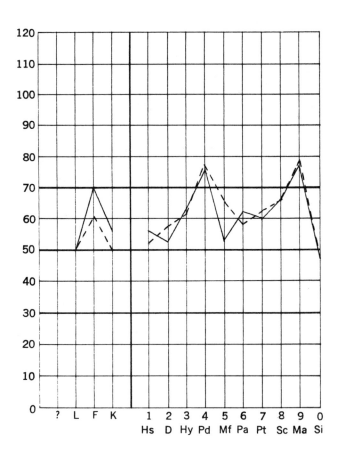

RULES
Scale 4: exceeds 69 T AND
      is higher than Scales 1, 2, 3, 6, 7, 9.
Scale 8: exceeds 69 T AND
      is higher than Scales 1, 2, 3, 6, 7, 9, use
      paragraphs 58 and 58-1.

RULES
Scale 4: exceeds 69 T AND
      is higher than Scales 1, 2, 3, 6, 7, 8.
Scale 9: exceeds 69 T AND
      is higher than Scales 1, 2, 3, 6, 7, 8, use
      paragraph 59.

(59) Individuals who obtain similar profiles are often described as extroverted, over active, impulsive and rather irresponsible. When this pattern is obtained during a psychiatric evaluation, these individuals are usually seen as hostile, socially shallow and superficial, and as having fluctuating morals and poor conscience development. Though their social skills may appear quite good, they eventually display lack of judgment, poor internal controls and neglect of obligations. They typically show flagrant excesses in their search for pleasure and self-stimulation. (6/50)

Paragraph 60 (6-7/7-6)

RULES
Scale 6: exceeds 69 T AND
  is higher than Scales 1-4, 8, 9.
Scale 7: exceeds 69 T AND
  is higher than Scales 1-4, 8, 9, use paragraphs 60 and 60-1.

(60) This is a statistically infrequent profile. Individuals who obtain similar profiles are often described as tense, anxious and rigid. A history of, as well as current dissatisfaction with, life's experiences results from an inability to appropriately interpret social stimuli, oversensitivity and the excessive use of projection. Similar patients are seen as somewhat suspicious and stubborn. They tend to brood and ruminate about real or imagined wrongs. Hostility is likely to be expressed in an indirect manner. (/2)

(60-1) Rule out paranoid trends.

Paragraph 61 (6-8/8-6)

Mean Female (—) (n=23) and Male (- -) (n=17) Profiles

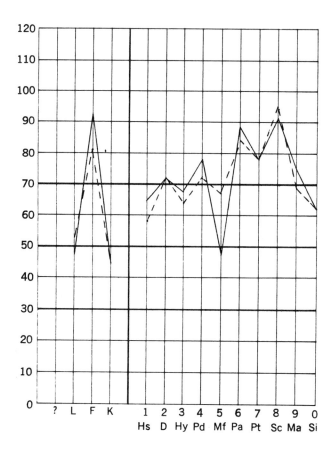

RULES
Scale 6: exceeds 69 T AND
  is higher than Scales 1-4, 7, 9.
Scale 8: exceeds 69 T AND
  is higher than Scales 1-4, 7, 9, use paragraphs 61 and 61-1.

NOTE: If Scale 6 exceeds Scale 7 by at least 10 T AND Scale 8 exceeds Scale 7 by at least 10 T, use paragraph 61A.
  If Scale 6 exceeds 79 T, use paragraph 61B.
  If Scale 8 exceeds 79 T, use paragraph 61C.

(61) Individuals who obtain similar profiles often display poor social skills and tend to withdraw from others during periods of stress. They are often preoccupied with abstract, theoretical or religious themes and present an unconventional cognitive approach. Excessive fantasy is often used as an escape from the direct expression of unacceptable impulses. In psychiatric populations, similar individuals are seen as depressed, tense and nervous. Their psychological discomfort is usually colored by a pervasive hostility and suspiciousness. (5/40)

(61-1) Thought processes should be carefully evaluated. Look for paranoid trends. In valid profiles, a diagnosis of paranoid schizophrenia should be considered.

(61A) This profile configuration suggests the presence of a serious personality disturbance. This patient may utilize projection to the degree where reality distortion takes the form of frankly delusional ego-syntonic features. (4/19)

(61B) In addition to suspiciousness and brooding, feelings of persecution and reference, feelings of maltreatment and fixed belief patterns are likely. (3/34)

(61C) Similar patients often display a general and pervasive apathy which accompanies behavior characterized by regression and disorganization. The presence of a thought disorder, confusion, strange thoughts, beliefs and actions are suggested. (7/35)

Paragraph 62 (6-9/9-6)

RULES
Scale 6: exceeds 69 T AND
is higher than Scales 1-4, 7, 8.
Scale 9: exceeds 69 T AND
is higher than Scales 1-4, 7, 8, use paragraphs 62 and 62-1.

(62) Individuals who obtain similar profiles often have a history of difficulty with social relations. Hostility within these situations is often openly manifest as well as suspiciousness and a pervasive distrust. They have difficulty expressing emotion in a modulated fashion, use projection to excess and tend to keep people at a distance. Similar psychiatric patients are often described as tense, anxious, irritable and jumpy. They over react to environmental stimuli and often exhibit poor behavioral controls and a heightened activity level. In some individuals lowered ability to concentrate and organize thinking in a goal directed manner is characteristic. Such patients tend to be ruminative, over-ideational and evidence ideas of reference. (/9)

(62-1) This profile pattern is seldom obtained from individuals who are not hospitalized and seriously disturbed. Consider paranoid schizophrenia and manic-depressive psychosis.

Paragraph 63 + 63A (7-8)

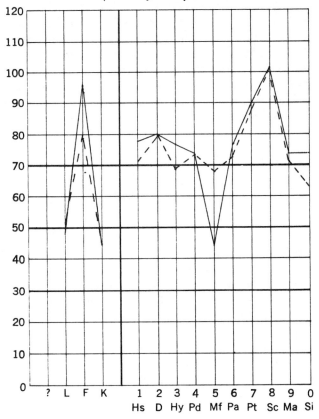

Paragraph 63 + 63B (8-7)

Mean Female (—) (n=8) and Male (--)
(n=40) Profiles

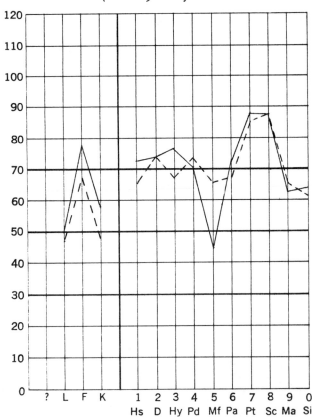

Paragraph 63 + 63C (7-8/8-7)

Mean Female (—) (n=5) and Male (--)
(n=45) Profiles

Scale 7: exceeds 69 T AND
is higher than Scales 1-4, 6, 9.

Scale 8: exceeds 69 T AND
is higher than Scales 1-4, 6, 9, use paragraph 63.

NOTE: If Scale 7 exceeds Scale 8 by at least 6 T, use paragraphs 63A and 63A-1.
If Scale 8 exceeds Scale 7 by at least 6 T, use paragraphs 63B and 63B-1.
If paragraphs 63A or 63B are not used, use paragraphs 63C and 63C-1.

(63) Individuals who obtain similar profiles are described as ruminative, obsessive and over-ideational. In relation to other people, they lack poise, assurance and dominance, and often have histories with few rewarding social experiences. Little common sense, a rich fantasy life and much daydreaming are characteristic. (5/104)

(63A) Similar patients often exhibit an unstable adjustment pattern, characterized by much anxiety, tension, agitation and struggle. These symptoms are seen as recognition of, and an attempt to work through, problems. Depression, withdrawal and obsessive-compulsive symptoms are likely. (/6)

(63A-1) Anti-anxiety medication is indicated. Psychotherapy may be beneficial. Rule out severe obsessive-compulsive. Evaluate for thought disorder. Suicide potential should be assessed.

(63B) Similar patients often present chronic, fixed patterns of behavior and thought. They are often schizoid or overtly psychotic. As these patients do not readily form stable relationships, they typically show poor response to psychotherapy. (8/48)

(63B-1) Rule out schizophrenic reaction. Supportive measures and anti-psychotic medication may be beneficial. Suicide potential should be assessed.

(63C) Similar patients with this test pattern are about evenly divided into neurotic and psychotic diagnoses. A passive-dependent adjustment and feelings of inadequacy, inferiority and insecurity may be present. Decompensation is a likelihood, especially if psychosomatic symptoms appear. (6/50)

(63C-1) Evaluate for thought disorder. Suicide potential should be assessed.

Paragraph 64 (7-9/9-7)

Scale 7: exceeds 69 T AND
is higher than Scales 1-4, 6, 8.

Scale 9: exceeds 69 T AND
is higher than Scales 1-4, 6, 8, use paragraphs 64 and 64-1.

(64) Individuals who obtain similar profiles are often described as tense, anxious, restless and agitated. They worry to an excess and often present symptoms which reflect chronic tension. A heightened energy level is suggested. Similar patients often experience periods of impulsivity and may, at times, display overactivity. These periods may be followed by feelings of guilt and obsessive self-condemnation. This patient may be somewhat self-centered and immature. (/4)

(64-1) Manic-depressive symptoms, though rare, may be present in current behavior or history. Chemotherapy may be beneficial.

Paragraph 65 (8-9/9-8)

Mean Female (−) (n=7) and Male (--) (n=38) Profiles

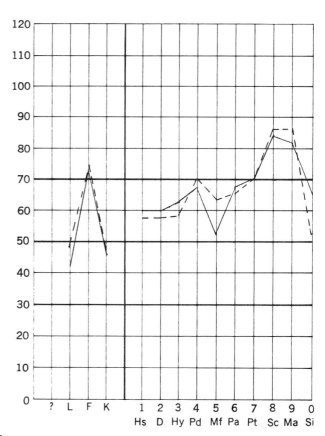

133

Scale 8: exceeds 69 T AND
　　　　 is higher than Scales 1-4, 6, 7.
Scale 9: exceeds 69 T AND
　　　　 is higher than Scales 1-4, 6, 7, use para-
　　　　 graphs 65 and 65-1.

(65) Individuals who obtain similar profiles are often described as hyperactive, restless and indecisive. They spend a great deal of time in fantasy and daydreaming, and usually display marginal, fluctuating reality testing at best. This patient may keep people at a distance and show poor social judgment. Projection, regression and inappropriate affect are often present. The majority of patients with this type of profile show evidence of paranoid mentation and a thought disorder. Onset is typically acute and accompanied by excitement, disorientation and general feelings of perplexity. Depression, anxiety and tension are usually found in combination with hostility, irritability and social withdrawal. (10/45)

(65-1) Schizophrenic reaction likely. Anti-psychotic medication may be beneficial. Rule out hallucinations and delusions.

SUBROUTINE SIGNIFICANT ELEVATIONS

This subroutine is used in all Type I & II Narratives. It is responsive to Subroutine Code as it excludes HP scales when they have already been used in this previous subroutine. This subroutine then considers the scales which remain (1-4, 6-9) in descending order and uses up to three additional one-scale paragraphs if all paragraph rules are met.

A conservative interpretive approach was attempted here by limitation of paragraph selection to a maximum of three as well as by specific rules which indicate elevation ranges for paragraph selection. This approach has resulted in moderate success, though the result, in terms of inaccuracy rates, is far less than optimum for Scales 1, 4 and 8. It is suggested that the clinician impose his own judgment on paragraph selection here whenever possible.

Sometimes selection of the paragraph from a lower elevation range will be appropriate, at other times a given scale interpretation would best be eliminated entirely.

The results for Scale 8 are likely to reflect the variable accuracy of this scale. The results for Scales 1 and 4 are less easily explained. Scale 4 statements appear after any Code paragraph and the effects of suppressor scales, such as Scale 3, are not taken into account. It is quite likely that Scale 4 paragraphs would be seen as more accurate when associated with certain codes than with others. The 17-19% inaccuracy rate for paragraphs 24A, 66 and 26A is more difficult to explain. Perhaps somatic complaints are less readily offered by patients during an interview, while this content cannot be avoided on the MMPI. Whatever the reason for the variable results of this subroutine, it is clear that more effort will be needed to improve this segment of the program.

SUBROUTINE SIGNIFICANT ELEVATIONS (Use in descending order up to 3 statements.)

SCALE 1

Paragraph 24A

RULES

Scale 1: 65-74 T AND
not an HP scale, use paragraph 24A.

(24A) This patient is expressing a greater than normal concern about body functioning. Though the exaggeration of symptoms based on actual ailments may be present, the control of unacceptable impulses through somatization defenses is suggested. Diffuse, non-specific physical complaints are likely. (17/126)

Paragraph 66

RULES

Scale 1: 74-84 T AND
not an HP scale, use paragraph 66.

(66) This patient is expressing a considerable number of physical complaints and displays, to an unusual degree, concern with body functions. Similar individuals are seen as very frustrating to their doctors as they often plead for treatment but reject any assistance and maintain a hopeless outlook. The ineffective use of somatization defenses is suggested. A sour, complaining attitude and the indirect expression of hostility often accompany physical symptoms which do not appear to have an organic basis. If actual physical findings are present, they do not account for the severity and intensity of the patient's complaints. (15/90)

Paragraph 26A

RULES

Scale 1: exceeds 84 T AND
not an HP scale, use paragraphs 26A and 26A-1.

(26A) This patient is expressing a great number of physical complaints and bodily preoccupations. Symptoms are likely fixed, organized and chronic. Somatization in similar individuals often leads to functional pain, fatigue and weakness. A review of symptoms often results in an "organ recital" in which physical complaints relate to body parts, head to toe. (7/37)

(26A-1) Rule out bizarre physical complaints and somatic delusions.

SCALE 2

Paragraph 67

RULES

Scale 2: 60-69 T AND
paragraph 38A not used, use paragraph 67.

(67) Such individuals are often mildly depressed, pessimistic and worried. They often feel discouraged and may have difficulty organizing or implementing new activities. (13/204)

Paragraph 68

RULES

Scale 2: 70-84 T AND
paragraph 38A not used AND
not an HP scale, use paragraphs 68 and 68-1.

(68) This patient is currently depressed, worried and pessimistic. Feelings of self-depreciation and inadequacy are characteristic. Suicidal ideation and tendencies should be ruled out, especially when behavioral depression is limited or absent. (14/174)

(68-1) Chemotherapy should be considered for depression.

Paragraph 69

RULES

Scale 2: exceeds 84 T AND
paragraph 38A not used AND
not an HP scale, use paragraphs 69 and 69-1.

(69) This patient is severely depressed, worrying, indecisive and pessimistic. Feelings of self-depreciation and inadequacy are characteristic. Withdrawal, feelings of lack of worth which may have a delusional quality, apathy, lethargy and motor retardation may be present. (9/54)

(69-1) Chemotherapy should be considered for depression.

SCALE 3

Paragraph 70

RULE

Scale 3: 65-69 T, use paragraph 70.

(70) This patient utilizes repression and denial to deal with psychological conflicts. Functional physical complaints may result from periods of prolonged emotional stress. Insight is probably limited and acceptance of psychological explanations for difficulties is unlikely.

[NOTE: The decision rule that generated paragraph 70 in the first evaluation study was Scale 3: 60-69 T. (31/325)]

Paragraph 71

RULES

**Scale 3: 70-84 T AND
not an HP scale, use paragraph 71.**

(71) This patient's use of repression and denial is either ineffective, or at best, wards off psychological discomfort at the cost of considerable psychic energy and resultant rigidity. Functional physical complaints are likely. Such individuals are often described as insightless, immature, dependent, egocentric, suggestible and demanding. (9/161)

Paragraph 72

RULES

**Scale 3: exceeds 84 T AND
not an HP scale, use paragraph 72.**

(72) A long history of insecurity, immaturity and a well established proclivity to physical complaint are characteristic. An amazing capacity for repression and denial is often seen combined with fixed notions as to organic basis for physical complaints. Insight is virtually impossible. Watch for subtle manipulation. (3/43)

SCALE 4

Paragraph 73

RULE

Scale 4: 65-74 T, use paragraph 73.

(73) Such individuals are often mildly independent, nonconforming and may have difficulty expressing hostility in a modulated fashion. They are often energetic and active, but may have poor behavioral controls and a history of minor run-ins with societal limits.

[NOTE: The decision rule that generated paragraph 73 in the first evaluation study was Scale 4: 60-69 T. (51/298)]

Paragraph 74

RULES

**Scale 4: 75-84 T, AND
not an HP scale, use paragraph 74.**

(74) Similar patients are usually seen as somewhat rebellious, resentful and nonconforming. Conflicts with society and authority figures are likely evident in history and current behavior. The presence of acting-out tendencies suggest a significant probability of highly visible behavioral correlates for current psychological conflicts. These individuals are sometimes described as impulsive and lacking in frustration tolerance. They are often dissatisfied with social relations and shy away from close personal ties.

[NOTE: The decision rule that generated paragraph 74 in the first evaluation study was Scale 4: 70-79 T and not an HP scale. (23/151)]

Paragraph 75

RULES

**Scale 4: exceeds 84 T AND
not an HP scale, use paragraph 75.**

(75) Similar patients are often described as highly rebellious and nonconforming individuals. Poor social judgment and inability to profit from experience are frequent characteristics. Psychological conflict is clearly manifest in highly visible behavioral correlates. Similar individuals often display conflict with authority figures, antisocial acts and manipulative interpersonal stratagems. They may be able to form only superficial and shallow relationships.

[NOTE: The decision rule that generated paragraph 75 in the first evaluation study was Scale 4: exceeds 79 T and not an HP scale. (14/100)]

SCALE 6

Paragraph 76

RULE

Scale 6: 60-69 T, use paragraph 76.

(76) Similar individuals are often described as somewhat oversensitive and rigid. They often feel pressed by social and vocational aspects of their life space. Suspiciousness, distrust, brooding and resentment may be characteristic. Indirect expression of hostility is likely. (25/241)

Paragraph 77

RULES

**Scale 6: 70-79 T AND
not an HP scale, use paragraph 77.**

(77) This patient may utilize projection of blame and hostility and is likely seen as rigid, stubborn, touchy, difficult and oversensitive. Individuals who obtain similar results tend to chronically misinterpret the words and actions of others. This tendency often leads to interpersonal difficulties. (5/88)

Paragraph 78

RULES

**Scale 6: exceeds 79 T AND
not an HP scale, use paragraph 78.**

(78) Similar individuals are often seen as very resentful and suspicious of others. It is likely that this patient feels frequently mistreated. A careful appraisal should differentiate between reality situations and fixed beliefs which may have delusional qualities. Projection is a prominent defense mechanism. Feelings of persecution and ideas of reference may be present. The open expression of hostility and anger is likely. (10/67)

SCALE 7

Paragraph 79

RULES

**Scale 7: 60-74 T AND
   not an HP scale, use paragraph 79.**

(79) Such individuals are often seen as orderly, self-critical and rigid. They tend to worry over minor problems and often evidence anxiety, tension and indecision. Similar psychiatric patients evidence some inefficiency in living. Rationalization and intellectualization are common defense mechanisms. (34/369)

Paragraph 80

RULES

**Scale 7: 75-84 T AND
   not an HP scale, use paragraph 80.**

(80) Moderate to severe levels of anxiety and tension make simple routine life tasks difficult for this patient. Such individuals are often described as chronically worrisome, apprehensive, rigid and meticulous. Phobias, compulsions and obsessive rumination are often characteristic. (13/123)

Paragraph 81

RULES

**Scale 7: exceeds 84 T AND
   not an HP scale, use paragraph 81.**

(81) Severe levels of anxiety and tension may make simple routine life tasks impossible. Agitated rumination, fearfulness, obsessions, compulsions and phobias are likely. Similar patients use intellectualization, isolation and rationalization but obtain no relief from chronic tension and guilt feelings. Constant rehashing of troubles and their possible solutions leads only to the continuation of present levels of misery. (5/78)

SCALE 8

Paragraph 82

RULES

**Scale 8: 65-74 T AND
   not an HP scale, use paragraph 82.**

(82) Similar individuals tend to stress abstract interests to the neglect of involvement with people and practical matters. There may be some qualities in this patient's thinking which represent an original or unconventional orientation or schizoid tendencies. Further evaluation will be necessary to make this differentiation. (30/190)

Paragraph 83

RULES

**Scale 8: exceeds 74 T AND
   not an HP scale, use paragraph 83.**

(83) Some original, unusual, or eccentric qualities may be present in this patient's thinking. These patients are often seen as relating poorly and tend to escape from reality pressures and their own unacceptable impulses through withdrawal and need-fulfillment fantasies. A thorough evaluation to rule out a thought disorder is suggested.

[NOTE: The decision rule that generated paragraph 83 in the first evaluation study was Scale 8: 75-84 T and not an HP scale. (11/101)]

Paragraph 84—Deleted

RULES

**Scale 8: exceeds 84 T AND
   not an HP scale, use paragraph 84.**

[(84) Such individuals are often at a loss to know what is expected of them in the simplest of interpersonal situations. They are socially introverted, relate poorly and tend to escape from reality pressures and their own unacceptable impulses into need-fulfillment fantasies. Similar patients evidence schizoid mentation and social incapacity. The presence of a thought disorder, confusion, strange thoughts, beliefs and actions is suggested. A thorough evaluation to rule out a thought disorder is indicated. (11/39)]

[NOTE: The high % inaccuracy of paragraph 84 suggested that the rule for paragraph 83 be changed to "Scale 8 exceeds 74 T . . . " and paragraph 84 deleted.]

SCALE 9

Paragraph 33A

RULES

**Scale 9: 65-74 T AND
   not an HP scale, use paragraph 33A.**

(33A) An individual who is full of plans and tends to be somewhat restless and impulsive is suggested. In psychiatric populations these individuals often display low frustration tolerance and perhaps ineffective hyperactivity of thought and action. (25/189)

Paragraph 34A

Scale 9: exceeds 74 T AND
not an HP scale, use paragraph 34A.

(34A) Similar individuals are often seen as talkative, distractible and restless. A low frustration tolerance and an insufficient capacity for delay is often accompanied by irritability and maladaptive hyperactivity of thought and action. (3/80)

SUBROUTINE CONFIGURATION

This subroutine represents several small operations which have been grouped together here because they do not fit elsewhere. Each rule should be considered separately. All appropriate paragraphs are printed. This subroutine includes:

1. Configural statements

   Paragraph

   85   Conversion "V" interpretation, within normal limits or secondary when paragraph 38 not used.

   86   Low energy level (moderate Scale 2 elevation, Scale 9 less than 45 T)

   87   Scale 4 minus Scale 5 sexual acting out index for females

   88   Passive-aggressive "V" (4-6/6-4) within normal limits or secondary when paragraph 56A not used (females only).

2. Sex role interest pattern (Scale 5)

   Paragraph

   89   Female patient, Scale 5 less than 41 T
   90   Female patient, Scale 5 more than 59 T
   91   Male patient, Scale 5 less than 41 T
   92   Male patient, Scale 5 60-69 T
   93   Male patient, Scale 5 more than 6 9T

3. Social orientation (Scale 0)

   Paragraph

   94   Scale 0 less than 45 T (Type III Narrative only.)
   95   Scale 0 60-69 T
   96   Scale 0 exceeds 69 T

4. Miscellaneous depression

   Paragraph

   97   Suggests depression in COMMENTS section when Scale 2 exceeds 69 T, but for configural reasons is not noted.

Paragraph 85

RULES

Paragraph 38 not used.

Scale 1: exceeds 59 T AND
     exceeds Scale 2 by at least 10 T.
Scale 3: exceeds 59 T AND
     exceeds Scale 2 by at least 10 T, use paragraph 85.

(85) This individual has a tendency to develop physical symptoms in response to periods of prolonged stress. These symptoms, such as fatigue and headache, when present, may represent psychological conflicts of which this patient is unaware. Conservative medical treatment of physical complaints is suggested. (8/44)

Paragraph 86

RULES

Scale 2: exceeds 59 T.
Scale 9: less than 45 T, use paragraph 86.

(86) This individual currently displays a low energy level and activity level, and may be difficult to motivate. Apathy, inertia and underlying depression may be present. (3/60)

Paragraph 87

RULES

Scale 4: **exceeds 69 T AND**
     exceeds Scale 5 by at least 30 T, use paragraph 87.

NOTE: patient female.

(87) She has a tendency to act out impulsively sexual conflicts and wishes. This characteristic is dependent for its manifestation on several variables such as occasion for action, age and social status.

[NOTE: The decision rule that generated paragraph 87 in the first evaluation study was Scale 4: exceeds 59 T and exceeds Scale 5 by at least 20 T. (37/185)]

Paragraph 88

RULES

Paragraph 56 A not used.
Scale 4: exceeds 59 T AND
     exceeds Scale 3 by at least 10 T AND
     exceeds Scale 5 by at least 10 T.
Scale 6: exceeds 59 T AND
     exceeds Scale 5 by at least 10 T AND
     exceeds Scale 7 by at least 10 T, use paragraph 88.

NOTE: patient female.

(88) She may be seen as passive-dependent and manipulative in interactions with men. Similar women express their anger in indirect ways and are suspicious of men. She may be seen as narcissistic and demanding. (/12)

Paragraph 89

RULES

Scale 5: less than 41 T AND
     patient female, use paragraph 89.

(89) She appears to place a great deal of emphasis on feminine interests. Similar women are often seen as passive, submissive and yielding. They are often highly constricted, self-pitying and fault-finding individuals. (6/68)

Paragraph 90

RULES
Scale 5: exceeds 59 T AND
    patient female, use paragraph 90.

(90) She is inclined toward masculine patterns of interests and activities. Similar women are sometimes rather assertive, confident and active in relations with others. (8/23)

[NOTE: This data suggests that this is both an infrequent and rather inaccurate descriptor for female patients. Clinicians may wish to exclude this narrative paragraph.]

Paragraph 91

RULES
Scale 5: less than 41 T AND
    patient male, use paragraph 91.

(91) He tends to emphasize masculine interests and may be seen as easygoing and adventurous. Similar individuals are often described as rather coarse, noncontemplative, practical and unoriginal in approach. (/8)

Paragraph 92

RULES
Scale 5: 60-69 T AND
    patient male, use paragraph 92.

(92) His interest patterns are somewhat different from those of the average male and may reflect a passive, noncompetitive personality. Those who have obtained more than a high school education may have esthetic interests and may be seen by others as sensitive and socially perceptive.

[NOTE: In its original format, this paragraph read: (92) He appears to be inclined toward esthetic interests. Others may see him as sensitive and socially perceptive. His interest patterns are somewhat different from those of the average male and may reflect a passive, non-competitive personality. (64/339) This high % inaccuracy rating prompted revision to the current paragraph.]

Paragraph 93

RULES
Scale 5: exceeds 69 T AND
    patient male, use paragraph 93.

(93) He is likely to be imaginative, sensitive and introspective, and have a wide range of interests. His interest pattern suggests nonidentification with the socially stereotyped masculine role and a passive and submissive orientation. In men with broad educational and cultural backgrounds, these findings are common and are usually of little concern. (31/215)

Paragraph 94

RULES
Scale 0: less than 45 T AND
    paragraph 16 used, use paragraph 94.

(94) This individual may be rather superficial and flighty in social interactions. Such persons are notably extroverted and are adept at making positive social contacts with many people, but operate on a superficial and rather insincere level. Social dependency and a high need for social approval are suggested. (6/25)

Paragraph 95

RULE
Scale 0: 60-69 T, use paragraph 95.

(95) This individual is likely to be reserved and somewhat uncomfortable in unfamiliar social situations and rather hard to "get to know." Similar persons are often described as shy, timid and retiring. (16/283)

Paragraph 96

RULE
Scale 0: exceeds 69 T, use paragraph 96.

(96) This person is likely to experience significant discomfort in social situations. Social introversion, shyness and poor social skills are often characteristic. Worry, lack of confidence and moodiness may be present. (9/191)

Paragraph 97

RULES
Scale 2: exceeds 69 T AND
    not used in a HP code AND
    not used in a significant elevations statement.
Paragraph 38A: not used, use pargraph 97 in COMMENTS section.
Paragraph 86: not used.

(97) Evidence of clinical depression is suggested. (2/39)

EXAMPLES OF NARRATIVES

Example of Type I Narrative

This profile was obtained from a sixty-year-old married female who was hospitalized for treatment of depression:

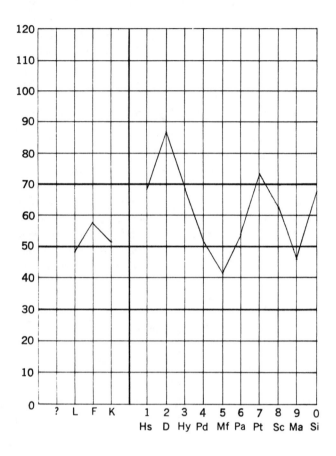

This MMPI interpretation should be viewed as a series of hypotheses which may require further investigation. This report is confidential and should not be shared with the patient.

Code: (2″7′ 1038-64/95: L:F/K/)

(14) This is a valid profile. It appears that this patient has made an attempt to follow instructions and read the items carefully. The responses appear to be realistically truthful and are likely to reflect this individual's current status.

(47) Individuals who obtain similar profiles are seen as manifesting multiple neurotic symptoms which include depression, nervousness, anxiety, weakness, fatigue, lack of initiative and a pervasive lack of self-esteem and self-confidence. Insomnia and decreased appetite may accompany psychic conflicts which are represented in hypochondriacal tendencies and somatic complaints. Sexual adjustment may be poor. These patients are likely to be pessimistic worriers, guilt-ridden and intropunitive, generally fearful and obsessively preoccupied with their personal deficiencies. When their need for achievement is frustrated, they usually respond by self-blame and neurotic guilt feelings.

(24A) This patient is expressing a greater than normal concern about body functioning. Though the exaggeration of symptoms based on actual ailments may be present, the control of unacceptable impulses through somatization defenses is suggested. Diffuse, non-specific physical complaints are likely.

(70) This patient utilizes repression and denial to deal with psychological conflicts. Functional physical complaints may result from periods of prolonged emotional stress. Insight is probably limited and acceptance of psychological explanations for difficulties is unlikely.

(95) This individual is likely to be reserved and somewhat uncomfortable in unfamiliar social situations and rather hard to "get to know." Similar persons are often described as shy, timid and retiring.

— COMMENTS —

(47-1) Consider psychotherapy and chemotherapy. Diagnostic possibilities include anxiety reaction, depressive reaction and obsessive-compulsive neurosis. Rule out suicidal ideation.

Example of Type II Narrative

This profile was obtained from an eighteen-year-old single male who was hospitalized on a general medical service:

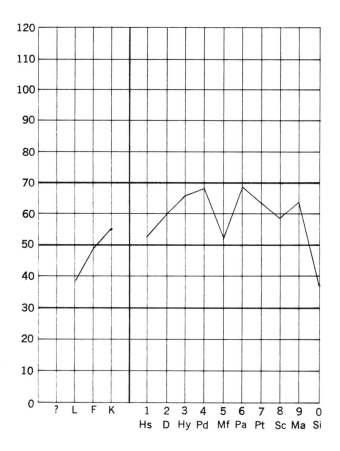

This MMPI interpretation should be viewed as a series of hypotheses which may require further investigation. This report is confidential and should not be shared with the patient.

Code: (643792—815/0# L#F:K/)

(14) This is a valid profile. It appears that this patient has made an attempt to follow instructions and read the items carefully. The responses appear to be realistically truthful and are likely to reflect this individual's current status.

(15) This profile is essentially within normal limits. There are, however, certain scale elevations which suggest personality characteristics which may be of clinical interest.

(76) Similar individuals are often described as somewhat oversensitive and rigid. They often feel pressed by social and vocational aspects of their life space. Suspiciousness, distrust, brooding and resentment may be characteristic. Indirect expression of hostility is likely.

(73) Such individuals are often mildly independent, non-conforming and may have difficulty expressing hostility in a modulated fashion. They are often energetic and active, but may have poor behavioral controls and a history of minor run-ins with societal limits.

(70) This patient utilizes repression and denial to deal with psychological conflicts. Functional physical complaints may result from periods of prolonged emotional stress. Insight is probably limited and acceptance of psychological explanations for difficulties is unlikely.

Example of Type III Narrative

This profile was obtained from a twenty-one-year-old single female who was hospitalized on a general medical service:

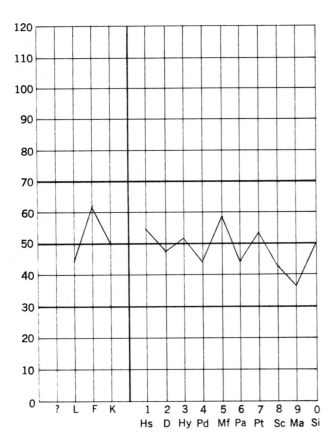

This MMPI interpretation should be viewed as a series of hypotheses which may require further investigation. This report is confidential and should not be shared with the patient.

Code: (51730/2468:9# L:F-K/)

(14) This is a valid profile. It appears that this patient has made an attempt to follow instructions and read the items carefully. The responses appear to be realistically truthful and are likely to reflect this individual's current status.

(16) This profile is within normal limits. Although this is a profile often associated with individuals whose personalities are without significant pathology, it is essential that this individual be evaluated carefully to rule out deviant behavior and experiences.

(23) Strong interest in people and practical matters is suggested. Similar individuals are often described as compliant, controlled, concrete, and unimaginative.

(21) Similar individuals may be rather distrustful of others, and tend to present only socially acceptable behavior. They may be seen as cautious, stubborn and touchy. Interpersonal antagonism may be present.

(20) This individual is likely to be seen as quite conventional and conforming. A passive, non-assertive orientation is suggested. Such individuals often lack heterosexual aggressiveness and tend to possess a narrow range of interests.

BIBLIOGRAPHY

Aaronson, B. S. Age and sex influences on MMPI profile peak distributions in an abnormal population. *Journal of Consulting Psychology*, 1958, 22, 203-206.

Berzins, J. I., Ross, W. F., & Monroe, J. J. A multivariate study of the personality characteristics of hospitalized narcotic addicts on the MMPI, *Journal of Clinical Psychology*, 1971, 27, 174-181.

Blumberg, S. MMPI F scale as an indicator of severity of psychopathology. *Journal of Clinical Psychology*, 1967, 23, 96-99.

Briggs, P. F., Taylor, M., & Tellegen, A. A study of the Marks and Seeman MMPI profile types as applied to a sample of 2,875 psychiatric patients. Report No. PR-66-5, November 15, 1966, Department of Psychiatry, University of Minnesota.

Butcher, J., Ball, B., & Ray, E. Effects of socio-economic level on MMPI differences in Negro-white college students. *Journal of Counseling Psychology*, 1964, 11, 83-87.

Calden, G., & Hokanson, J. E. The influence of age on MMPI responses. *Journal of Clinical Psychology*, 1959, 15, 194-195.

Carson, R. C. Interpretive manual to the MMPI. In J. N. Butcher (Ed.), *MMPI: Research developments and clinical applications*, New York: McGraw-Hill, 1969.

Comrey, A. L. A factor analysis of items on the MMPI psychasthenia scale. *Educational and Psychological Measurement*, 1958, 18, 293-300.

Cooke, G. The court study unit: Patient characteristics and differences between patients judged competent and incompetent. *Journal of Clinical Psychology*, 1969, 25, 140-143.

Costello, R. M., Tiffany, D. W., & Gier, R. H. Methodological issues and racial (black-white) comparisons on the MMPI. *Journal of Consulting and Clinical Psychology*, 1972, 38, 161-168.

Dahlstrom, W. G., Welsh, G. S., & Dahlstrom, L. E. *An MMPI handbook. Volume I. Clinical interpretation*. Minneapolis: University of Minnesota Press, 1972.

Davis, K. R., & Sines, J. O. An antisocial behavior pattern associated with a specific MMPI profile. *Journal of Consulting and Clinical Psychology*, 1971, 36, 229-234.

Drake, L. E. A social I.E. scale for the MMPI. *Journal of Applied Psychology*, 1946, 30, 51-54.

Drake, L. E., & Oetting, E. R. *An MMPI codebook for counselors*. Minneapolis: University of Minnesota Press, 1959.

Drake, L. E., & Thiede, W. B. Further validation of the social I.E. scale for the MMPI. *Journal of Educational Research*, 1948, 41, 551-556.

Eichman, W. J. (MMPI) Computerized scoring and interpreting services. In O. K. Buros (Ed.), *The seventh mental measurements yearbook*. Highland Park, New Jersey: The Gryphon Press, 1972 (pp. 250-262).

Fowler, R. D., & Athey, E. B. A cross-validation of Gilberstadt and Duker's 1-2-3-4 profile type. *Journal of Clinical Psychology*, 1971, 27, 483-486.

Fowler, R. D., & Coyle, F. A., Jr. A comparison of two MMPI actuarial systems used in classifying an alcoholic out-patient population. *Journal of Clinical Psychology*, 1968, 24, 434-435.

Gauron, E., Severson, R., & Engelhart, R. MMPI F scores and psychiatric diagnosis. *Journal of Consulting Psychology*, 1962, 26, 488.

Gilberstadt, H. *Comprehensive MMPI code book for males*. Washington, D.C.: U.S. Government Printing Office, 1970.

Gilberstadt, H., & Duker, J. Case history correlates of three MMPI profile types. *Journal of Consulting Psychology*. 1960, 24, 361-367.

Gilberstadt, H., & Duker, J. *A handbook for clinical and actuarial MMPI interpretation*. Philadelphia: W. B. Saunders, 1965.

Gilberstadt, H., & Jancis, M. "Organic" vs. "functional" diagnoses from 1-3 MMPI profiles. *Journal of Clinical Psychology*, 1967, 23, 480-483.

Gilbert, J. G. & Lombardi, D. N. Personality characteristics of young male narcotic addicts. *Journal of Consulting Psychology*. 1967, 31, 536-538.

Goldberg, L. R. Diagnosticians vs. diagnostic signs: The diagnosis of psychosis vs. neurosis from the MMPI. *Psychological Monographs*, 1965, 79 (Whole No. 602), 29 pp.

Gough, H. G. The F minus K dissimulation index for the MMPI. *Journal of Consulting Psychology*, 1950, 14, 408-413.

Graham, J. R. Behavioral correlates of simple MMPI code types. Presented at the Eighth Annual MMPI Symposium, New Orleans, February 1973.

Graham, J. R., Schroeder, H. E., & Lilly, R. S. Factor analysis of items on the social introversion and masculinity-femininity scales of the MMPI. *Journal of Clinical Psychology*, 1971, 27, 367-372.

Gross, L. R. MMPI L-F-K relationships with criteria of behavioral disturbance and social adjustment in a schizophrenic population. *Journal of Consulting Psychology*, 1959, 23, 319-323.

Gynther, M. D. The clinical utility of "invalid" MMPI F scores. *Journal of Consulting Psychology*, 1961, 25, 540-542.

Gynther, M. D. A new replicated actuarial program for interpreting MMPIs of state hospital patients. Presented at the Seventh Annual MMPI Symposium, Mexico City, February 1972(a).

Gynther, M. D. White norms and black MMPIs: A prescription for discrimination? *Psychological Bulletin*, 1972, 78, 386-402(b).

Gynther, M. D., Altman, H., & Sletten, I. W. Replicated correlates of MMPI two-point code types: The Missouri actuarial system. *Journal of Clinical Psychology Monographs*, 1973, 29, 263-289.

Gynther, M. D., Fowler, R. D., & Erdberg, P. False positives galore: The application of standard MMPI critial to a rural, isolated, Negro sample. *Journal of Clinical Psychology*, 1971, 27, 234-237.

Gynther M. D., & Shimkunas, A. M. More data on MMPI F>16 scores. *Journal of Clinical Psychology*, 1965, 21, 275-277.

Gynther M. D., & Shimkunas, A. M. Age and MMPI performance, *Journal of Consulting Psychology*, 1966, 30, 118-121.

Halbower, C. C. A comparison of actuarial versus clinical prediction to classes discriminated by MMPI. Ph.D. dissertation, University of Minnesota, 1955. (Also in *Dissertation Abstracts*, 1955, 15, 1115.)

Harris, R. E., & Lingoes, J. C. Subscales for the MMPI: an aid to profile interpretation. Mimeographed materials. Department of Psychiatry, University of California, 1955. (Corrected version, 1968.) Citation: Dahlstrom, Welsh & Dahlstrom, 1972.

Harrison, R. H., & Kass, E. H. Differences between Negro and white pregnant women on the MMPI. *Journal of Consulting Psychology*, 1967, 31, 454-463.

Hathaway, S. R. Scales 5 (masculinity-femininity), 6 (paranoia), and 8 (schizophrenia). In G. S. Welsh & W. G. Dahlstrom (Eds.), *Basic readings on the MMPI in psychology and medicine*. Minneapolis: University of Minnesota Press, 1956.

Hathaway, S. R., & McKinley, J. C. A multiphasic personality schedule (Minnesota). III. The measurement of symptomatic depression. *Journal of Psychology*, 1942, 14, 73-84.

Hathaway, S. R., & Meehl, P. E. *An atlas for the clinical use of the MMPI*. Minneapolis, University of Minnesota Press, 1951.

Hokanson, J. E., & Calden, G. Negro-white differences on the MMPI. *Journal of Clinical Psychology*, 1960, 16, 32-33.

Hovey, H. B., & Lewis, E. G. Semiautomatic interpretation of the MMPI. *Journal of Clinical Psychology*, 1967, 23, 123-134.

Huff, F. W. Use of actuarial description of personality in a mental hospital. *Psychological Reports*, 1965, 17, 224.

King, G. F., & Schiller, M. A. A research note on the K scale of the MMPI and "defensiveness." *Journal of Clinical Psychology*, 1959, 15, 305-306.

Lachar, D. MMPI two-point code-type correlates in a state hospital population. *Journal of Clinical Psychology*, 1968, 24, 424-427.

Lushene, R. E., & Gilberstadt, H. Validation of VA MMPI computer-generated reports. Presented at the VA Cooperative Studies Conference, St. Louis, March 1972.

Manosevitz, M. Education and MMPI Mf scores in homosexual and heterosexual males. *Journal of Consulting and Clinical Psychology*, 1971, 36, 395-399.

Marks, P. A., & Seeman, W. *The actuarial description of abnormal personality*. Baltimore: Williams and Wilkins, 1963.

McDonald, R. L., & Gynther, M. D. MMPI differences associated with sex, race, and class in two adolescent samples. *Journal of Consulting Psychology*, 1963, 27, 112-116.

McKinley J. C., & Hathaway, S. R. A multiphasic schedule (Minnesota): II. A differential study of hypochondriasis. *Journal of Psychology*, 1940, 10, 255-268.

McKinley, J. C., & Hathaway, S. R. a multiphasic personality schedule (Minnesota): IV Psychasthenia. *Journal of Applied Psychology*, 1942, 28, 153-174.

McKinley, J. C., & Hathaway, S. R. The MMPI: V. Hysteria, hypomania and psychopathic deviate. *Journal of Applied Psychology*, 1944, 28, 153-174.

McKinley, J. C. Hathaway, S. R., & Meehl, P. E. The MMPI: VI The K scale. *Journal of Consulting Psychology*, 1948, 12, 20-31.

Meehl, P. E. Profile analysis of the MMPI in differential diagnosis. *Journal of Applied Psychology*, 1946, 30, 517-524.

Meehl, P. E. Wanted — a good cookbook. *American Psychologist*, 1956, 11, 263-272.

Meikle, S., & Gerritse, R. MMPI "cookbook" pattern frequencies in a psychiatric unit. *Journal of Clinical Psychology*, 1970, 26, 82-84.

Miller, C., Knapp, S. C., & Daniels, C. W. MMPI study of Negro mental hygiene clinic patients. *Journal of Abnormal Psychology*, 1968, 73, 168-173.

Newmark, C. S., & Sines, L. K. Characteristics of hospitalized patients who produce the "floating" MMPI profiles. *Journal of Clinical Psychology*, 1972, 28, 74-76.

Owen, D. R. Classification of MMPI profiles from non-psychiatric populations using two cookbook systems. *Journal of Clinical Psychology*, 1970, 26, 84-86.

Panton, J. H. The identification of habitual criminalism with the MMPI. *Journal of Clinical Psychology*, 1962, 18, 137-139 (a).

Panton, J. H. The identification of predispositional factors in self-mutilation within a state prison population. *Journal of Clinical Psychology*, 1962, 18, 63-67 (b).

Pauker, J. D. Identification of MMPI profile types in a female, inpatient, psychiatric setting using the Marks and Seeman rules. *Journal of Consulting Psychology*, 1966, 30, 90.

Payne, F. D., & Wiggins, J. S. Effects of rule relaxation and system combination on classification rates in two MMPI "cookbook" systems. *Journal of Consulting and Clinical Psychology*, 1968, 32, 734-736.

Pepper, L. J., & Strong, P. N. Judgemental subscales for the Mf scale of the MMPI. Unpublished materials, 1958. Citation: Dahlstrom, Welsh & Dahlstrom, 1972.

Persons, R. W., & Marks, P. A. The violent 4-3 MMPI personality type. *Journal of Consulting and Clinical Psychology*, 1971, 36, 189-196.

Porier, G. W., & Smith, R. C. MMPI "cookbooks": Are rule relaxation and system combination procedures an answer to low classification rates? *Journal of Clinical Psychology*, 1971, 27, 96-101.

Postema, L. J., & Schell, R. E. Aging and psychopathology: Some MMPI evidence for seemingly greater neurotic behavior among older people. *Journal of Clinical Psychology*, 1967, 23, 140-143.

Randolph, M. H., Richardson, H., & Johnson, R. C. A comparison of social and solitary male delinquents. *Journal of Consulting Psychology*, 1961, 25, 293-295.

Ries, H. A. The MMPI K scale as a predictor of prognosis. *Journal of Clinical Psychology*, 1966, 22, 212-213.

Schwartz, M. S., & Krupp, N. E. The MMPI "conversion V" among 50,000 medical patients: A study of incidence, criteria, and profile elevation. *Journal of Clinical Psychology*, 1971, 27, 89-95.

Schwartz, M. S., Osborne, D., & Krupp, N. E. Moderating effects of age and sex on the association of medical diagnoses and 1-3/3-1 MMPI profiles. *Journal of Clinical Psychology*, 1972, 28, 502-505.

Shaw, D. J., & Mathews, C. G. Differential MMPI performance of brain-damaged vs. pseudo-neurologic groups. *Journal of Clinical Psychology*, 1965, 21, 405-408.

Shultz, T. D., Gibeau, P. J., & Barry, S. M. Utility of MMPI "cookbooks." *Journal of Clinical Psychology*, 1968, 24, 430-433.

Sines, I. O. Actuarial methods in personality assessment. In B. A. Maher (Ed.), *Progress in experimental personality research*. Vol. 3. New York: Academic Press, 1966.

Singer, M. I. Comparison of indicators of homosexuality on the MMPI. *Journal of Counsulting and Clinical Psychology*, 1970, 34, 15-18.

Spiegel, D., Hadley, P. A., & Hadley, R. G. Personality test patterns of rehabilitation center alcoholics, psychiatric inpatients and normals. *Journal of Clinical Psychology*, 1970, 26, 366-371.

Sweetland, A., & Quay, H. A note on the K scale of the Minnesota Multiphasic Personality Inventory. *Journal of Consulting Psychology*, 1953, 17, 314-316.

Swenson, W. M. Structured personality testing in the aged: An MMPI study of the gerontic population. *Journal of Clinical Psychology*, 1961, 17, 302-304..

Vestre, N. D., & Klett, W. G. Classification of MMPI profiles using the Gilberstadt-Duker rules. *Journal of Clinical Psychology*, 1969, 25, 284-286.

146

Webb, J. T. The relation of MMPI two-point codes to age, sex, and educational level in a representative nationwide sample of psychiatric outpatients. Presented at the Southeastern Psychological Association, Louisville, April 1970.

Webb, J. T. Regional and sex differences in MMPI scale high-point frequencies of psychiatric patients. *Journal of Clinical Psychology*, 1971, 27, 483-486.

Welsh, G. S. An extension of Hathaway's MMPI profile coding system. *Journal of Consulting Psychology*, 1948, 12, 343-344.

Wiener, D. N. Subtle and obvious keys for the MMPI. *Journal of Consulting Psychology*, 1948, 12, 164-170.

Appendix A. Adult Norms

CONVERTING RAW SCORES TO T SCORES WHEN THE K FACTOR HAS BEEN ADDED TO THE RAW SCORES OF FIVE OF THE CLINICAL VARIABLES

Raw Scores — Five of the Variables With K Added

T or Tc	?	L	F	K	Hs+.5K M	Hs+.5K F	D M	D F	Hy M	Hy F	Pd+.4K	Mf M	Mf F	Pa	Pt+1K M	Pt+1K F	Sc+1K M	Sc+1K F	Ma+.2K	Si	T or Tc
120							46				48			32	57						120
119							45		54						56		58				119
118					38			54						31				67			118
117							44		53		47						57	66			117
116					37										55						116
115								53	52								56	65			115
114											46			30	54			64			114
113					36		43	52	51								55				113
112										54					53			63			112
111					35	43	42	51	50		45			29			54	62			111
110			31							53		51			52						110
109			30			42		50	49	52	44						53	61			109
108					34		41		48	51		50		28					40		108
107						41		49	47		43				51	60	52	60			107
106			29		33		40					49				59		59	39		106
105			28			40		48	46	50	42			27	50		51	58			105
104						39	39					48			49	58	50	57	38		104
103			27		32		38	47		49	41	47				57					103
102						38			45					26	48	56	49	56	37		102
101						38		46		48											101
100			26		31		37	45	44	47	40	46		25	47	55	48	55			100
99						37		44		46								54			99
98			25		30				43		39	45		24	46	54	47	53	36		98
97						36		43	42	45						53	46			70	97
96			24				36					44			45			52		69	96
95					29	35	35		41		38		15	23	45	52	45	51		68	95
94			23		28	34	34	42		44	37	43			44	51	44	50	34	67	94
93						33		41	40	43			16					49		66	93
92			22						39	42		42			43	50			33	65	92
91														22						64	91
90			21		27			40	38	41	36	41	17		42	49	43	48		63	90
89			20			32	33	39			35	40	18	21		48	42		32	62	89
88					26				37	40	34	39	19		41	47	41	47		61	88
87						31	32	38	36	39								46	31	60	87
86		15	19																	59	86
85					25	30			35	38		38	20	20	40	46	40	45		58	85
84		14	18	30			31	37	34	37	33				39	45	39	44	30	57	84
83			17	29			30	36				37	21	19				43		56	83
82					24	29					32				38	44			29	55	82
81																	38	42		54	81
80	130+	13	16	28	23	28	29	35	33	36	31	36	22		37	43				53	80
79			15			27		34	32	35		35	23	18		42	37	41	28	52	79
78				27	22		28	34						17	36			40		51	78
77						26		33	31	34	30	34	24			41	36			50	77
76	120	12	14		21	25	27	32	30	33	29				35	40	35	39	27	49	76
75			13	26								33	25	16	34	39	34	38	26	48	75
74		11		25	20	24	26	31	29	32	28	32	26		33	38	33	37		47	74
73	110			24					28	31								36		46	73
72								30												45	72
71										30										44	71

| T or Tc | ? | L | F | K | Hs+.5K M | Hs+.5K F | D M | D F | Hy M | Hy F | Pd+.4K | Mf M | Mf F | Pa | Pt+1K M | Pt+1K F | Sc+1K M | Sc+1K F | Ma+.2K | Si | T or Tc |

Converting Raw Scores to T Scores When the K Factor Has Been Added to the Raw Scores of Five of the Clinical Variables

Raw Scores — Five of the Variables With K Added

T or Tc	?	L	F	K	Hs+.5K M	Hs+.5K F	D M	D F	Hy M	Hy F	Pd+.4K	Mf M	Mf F	Pa	Pt+1K M	Pt+1K F	Sc+1K M	Sc+1K F	Ma+.2K	Si	T or Tc
	M&F	M&F	M&F	M&F	M	F	M	F	M	F	M&F	M	F	M&F	M	F	M	F	M&F	M&F	
70		10	12	23	19	23	25			30				15					25	43	70
69	100							29	27		27	30	27		32	37	32	35		42	69
68			11	22		22	24	28		29			28			36		36	24	41	68
67					18	21			26			29		14			31	34		40	67
66	90	9	10	21						28	26		29		31	35		33		39	66
65					17		23	27	25			28		13		34	30		23	38	65
64	80		9	20		20	22	26	24	27	25				30			32		37	64
63		8		19	16	19			23	26		27	30			33	29	31	22	36	63
62			8								24			12	29					35	62
61	70			18				25		25		26	31			32	28	30		34	61
60		7	7			18	21		22		23				28	31		29	21	33	60
59				17	15			24		24		25	32	11			27				59
58	60		6			17	20		21	23					27	30		28	20	32	58
57				16	14			23			22	24	33				26	27			57
56	50	6				16	19		20	22				10	26	29				31	56
55			5	15				22	19		21	23	34			28	25	26	19	30	55
54				14	13	15				21					25			25		29	54
53	40	5	4		12	14	18	21	18	20	20	22	35	9		27	24		18	28	53
52															24			24		27	52
51				13			17	20	17			21	36			26	23	23		26	51
50	30	4	3			13		19		19	19	20	37	8	23	25	22		17	25	50
49				12	11		16		16	18								22		24	49
48			2	11		12	16				18				22	24	21		16	23	48
47	20				10			18	15	17		19	38	7				21		22	47
46		3	1	10		11	15	17			17				21	23	20	20		21	46
45					9	10	14	16	14	16		18	39	6		22		22	15	20	45
44	10	2	0	9				15	13						20		19	19		19	44
43						9	13			15	16	17	40			21		18	14	18	43
42				8	8				12	14					19		18			17	42
41	0										15	16	41	5		20		17		16	41
40		1		7				14	11	13					18	19	17	16	13	15	40
39				6	7	8	12	13			14	15	42							14	39
38									10	12				4	17	18	16	15	12	13	38
37						7						14	43					14		12	37
36		0		5	6		11	12	9	11	13				16	17	15		11	11	36
35				4	5	6			8	10	12	13		3		16		13	11	10	35
34							10	11		9		12	44		15		14	12	10	9	34
33				3		5	9	10		9	11			2		15			10	8	33
32				2	4	4						11	45		14	14	13	11		7	32
31										8								10			31
30					3	3		9			10	10	46	1	13	13	12		9	6	30
29				1			8	8		7		9	47					9		5	29
28						2					9				12	12	11		8	4	28
27				0	2					6		8	48	0		11		8		3	27
26										5					11		10	7	7	2	26
25						1										10	9			1	25
24										4	8		49					6	6		24
23					1	0									10	9	8	5			23
22											7		50		9	8					22
21					0											7			5		21
20											6		51								20
T or Tc	?	L	F	K	Hs+.5K M	Hs+.5K F	D M	D F	Hy M	Hy F	Pd+.4K	Mf M	Mf F	Pa	Pt+1K M	Pt+1K F	Sc+1K M	Sc+1K F	Ma+.2K	Si	T or Tc
	M&F	M&F	M&F	M&F	M	F	M	F	M	F	M&F	M	F	M&F	M	F	M	F	M&F	M&F	

Converting Raw Scores to T Scores When the K Factor Has Not Been Added to the Raw Scores of Five Clinical Variables

Raw Scores

T	Hs M	Hs F	Pd M	Pd F	Pt M	Pt F	Sc M	Sc F	Ma M & F	T
120				43						120
119			41							119
118										118
117				42			59			117
116			40							116
115	33			41			58			115
114			39				57			114
113	32			40			56			113
112										112
111			38				55	59		111
110	31			39			54			110
109							53	58		109
108	30		37	38				57		108
107							52	56		107
106	29		36	37			51	55	39	106
105							50			105
104	28							54	38	104
103			35	36	48		49	53		103
102					47		48	52		102
101	27		34	35			47	51	37	101
100					46					100
99	26	33		34	45		46	50	36	99
98			33		44		45	49		98
97	25	32			43		44	48	35	97
96		31	32	33				47		96
95					42	48	43		34	95
94	24	30		32		47	42	46		94
93			31		41	46		45	33	93
92	23	29			40		41	44		92
91			30	31	39	45	40	43		91
90	22	28				44	39		32	90
89				30	38	43		42		89
88	21	27	29		37	42	38	41	31	88
87				29			37	40		87
86		26	28		36	41	36	39	30	86
85	20				35	40				85
84		25		28	34	39	35	38	29	84
83	19		27		33	38	34	37		83
82		24		27	32	37	33	36		82
81	18		26						28	81
80		23		26		36	32	35	27	80
79		22			31		31	34		79
78	17		25	25	30	35	30	33		78
77		21			29	34		32	26	77
76	16					33	29			76
75		20	24	24	28	32	28	31	25	75
74	15		23	23	27		27	30		74
73		19			26	31		29	24	73
72	14					30	26	28		72
71		18			25	29	25			71

Raw Scores

T	Hs M	Hs F	Pd M	Pd F	Pt M	Pt F	Sc M	Sc F	Ma M & F	T
70			22	22	24		24	27	23	70
69	13	17				28		26		69
68			21	21	23	27	23	25	22	68
67	12	16			22	26	22	24		67
66					21				21	66
65	11	15	20	20		25	21	23		65
64					20	24	20	22		64
63		14	19	19	19	23	19	21	20	63
62	10	13				22		20		62
61				18	18		18		19	61
60	9	12	18		17	21	17	19		60
59					16	20	16	18	18	59
58	8	11	17	17		19		17		58
57					15	18	15	16	17	57
56	7	10		16			14			56
55			16		14	17	13	15		55
54		9			13	16	12	14	16	54
53	6		15	15	12		11	13		53
52		8			11	15		12	15	52
51	5					14	10	11		51
50		7	14		10	13		10	14	50
49	4			13	9	12	9	10	13	49
48		6			8		8	9		48
47	3		13	12		11	7	8		47
46					7	10				46
45		4	12		6	9	6	7	12	45
44	2			11			5	6		44
43		3			5	8	4	5	11	43
42	1		11	10	4	7	3	4	10	42
41		2			3	6				41
40	0		10	9	2	5	2	3		40
39		1						2	9	39
38					1	4	1	1		38
37		0	9	8	0	3	0	0	8	37
36					0	2				36
35			8	7						35
34						1			7	34
33						0				33
32			7	6					6	32
31										31
30			6	5					5	30
29										29
28				4					4	28
27			5							27
26										26
25			4	3					3	25
24										24
23				2					2	23
22			3							22
21				1						21
20			2							20

Appendix B. Adolescent Norms

T-Score Conversions for Basic Scales without K Corrections for Minnesota Adolescents Age 14 and Below

Raw Score	Males														Females														Raw Score
	?	L	F	K	1 (Hs)	2 (D)	3 (Hy)	4 (Pd)	5 (Mf)	6 (Pa)	7 (Pt)	8 (Sc)	9 (Ma)	0 (Si)	?	L	F	K	1 (Hs)	2 (D)	3 (Hy)	4 (Pd)	5 (Mf)	6 (Pa)	7 (Pt)	8 (Sc)	9 (Ma)	0 (Si)	
78												116																		78
77												115																		77
76												114																		76
75												113																		75
74												112																		74
73												111																		73
72												110															120			72
71												108															119			71
70	62											107		106	62											118		102	70
69												106		104													117		101	69
68												105		103													115		100	68
67												104		102													114		99	67
66												103		100													113		97	66
65												102		99													112		96	65
64												101		98													110		95	64
63												100		96													109		94	63
62												99		95													108		92	62
61												98		93													107		91	61
60	58											97		92	58											106		90	60
59												96		91													104		88	59
58												95		89													103		87	58
57												93		88													102		86	57
56												92		87													101		85	56
55												91		85													99		83	55
54												90		84													98		82	54
53												89		83													97		81	53
52												88		81							120						96		80	52
51												87		80							118	120					95		78	51
50	56								119			86		79	56						116	118					93		77	50
49						119	120		117			85		77							114	115	119	20			92		76	49
48						117	118	120	114		96	84		76							112	113	117	22		97	91		75	48
47						115	115	118	112		95	83		75							110	111	115	24		96	90		73	47
46						112	113	116	109		93	82	105	73							108	109	113	26		94	88	113	72	46
45						110	111	113	107		92	81	103	72							106	106	111	29		93	87	110	71	45
44						108	109	111	105		91	80	101	70							104	104	109	31		92	86	108	69	44
43						106	107	109	102		89	78	100	69							102	102	107	33		90	85	106	68	43
42			119			103	104	106	100		88	77	98	68							99	100	104	35		89	84	104	67	42
41			117			101	102	104	98		86	76	96	66							97	98	102	37		87	82	102	66	41
40	53		115			99	100	102	95		85	75	94	65	53						95	95	100	40	115	86	81	100	64	40
39			113			97	98	100	93		84	74	92	64							93	93	98	42	113	84	80	98	63	39
38			111			95	95	97	91		82	73	90	62							91	91	94	44	110	83	79	96	62	38
37			109			92	93	95	88		81	72	88	61							89	89	94	46	108	82	77	94	61	37
36			107			90	91	93	86	120	80	71	86	60							87	86	92	48	106	80	76	91	59	36
35			105			88	89	90	83	117	78	70	84	58							85	84	89	51	104	79	75	89	58	35
34			103			86	87	88	81	114	77	69	82	57							83	82	87	53	102	77	74	87	57	34
33			101			83	84	86	79	112	75	68	80	56			119		118	80	80	85	55	99	76	73	85	56	33
32			99			81	82	83	76	109	74	67	78	54			116		116	78	78	83	57	97	74	71	83	54	32
31			97			79	80	81	74	106	73	66	76	53			114		113	76	75	81	59	95	73	70	81	53	31
30	50		95	85	123	77	78	79	72	104	71	65	74	51	50		111	87	111	74	73	79	62	93	72	69	79	52	30
29			93	83	120	75	75	76	69	101	70	63	72	50			109	85	109	72	71	76	64	91	70	68	77	51	29
28			91	81	117	72	73	74	67	98	69	62	70	49			106	82	106	70	69	74	66	89	69	67	75	49	28
27			89	79	114	70	71	72	65	95	67	61	68	47			104	80	104	68	66	72	68	86	67	65	72	48	27
26			87	76	111	68	69	69	62	93	66	60	66	46			101	78	101	66	64	70	70	84	66	64	70	47	26

L F K 1 2 3 4 5 6 7 8 9 0

T-Score Conversions for Basic Scales without K Corrections for Minnesota Adolescents Age 14 and Below—continued

Left block = **Males**, right block = **Females**.

Raw Score	?	L	F	K	1 (Hs)	2 (D)	3 (Hy)	4 (Pd)	5 (Mf)	6 (Pa)	7 (Pt)	8 (Sc)	9 (Ma)	0 (Si)	?	L	F	K	1 (Hs)	2 (D)	3 (Hy)	4 (Pd)	5 (Mf)	6 (Pa)	7 (Pt)	8 (Sc)	9 (Ma)	0 (Si)	Raw Score
25		85	74	108	66	67	67		60	90	65	59	64	45		99	76	99	64	62	68		73	82	64	63	68	45	25
24		83	72	105	63	64	65		57	87	63	58	62	43		96	73	96	62	60	66		75	80	63	62	66	44	24
23		81	70	102	61	62	62		55	84	62	57	60	42		94	71	94	59	58	64		77	78	62	60	64	43	23
22		79	68	99	59	60	60		53	82	60	56	58	41		91	69	91	57	55	61		79	75	60	59	62	42	22
21		77	66	96	57	58	58		50	79	59	55	56	40		89	67	89	55	53	59		81	73	59	58	60	40	21
20	47	75	64	93	55	56	56		48	76	58	54	54	38	47	86	65	86	53	51	57		84	71	57	57	58	39	20
19		73	62	90	52	53	53		46	74	56	53	52	37		84	62	84	51	49	55		86	69	56	56	56	38	19
18		71	60	87	50	51	51		43	71	55	52	50	35		81	60	81	49	46	53		88	67	54	54	54	37	18
17		70	58	84	48	49	49		41	68	54	51	49	34		79	58	79	47	44	51		90	65	53	53	51	35	17
16		68	56	82	46	47	46		38	65	52	50	47	33		76	56	76	45	42	49		92	62	52	52	49	34	16
15	105	66	54	79	43	44	44		36	63	51	48	45	31	101	74	53	74	43	40	46		95	60	50	51	47	33	15
14	100	64	52	76	41	42	42		34	60	49	47	43	30	97	71	51	71	41	38	44		97	58	49	49	45	32	14
13	95	62	50	73	39	40	39		31	57	48	46	41	28	92	69	49	69	38	35	42		99	56	47	48	43	30	13
12	90	60	48	70	37	38	37		29	55	47	45	39	27	87	66	47	66	36	33	40		100	54	46	47	41	29	12
11	85	58	45	67	35	36	35		27	52	45	44	37	26	83	64	44	64	34	31	38		102	51	44	46	39	28	11
10	80	56	43	64	32	33	32		24	49	44	43	35	24	78	61	42	61	32	29	36		104	49	43	45	37	26	10
9	76	54	41	61	30	31	30		22	46	43	42	33	23	73	59	40	59	30	27	34		107	47	42	43	35	25	9
8	71	52	39	58	28	29	28		20	44	41	41	31	22	69	56	38	56	28	24	31		109	45	40	42	32	24	8
7	66	50	37	55	26	27	25			41	40	40	29	20	64	54	35	54	26	22	29		111	43	39	41	30	23	7
6	61	48	35	52	23	25	23			38	38	39	27		59	51	33	51	24	20	27		113	40	37	40	28	21	6
5	56	46	33	49	21	22	21			35	37	38	25		55	49	31	49	22		25		115	38	36	38	26	20	5
4	51	44	31	46		20				33	36	37	23		50	46	29	46	20		23		118	36	34	37	24		4
3	46	42	29	43						30	34	36	21		46	44	27	44			21		120	34	33	36	22		3
2	42	40	27	40						27	33	35			41	41	24	41						32	32	35	20		2
1	37	38	25	37						25	32	33			36	39	22	39						30	30	34			1
0	32	36	23	34						23	30	32			31	36		36						28	29	32			0

T-Score Conversions for Basic Scales without K Corrections for Minnesota Adolescents Age 15

Left block = **Males**, right block = **Females**.

Raw Score	?	L	F	K	1 (Hs)	2 (D)	3 (Hy)	4 (Pd)	5 (Mf)	6 (Pa)	7 (Pt)	8 (Sc)	9 (Ma)	0 (Si)	?	L	F	K	1 (Hs)	2 (D)	3 (Hy)	4 (Pd)	5 (Mf)	6 (Pa)	7 (Pt)	8 (Sc)	9 (Ma)	0 (Si)	Raw Score
78												111														117			78
77												110														116			77
76												109														115			76
75												108														114			75
74												107														113			74
73												106														112			73
72												105														110			72
71												104														109			71
70	62											103		105	62											108		103	70
69												102		103												107		102	69
68												101		102												106		101	68
67												100		101												105		99	67
66												99		99												104		98	66
65												98		98												103		97	65
64												97		97												102		95	64
63												96		95												101		94	63
62												95		94												100		93	62
61												94		93												99		92	61
60	58											93		91	58											98		90	60
59												92		90												97		89	59
58												91		89												95		88	58
57												90		87												94		86	57
56												89		86												93		85	56

T-Score Conversions for Basic Scales without K Corrections for Minnesota Adolescents Age 15—continued

Raw Score	Males ?	L	F	K	1 (Hs)	2 (D)	3 (Hy)	4 (Pd)	5 (Mf)	6 (Pa)	7 (Pt)	8 (Sc)	9 (Ma)	0 (Si)	Females ?	L	F	K	1 (Hs)	2 (D)	3 (Hy)	4 (Pd)	5 (Mf)	6 (Pa)	7 (Pt)	8 (Sc)	9 (Ma)	0 (Si)	Raw Score
55									120			88		85												92		84	55
54									118			87		83							120					91		82	54
53									116			86		82							118					90		81	53
52							120		114			85		81							115					89		80	52
51							118		112			84		79			119			113						88		79	51
50	56		120			116	118		110			83		78	56					116	111	118				87		77	50
49			119			120	114	116	108			82		77						114	109	115	20			86		76	49
48			117				112	114	106		98	81		75						112	107	113	22		94	85		75	48
47			115			115	110	111	104		96	80		74						110	105	111	24		93	84		73	47
46			114			113	108	109	101		95	79	103	73						108	103	109	26		91	83	104	72	46
45			112			111	106	107	99		93	78	101	71						106	101	107	28		90	82	102	71	45
44			110			108	104	105	97		92	77	99	70						103	99	105	30		89	80	100	70	44
43			108			106	102	103	95		90	76	97	69						101	97	103	32		87	79	98	68	43
42			107			104	100	101	93		89	75	95	67						99	95	101	34		86	78	96	67	42
41			105			101	98	99	91		88	74	93	66						97	93	99	36		85	77	95	66	41
40	53		103			99	96	96	89	111	86	73	91	64	53					95	91	97	38	114	83	76	93	64	40
39			102			97	94	94	87	109	85	72	89	63						93	89	95	40	112	82	75	91	63	39
38			100			95	91	92	85	106	83	71	87	62						90	87	92	42	110	80	74	89	62	38
37			98			92	89	90	83	104	82	70	86	60			120			88	85	90	45	108	79	73	87	61	37
36			97			90	87	88	81	102	81	69	84	59			118			86	83	88	47	106	78	72	85	59	36
35			95			88	85	86	79	100	79	68	82	58			116			84	81	86	49	103	76	71	83	58	35
34			93			86	83	84	76	98	78	67	80	56			114			82	79	84	51	101	75	70	82	57	34
33			92		114	83	81	81	74	96	76	66	78	55			111		110	80	76	82	53	99	74	69	80	55	33
32			90		112	81	79	79	72	94	75	65	76	54			109		108	78	74	80	55	97	72	68	78	54	32
31			88		109	79	77	77	70	92	73	64	74	52			107		106	75	72	78	57	95	71	66	76	53	31
30	50		87	85	107	77	75	75	68	90	72	63	72	51	50		104	86	104	73	70	76	59	93	70	65	74	52	30
29			85	83	105	74	73	73	66	88	71	62	70	50			102	84	102	71	68	74	61	94	68	64	72	50	29
28			83	81	102	72	71	71	64	86	69	61	68	48			100	82	99	69	66	71	63	88	67	63	70	49	28
27			82	78	100	70	69	69	62	83	68	60	66	47			98	80	97	67	64	69	65	86	66	62	69	48	27
26			80	76	98	67	67	66	60	81	66	59	65	46			95	77	95	65	62	67	67	84	64	61	67	46	26
25			78	74	95	65	65	64	58	79	65	58	63	44			93	75	93	62	60	65	69	82	63	60	65	45	25
24			77	72	93	63	63	62	56	77	64	57	61	43			91	73	90	60	58	63	71	79	62	59	63	44	24
23			75	70	91	61	61	60	53	75	62	56	59	42			89	71	88	58	56	61	73	77	60	58	61	42	23
22			73	68	88	58	59	58	51	73	61	55	57	40			86	69	86	56	54	59	75	75	59	57	59	41	22
21			72	66	86	56	57	56	49	71	59	54	55	39			84	67	84	54	52	57	77	73	58	56	57	40	21
20	47		70	64	84	54	54	54	47	69	58	53	53	38	47		82	64	81	52	50	55	79	71	56	55	56	39	20
19			68	62	81	52	52	52	45	67	56	52	51	36			79	62	79	49	48	53	82	68	55	54	54	37	19
18			67	60	79	49	50	49	43	65	55	51	49	35			77	60	77	47	46	51	84	66	53	53	52	36	18
17			65	58	76	47	48	47	41	63	54	50	47	34			75	58	75	45	44	48	86	64	52	51	50	35	17
16			63	55	74	45	46	45	39	60	52	49	45	32			73	56	72	43	42	46	88	62	51	50	48	33	16
15		98	62	53	72	43	44	43	37	58	51	48	43	31		96	70	53	70	41	39	44	90	60	49	49	46	32	15
14		93	60	51	69	40	42	41	35	56	49	47	42	30		92	68	51	68	39	37	42	92	58	48	48	44	31	14
13		89	58	49	67	38	40	39	33	54	48	46	40	28		88	66	49	66	37	35	40	94	55	47	47	42	30	13
12		85	57	47	65	36	38	37	31	52	46	45	38	27		83	63	47	64	34	33	38	96	53	45	46	41	28	12
11		80	55	45	62	33	36	34	28	50	45	44	36	25		79	61	45	61	32	31	36	98	51	44	45	39	27	11
10	44	76	53	43	60	31	34	32	26	48	44	43	34	24	44	75	59	42	59	30	29	34	100	49	43	44	37	26	10
9		72	52	41	58	29	32	30	24	46	42	42	32	23		70	57	40	57	28	27	32	101	47	41	43	35	24	9
8		67	50	39	55	27	30	28	22	44	41	41	30	21		66	54	38	55	26	25	30	103	44	40	42	33	23	8
7		63	48	37	53	24	28	26	20	42	39	40	28	20		62	52	36	52	24	23	27	105	42	39	41	31	22	7
6		59	46	34	51	22	26	24		40	38	39	26			58	50	34	50	21	21	25	107	40	37	40	29	21	6
5		55	45	32	48	20	24	22		37	37	38	24			53	47	32	48			23	109	38	36	39	28		5
4		50	43	30	46		22			35	35	37	22			49	45	29	46			21	111	36	35	37	26		4
3		46	41	28	44		20			33	34	36	21			45	43	27	43				113	33	33	36	24		3
2		42	40	26	41					31	32	35				40	41	25	41				115	31	32	35	22		2
1		37	38	24	39					29	31	34				36	38	23	39				118	29	31	34	20		1
0	41	32	37	22	36					27	29	33			41	31	36	21	37				120	26	29	32			0

153

T-Score Conversions for Basic Scales without K Corrections for Minnesota Adolescents Age 16

	Males														Females														
Raw Score	?	L	F	K	1 (Hs)	2 (D)	3 (Hy)	4 (Pd)	5 (Mf)	6 (Pa)	7 (Pt)	8 (Sc)	9 (Ma)	0 (Si)	?	L	F	K	1 (Hs)	2 (D)	3 (Hy)	4 (Pd)	5 (Mf)	6 (Pa)	7 (Pt)	8 (Sc)	9 (Ma)	0 (Si)	Raw Score
78												116														114			78
77												115														113			77
76												114														112			76
75												112														111			75
74												111														110			74
73												110														109			73
72												109														108			72
71												108														107			71
70	62											107		107	62											106		98	70
69												106		106												105		96	69
68												105		105												104		95	68
67												104		103												103		94	67
66												103		102												102		93	66
65												102		100												101		91	65
64												101		99												100		90	64
63												99		98												99		89	63
62												98		96												98		88	62
61												97		95												97		86	61
60	58											96		93	58											95		85	60
59												95		92												94		84	59
58												94		90												93		83	58
57												93		89												92		82	57
56												92		88												91		80	56
55												91		86						120	119					90		79	55
54												90		85						118	117					89		78	54
53												89		83						116	115					88		77	53
52												88		82						114	113					87		75	52
51												86		81						112	111					86		74	51
50	56						120	118	119			85		79	56					110	109					85		73	50
49			120			119	117	116	117			84		78						108	107	119				84		72	49
48			118			116	115	114	114		99	83		76						106	105	116			91	83		70	48
47			117			114	113	112	112		98	82		75						104	103	114	20		90	82		69	47
46			115			112	111	110	110		96	81	109	73						102	101	112	22		89	81	115	68	46
45			113			110	109	107	107		95	80	107	72						100	99	110	24		87	80	113	67	45
44			112			107	106	105	105		93	79	105	71						98	97	108	27		86	79	111	65	44
43			110			105	104	103	103		92	78	103	69						96	95	106	29		85	78	109	64	43
42			108			103	102	101	100		90	77	100	68						94	93	103	31		83	77	106	63	42
41			106			101	100	99	98		89	76	98	66						92	91	101	34		82	75	104	62	41
40	53		105			98	98	97	95	92	87	75	96	65	53					89	89	99	36		81	74	102	60	40
39			103			96	96	95	93	91	86	74	94	63						87	87	97	38		79	73	100	59	39
38			101			94	93	92	91	89	85	72	92	62			120			85	85	95	40	120	78	72	98	58	38
37			99			92	91	90	88	88	83	71	90	61			118			83	83	92	43	118	77	71	95	57	37
36			98			89	89	88	86	86	82	70	88	59			116			81	81	90	45	115	75	70	93	55	36
35			96			87	87	86	84	85	80	69	85	58			113			79	79	88	47	112	74	69	91	54	35
34			94			85	85	84	81	83	79	68	83	56			111			77	77	86	50	110	73	68	89	53	34
33			92			83	82	82	79	82	77	67	81	55			109		112	75	75	84	52	107	71	67	86	52	33
32			91			80	80	79	76	80	76	66	79	54			107		109	73	73	82	54	105	70	66	84	51	32
31			89			78	78	77	74	79	74	65	77	52			104		107	71	71	79	57	102	69	65	82	49	31
30	50		87	88	118	76	76	75	72	77	73	64	75	51	50		102	88	105	69	69	77	59	99	67	64	80	48	30
29			86	85	115	74	74	73	69	76	71	63	73	49			100	85	102	67	67	75	61	97	66	63	77	47	29
28			84	83	112	71	71	71	67	74	70	62	70	48			98	83	100	65	65	73	64	94	65	62	75	46	28
27			82	81	109	69	69	69	65	73	68	61	68	46			95	81	98	63	63	71	66	92	64	61	73	44	27
26			80	79	107	67	67	66	62	71	67	59	66	45			93	79	95	61	61	68	68	89	62	60	71	43	26
25			79	76	104	65	65	64	60	70	65	58	64	44			91	77	93	59	59	66	70	87	61	59	68	42	25
24			77	74	101	63	63	62	57	68	64	57	62	42			89	74	91	57	57	64	73	84	60	58	66	41	24
23			75	72	98	60	61	60	55	67	62	56	60	41			86	72	88	55	56	62	75	81	58	56	64	39	23
22			73	70	95	58	58	58	53	66	61	55	58	39			84	70	86	53	54	60	77	79	57	55	62	38	22
21			72	67	93	56	56	56	50	64	59	54	55	38			82	68	84	51	52	57	80	76	56	54	59	37	21

T-Score Conversions for Basic Scales without K Corrections for Minnesota Adolescents Age 16—continued

Raw Score	Males														Females														Raw Score
	?	L	F	K	1 (Hs)	2 (D)	3 (Hy)	4 (Pd)	5 (Mf)	6 (Pa)	7 (Pt)	8 (Sc)	9 (Ma)	0 (Si)	?	L	F	K	1 (Hs)	2 (D)	3 (Hy)	4 (Pd)	5 (Mf)	6 (Pa)	7 (Pt)	8 (Sc)	9 (Ma)	0 (Si)	
20	47		70	65	90	54	54	53	48	63	58	53	53	37	47		80	66	81	49	50	55	82	74	54	53	57	36	20
19			68	63	87	51	52	51	46	61	56	52	51	35			77	63	79	47	48	53	84	71	53	52	55	34	19
18			66	60	84	49	50	49	43	60	55	51	49	34			75	61	77	45	46	51	87	68	52	51	53	33	18
17			65	58	81	47	47	47	41	58	54	50	47	32			73	59	74	43	44	49	89	66	50	50	50	32	17
16			63	56	78	45	45	45	39	57	52	49	45	31			71	57	72	40	42	47	91	63	49	49	48	31	16
15		99	61	54	76	42	43	43	36	55	51	48	43	29		95	68	55	70	38	40	44	94	61	48	48	46	29	15
14		94	60	51	73	40	41	41	34	54	49	46	40	28		91	66	52	67	36	38	42	96	58	46	47	44	28	14
13		89	58	49	70	38	39	38	31	52	48	45	38	27		86	64	50	65	34	36	40	98	55	45	46	41	27	13
12		85	56	47	67	36	37	36	29	51	46	44	36	25		82	62	48	63	32	34	38	100	53	44	45	39	26	12
11		80	54	45	64	33	34	34	27	49	45	43	34	24		78	59	46	61	30	32	36	102	50	42	44	37	24	11
10	44	76	53	42	62	31	32	32	24	48	43	42	32	22	44	73	57	44	58	28	30	33	104	48	41	43	35	23	10
9		71	51	40	59	29	30	30	22	46	42	41	30	21		69	55	41	56	26	28	31	106	45	40	42	32	22	9
8		67	49	38	56	27	28	28	20	45	40	40	28	20		64	53	39	54	24	26	29	109	42	38	41	30	21	8
7		62	47	36	53	24	26	25		43	39	39	25			60	50	37	51	22	24	27	111	40	37	40	28	20	7
6		58	46	33	50	22	23	23		42	37	38	23			56	48	35	49	20	22	25	113	37	36	39	26		6
5		53	44	31	47	20	21	21		40	36	37	21			51	46	33	47		20	23	116	35	34	38	23		5
4		49	42	29	45					39	34	36				47	44	30	44			20	118	32	33	36	21		4
3		44	40	27	42					37	33	35				42	41	28	42				120	29	32	35			3
2		40	39	24	39					36	31	33				38	39	26	40					27	30	34			2
1		35	37	22	36					35	30	32				34	37	24	37					24	29	33			1
0	41	31	35	20	33					34	28	30			41	29	35	22	35					21	27	32			0

T-Score Conversions for Basic Scales without K Corrections for Minnesota Adolescents Age 17

Raw Score	Males														Females														Raw Score
	?	L	F	K	1 (Hs)	2 (D)	3 (Hy)	4 (Pd)	5 (Mf)	6 (Pa)	7 (Pt)	8 (Sc)	9 (Ma)	0 (Si)	?	L	F	K	1 (Hs)	2 (D)	3 (Hy)	4 (Pd)	5 (Mf)	6 (Pa)	7 (Pt)	8 (Sc)	9 (Ma)	0 (Si)	
78												116														119			78
77												115														118			77
76												114														117			76
75												113														116			75
74												112														114			74
73												111														113			73
72												109														112			72
71												108														111			71
70	62											107		112	62											110		101	70
69												106		110												109		99	69
68												105		109												108		98	68
67												104		107												106		97	67
66												103		106												105		95	66
65												102		104												104		94	65
64												101		103												103		93	64
63												100		101												102		91	63
62												99		100												101		90	62
61												97		98												100		89	61
60	58											96		97	58											98		87	60
59												95		95												97		86	59
58												94		94												96		85	58
57						118						93		92												95		83	57
56						117	120					92		91							119					94		82	56

T-Score Conversions for Basic Scales without K Corrections for Minnesota Adolescents Age 17—continued

	Males														Females														
Raw Score	?	L	F	K	1 (Hs)	2 (D)	3 (Hy)	4 (Pd)	5 (Mf)	6 (Pa)	7 (Pt)	8 (Sc)	9 (Ma)	0 (Si)	?	L	F	K	1 (Hs)	2 (D)	3 (Hy)	4 (Pd)	5 (Mf)	6 (Pa)	7 (Pt)	8 (Sc)	9 (Ma)	0 (Si)	Raw Score
55						115	118					91		89							117					93		81	55
54						113	116					90		88						120	115					92		79	54
53						112	114		120			89		86						118	113					90		78	53
52						110	112		118			88		85						116	111					89		77	52
51						108	110		116			86		83						114	109					88		75	51
50	56					106	108		114			85		82	56					112	107					87		74	50
49						104	107	119	111			84		80						110	105					86		73	49
48						102	105	117	109		101	83		79						108	103	118			95	85		71	48
47						101	103	114	107		99	82		77						105	101	116	20		94	84		70	47
46						99	101	112	105		98	81	109	76						103	99	114	22		93	82	114	69	46
45						97	99	110	103		96	80	107	74						101	97	111	24		91	81	112	67	45
44						95	97	108	100		95	79	105	73						99	95	109	27		90	80	110	66	44
43						93	95	105	98		93	78	103	71						97	93	107	29		88	79	108	65	43
42						92	93	103	96		92	77	101	70						95	91	104	31		87	78	106	63	42
41						90	91	101	94		90	75	99	68						93	89	102	33		85	77	104	62	41
40	53		119			88	89	98	92		89	74	96	67	53					90	87	100	36		84	76	101	61	40
39			117			86	87	96	90		87	73	94	65						88	85	98	38		82	74	99	59	39
38			115			84	86	94	87		86	72	92	64						86	83	95	40		81	73	97	58	38
37			113			83	84	91	85		84	71	90	62						84	81	93	42		79	72	95	57	37
36			110			81	82	89	83		82	70	88	61			118			82	79	91	44		78	71	93	55	36
35			108			79	80	87	81		81	69	86	59			118			80	77	88	47		77	70	91	54	35
34			106			77	78	85	79	120	79	68	84	58			116			78	75	86	49	119	75	69	89	53	34
33			104		118	75	76	82	77	117	78	67	82	56			113		107	75	73	84	51	116	74	68	86	51	33
32			102		115	73	74	80	74	114	76	66	79	55			111		105	73	71	81	53	113	72	66	84	50	32
31			100		113	72	72	78	72	111	75	64	77	53			109		103	71	69	79	56	110	71	65	82	49	31
30	50		97	86	110	70	70	75	70	108	73	63	75	52	50		106	94	100	69	67	77	58	108	69	64	80	47	30
29			95	84	108	68	68	73	68	105	72	62	73	50			104	91	98	67	65	74	60	105	68	63	78	46	29
28			93	82	105	66	67	71	66	102	70	61	71	49			101	89	96	65	63	72	62	102	66	62	76	45	28
27			91	80	103	64	65	69	63	99	69	60	69	47			99	86	93	62	61	70	65	99	65	61	73	43	27
26			89	78	100	63	63	66	61	96	67	59	67	45			96	84	91	60	59	67	67	96	63	60	71	42	26
25			87	75	98	61	61	64	59	93	65	58	65	44			94	81	89	58	57	65	69	93	62	58	69	41	25
24			84	73	95	59	59	62	57	90	64	57	62	42			91	79	87	56	55	63	71	90	60	57	67	39	24
23			82	71	93	57	57	59	55	87	62	56	60	41			89	76	84	54	53	61	74	87	59	56	65	38	23
22			80	69	90	55	55	57	53	84	61	55	58	39			86	74	82	52	51	58	76	84	58	55	63	37	22
21			78	67	88	54	53	55	50	81	59	53	56	38			84	71	80	50	49	56	78	82	56	54	60	35	21
20	47		76	64	85	52	51	52	48	78	58	52	54	36	47		81	69	77	47	47	54	80	79	55	53	58	34	20
19			73	62	83	50	49	50	46	75	56	51	52	35			79	66	75	45	45	51	83	76	53	52	56	33	19
18			71	60	80	48	48	48	44	72	55	50	50	33			77	64	73	43	43	49	85	73	52	50	54	31	18
17			69	58	78	46	46	46	42	70	53	49	48	32			74	61	71	41	41	47	87	70	50	49	52	30	17
16			67	56	75	44	44	43	40	67	52	48	45	30			72	59	68	39	39	44	89	67	49	48	50	29	16
15		93	65	53	73	43	42	41	37	64	50	47	43	29		91	69	56	66	37	37	42	92	64	47	47	47	27	15
14		88	63	51	70	41	40	39	35	61	48	46	41	27		87	67	54	64	35	35	40	94	61	46	46	45	26	14
13		84	60	49	68	39	38	36	34	58	47	45	39	26		83	64	51	61	32	33	37	96	59	44	45	43	25	13
12		80	58	47	65	37	36	34	31	55	45	44	37	24		79	62	49	59	30	31	35	98	56	43	44	41	23	12
11		76	56	45	63	35	34	32	29	52	44	43	35	23		74	59	46	57	28	29	33	100	53	42	43	39	22	11
10	44	72	54	42	60	34	32	29	26	49	42	41	33	21	44	70	57	44	55	26	27	31	102	50	40	41	37	21	10
9		68	52	40	58	32	30	27	24	46	41	40	31	20		66	54	41	52	24	25	28	104	47	39	40	34		9
8		63	50	38	55	30	29	25	22	43	39	39	28			62	52	38	50	22	23	26	106	44	37	39	32		8
7		59	47	36	53	28	27	23	20	40	38	38	26			58	49	36	48	20	21	24	108	41	36	38	30		7
6		55	45	34	50	26	25	20		37	36	37	24			54	47	33	45			21	111	38	34	37	28		6
5		51	43	31	48	24	23			34	35	36	22			49	45	31	43				113	35	33	36	26		5
4		47	41	29	45	23	21			31	33	35	20			45	42	28	41				115	33	31	35	24		4
3		43	39	27	43	21				28	32	34				41	40	26	38				117	30	30	32	22		3
2		38	36	25	40					25	30	33				37	37	23	36				120	27	28	32			2
1		34	34	23	38					22	28	32				33	35	21	34					24	27	31			1
0	41	30	32	20	35						27	31			41	28	32		31					21	25	29			0

The Minnesota Multiphasic Personality Inventory

Starke R. Hathaway and J. Charnley McKinley

Scorer's Initials_____

Female

Fractions of K

K	.5	.4	.2
30	15	12	6
29	15	12	6
28	14	11	6
27	14	11	5
26	13	10	5
25	13	10	5
24	12	10	5
23	12	9	5
22	11	9	4
21	11	8	4
20	10	8	4
19	10	8	4
18	9	7	4
17	9	7	3
16	8	6	3
15	8	6	3
14	7	6	3
13	7	5	3
12	6	5	2
11	6	4	2
10	5	4	2
9	5	4	2
8	4	3	2
7	4	3	1
6	3	2	1
5	3	2	1
4	2	2	1
3	2	2	1
2	1	1	0
1	1	1	0
0	0	0	0

Raw Score ___

K to be added ___

Raw Score with K ___

The Minnesota Multiphasic Personality Inventory

Starke R. Hathaway and J. Charnley McKinley

Scorer's Initials_____

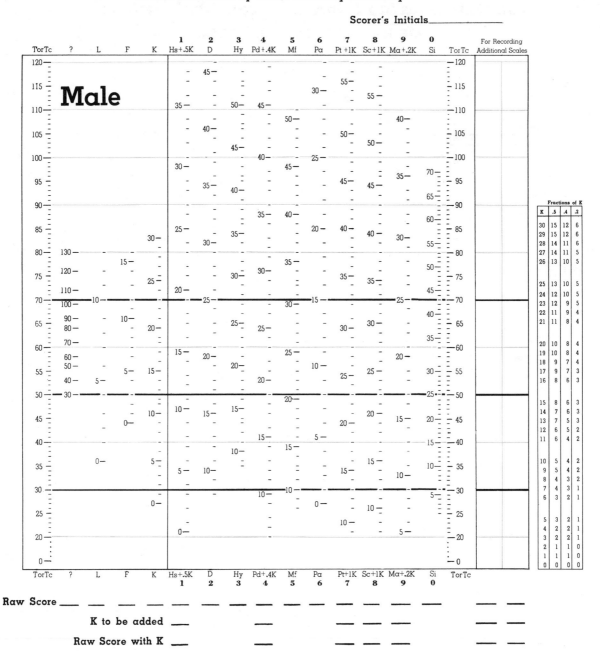

Raw Score ___ __ __ __ __ __ __ __ __ __ __ __ __

K to be added ___ __ __ __ __

Raw Score with K ___ __ __ __ __ __ __

Appendix D. Instructions for Evaluation of MMPI Narratives

We are asking you to read the computer print-out on your patients and evaluate the accuracy of each narrative paragraph.

Accuracy here indicates whether the material presented in the report *does not conflict* with the clinical data you have gathered.

If a statement is mostly accurate, consider the whole statement accurate, but feel free to comment on the back of the report concerning specific parts of a given paragraph. If a statement is mostly inaccurate (i.e., its basic substance is contradicted by the clinical picture), place an (X) by the paragraph number which heads that statement.

There are a few points you should remember:

(1) Psychological tests may provide rather limited data; therefore, a statement's accuracy does *not* deal with what is not said.

(2) If clinical data is not available covering a specific narrative paragraph, consider the paragraph accurate.

(3) We are certain that statements have *variable* accuracy. Some will be quite good, others quite poor. Do not *initially* come to an overall opinion of the report, just take each paragraph *separately* and *independently*.

(4) Evaluate the accuracy of paragraphs as they relate to the state of the patient *at the time of testing*, do not include characteristics which were not present until later in treatment.

At the end of the narrative there will be a place for you to make a judgment about the accuracy of the total report. Here consider the distance between numbers on the rating scale equal. At this point compare the relation between all paragraphs to the general clinical picture of the patient, keeping in mind the four points noted above.

The small additional time needed to read and evaluate these reports will greatly add to our isolation of "poor" or "weak" parts of the program. These data will, with luck, lead to the necessary modifications.